After about an hour the noises from the small trunk stopped. Now the boys worried that Reza's father didn't have enough air. They were still more than three hundred miles from Los Angeles, and having their captive die in transit wasn't part of the plan. Knowing he must act, Dean found a screwdriver and worked it through the sturdy trunk again and again until he had made more than a dozen air holes.

Around dusk the truck made an unscheduled stop just off the highway. The boys had been talking aimlessly for a while when they noticed that no noises had come from the trunk for some time. "You'd better check," Joe told Dean.

Dean tentatively unlatched the trunk and lifted the lid. He was met with a surge of heat. He slammed the lid back down.

"He's dead."

"I guess we blew it," Joe said quietly.

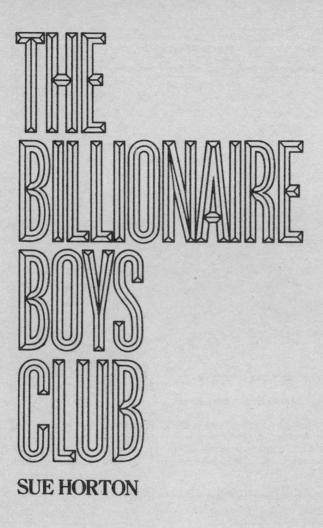

THE BILLIONAIRE BOYS CLUB

SUE HORTON

ST. MARTIN'S PAPERBACKS

THE BILLIONAIRE BOYS CLUB

Copyright © 1989 by Sue Horton.

Library of Congress Catalog Card Number: 89-4249

ISBN: 0-312-92232-9

Printed in the United States of America

St. Martin's Press hardcover edition published 1989
St. Martin's Paperbacks edition/April 1990

10 9 8 7 6 5 4 3 2 1

For Carl

Acknowledgments

During more than three and a half years of looking into the story of the BBC, I have become indebted to dozens of people who gave willingly of their time and energy. For their help and cooperation I am very grateful.

More than a hundred people agreed to open their lives to me through lengthy interviews. I wish to thank those people, without naming names, as many of them preferred to remain anonymous; they include BBC members, their families and friends, investors, and the friends and families of the two victims, Ron Levin and Hedayat Eslaminia.

Thanks are also due to the defense lawyers who represented the various BBC defendants for their willingness to assist in such ways as legal ethics allowed.

I owe both gratitude and admiration to the prosecution teams of John Vance and Oscar Breiling and Fred Wapner and Les Zoeller.

I wish to particularly thank Greg Critser, from whom I first heard about the BBC and with whom I first wrote about the group.

In addition, for their support, encouragement, and input, I wish to thank the following:

My editor, Toni Lopopolo, Kris Bell, Kathy Borgenicht, Carl Byker, Sam Byker, Samantha Campbell, Marcia Chambers, Stevie Chapple, Ed Cray, Karen Denne, Joe Domanick, Glenn Duncan, John Forker, Brenda Friend, Murray Fromson,

Lily Garrison, Nicholas Garrison, Peter Garrison, Molly Gingras, Richard Gingras, Marcy Gross, Joan Guerin, Joe Guerin, Mike Hamilburg, Lew Harris, Nancy Hill Holtzman, Denton Holland, Charles Horton, John Horton (both of them), Laura Horton, Margaret Horton, Robert Horton, Georgianne King, Margaret King, Zina Klapper, Jon Kotler, Jack Langguth, Donald March, the Marills (all of them), Cathy Medich, Chris Meindl, the Morains, Barbara Neely, Jim Neely, Jean O'Neill, Ron Ostroff, Scot Paltrow, Terry Pristin, Jan Raabe, Steve Randall, Aaron Rowland, Craig Rowland, Tom Shima, Lauren Taylor, Cleo Trumbo, David Webb, and Heidi Yorkshire.

Cast of Characters

Jon Allen
A BBC member who attended law school with Dean Karny.

Arthur Barens
One of Joe Hunt's lawyers at his trial for Ron Levin's murder.

Ron Bass
The lawyer from the California attorney general's office first assigned to Hedayat Eslaminia's murder.

Oscar Breiling
The investigator for California's Special Prosecutions Unit who handled the Eslaminia murder investigation.

Chester Brown
One of Joe Hunt's biggest investors and a cousin of Steve Weiss.

Gene Browning
A chemist and inventor who designed the rock-crushing machine the BBC attempted to market.

Richard Chier
With Arthur Barens, served as Joe Hunt's lawyer at his trial for the murder of Ron Levin.

Evan Dicker
An early member of the BBC and the son of a prominent Beverly Hills property lawyer.

Ben Dosti
With Dean Karny and Joe Hunt, one of the BBC's three Shadings and the son of a Los Angeles *Times* food critic.

Jerry Eisenberg
Recruited as a BBC member after his graduation from law school. Served as the group's lawyer and was the first to alert authorities to Hedayat Eslaminia's murder.

Hedayat Eslaminia — The father of BBC member Reza Eslaminia and the target of a BBC kidnapping, extortion, and murder plot.

Reza Eslaminia — A BBC member and the son of Hedayat Eslaminia.

Jack Friedman — The broker at the commodities trading firm of Clayton Brokerage Co. who unwittingly set up Levin's scam of Joe Hunt.

Greg Gamsky — Joe Hunt's brother.

Joe Gamsky — Joe Hunt's original name.

Kathy Gamsky — Joe Hunt's mother.

Larry Gamsky — Joe Hunt's father before he changed his name to Ryan Hunt.

Jim Graham — The name by which BBC members knew Jim Pittman, security director of the BBC.

Mina Hakimi — Reza Eslaminia's mother.

Joe Hunt — The leader and founder of the BBC. Born Joe Gamsky.

Ryan Hunt — Joe Hunt's father. Originally Larry Gamsky.

Kate Johnston — A pseudonym used in this book for Ben Dosti's girlfriend.

Dean Karny — With Joe Hunt and Ben Dosti, one of the BBC's three Shadings. The son of a successful Los Angeles developer.

Carol and Martin Levin — Ron Levin's parents.

Ron Levin — A Beverly Hills con man and the first victim of Joe Hunt.

Steve Lopez — A Singapore native of Indian descent who socialized with BBC members and put up significant amounts of money for Joe Hunt to trade in the commodities market.

Dave and Tom May	BBC members and adopted twin sons of wealthy May Company family member David May II.
Gary Merritt	One of Reza Eslaminia's lawyers in his trial for the murder of his father.
Tom Nolan	Ben Dosti's primary lawyer in his trial for the murder of Hedayat Eslaminia.
Jim Pittman	A security guard at the Wilshire Manning later recruited to be director of security for the BBC. Known to members as Jim Graham. Pittman was tried twice for the murder of Ron Levin, but both times the jury failed to reach a verdict. In the end, murder charges were dropped in exchange for guilty pleas to charges of being an accessory after the fact to the murder and carrying an illegal weapon.
Jeff Raymond	A BBC member who, with Dave May, was among the first to alert authorities to Ron Levin's murder.
Laurence Rittenband	The judge in Joe Hunt's Santa Monica trial for the murder of Ron Levin.
Bobby and Lynne Roberts	Brooke Roberts's parents. Put up bail for Joe Hunt and invited him to live in their Bel Air mansion while he awaited trial.
Brooke Roberts	The daughter of Hollywood producer Bobby Roberts and live-in girlfriend of Joe Hunt.
Bruce Swartout	An Orange County businessman whose dealings with the BBC turned sour. Later attacked outside his office.
Steve Taglianetti	A BBC member and former prep school classmate of the Mays, Joe Hunt, and Dean Karny.
John Vance	The Special Prosecutions Unit attorney who ultimately tried the various defendants in the Eslaminia murder case.

Fred Wapner

The lawyer from the Los Angeles County district attorney's office who prosecuted Hunt and Pittman for the murder of Ron Levin.

Steve Weiss

One of Joe Hunt's investors who ultimately brought in more than forty other investors for the BBC.

Les Zoeller

The Beverly Hills detective who investigated the Levin homicide.

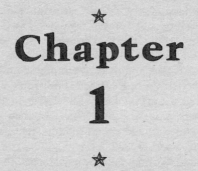

Chapter
1

There are only five people remaining alive who know for sure what happened to Hedayat Eslaminia on the afternoon of July 30, 1984. Each has a different version of the day's events. Police and prosecutors believe the story of Dean Karny, one of the young men involved in the Eslaminia affair. Karny says it happened this way:

At about two-thirty on that warm summer afternoon, Dean stepped off an airplane at the San Francisco airport. So far, everything was happening on schedule. By 3 P.M., Dean had alighted from a taxi at the Villa Motel, fifteen miles south of the airport in the San Francisco Peninsula town of Belmont. Dean was the last of the five young men scheduled to participate in the afternoon's events to arrive at the motel.

Dean was pleased to find everything under control in the room the others had rented. Joe Hunt, Dean's best friend and the clear-cut leader of the assembled group, was just giving final instructions to the participants in the operation they called Project Sam. Only a few last-minute details needed attending. Joe Hunt and another boy, Ben Dosti, still had to change clothes, trade their customary business suits for brown UPS uniforms. While they were dressing, Dean took a roll of brown paper and began wrapping an empty blue steamer trunk sitting on the floor. The trunk was just large enough to hold a person, Dean knew. He had tried it out himself back in Los Angeles. When he had finished the wrapping, he wrote an address on the top: Hedayat Eslaminia, 400 Davey Glen Road, #4322.

Their final tasks completed, the boys loaded the large parcel into the back of the yellow pickup truck Joe had borrowed from his father and driven up north. Everything was ready to go: they had packed the chloroform, the handcuffs, the pistol, and the trunk. It was time to put their carefully laid plans into action.

The five young men were an unlikely bunch for the job they were about to perform. Three of them—Ben, Dean, and their leader, Joe—had known each other since they were students at an exclusive Los Angeles prep school. Joe Hunt's last name was Gamsky back then. Reza Eslaminia, the handsome, exotic-looking son of the man whose name now appeared on the wrapped steamer trunk, had only been friends with the others for a month. He had attended prep school in northern California. Now in their early twenties, the young men were all part of a business and social group called the BBC, or the Billionaire Boys Club, as they sometimes called it in jest, which Joe Hunt had founded a year earlier.

Jim Graham was the only one of the BBC members assembled at the Villa who seemed remotely suited to the task at hand. He had met the boys the previous winter while working as a guard in the luxury condominium complex where Joe, Dean, and Ben lived. But his security work had hardly prepared him for what lay ahead.

Reza Eslaminia led the way to his father's apartment building in a late-model BMW owned by the group. Jim Graham rode with him. Joe Hunt followed in his father's pickup and camper with Dean Karny and Ben Dosti. Ten minutes after leaving the motel, they arrived at the huge complex in the hills overlooking the San Francisco Bay. Jim got out and went ahead to open the security door while the others parked. Then Joe, the self-appointed "master of torture" for the operation, and Ben, both in their UPS uniforms, unloaded the paper-wrapped trunk and carried it toward the door.

When the others had disappeared inside, Dean slid over into the driver's seat and began his anxious wait. Within minutes he heard what he thought were shrieks. He sat very still. Surely the neighbors must have heard the screams and would call the police. But after ten minutes his friends reappeared carrying the blue trunk, now paperless and clearly very heavy. Dean helped the boys stash their load in the pickup's camper and then climbed into the cab with Joe.

As the boys pulled away in their truck, followed by the others in the BMW, Joe told Dean what had happened inside Eslaminia's condominium. They had abducted the Iranian man, as they had come to northern California to do, but things hadn't gone exactly as planned. First, Jim, a well-muscled, streetwise black man, had actually had trouble subduing the much smaller Eslaminia. In the end it had taken all three boys to manage him.

Next, when Jim attempted to knock out the Iranian man with the chloroform they had brought, he had grown faint himself, spilling the contents of the bottle. "The strangest thing of all, though, was Ben," Joe told Dean. "Right in the middle of the abduction, he ran into the kitchen and washed his hands. It was an absolutely classic symbolic gesture of guilt." The way Joe told it, he alone of the three kidnappers had performed his duties flawlessly. But everything had worked out in the end, and now the boys had their captive. Back in Los Angeles, if all went according to plan, they would force him to sign over his assets to his son, Reza. Then, at least Joe, Ben, and Dean understood, they would kill him.

*   *   *

Ten minutes after the abduction, as the boys transferred the trunk into a U-Haul they had rented earlier for the rest of the seven-hour journey to Los Angeles, the reality of what they were doing became painfully clear. "Please, sir, let me out," the heavily accented voice wailed from inside the trunk. But things had gone too far for that.

After Jim Graham started up the truck, Dean Karny, in back with the trunk, realized that the U-Haul's back doors were not shut. For the next forty-five minutes he crouched near the doors, holding them shut and listening to Eslaminia knock and plead for his release. When the truck made a stop, Ben Dosti joined Dean, and the boys shut the doors securely, but Dean remained very rattled.

By now Eslaminia was gasping between pleas, and Dean and Ben, alone with the trunk in the dark truck, were beginning to panic. Ben was carrying a bottle of chloroform and a .25 caliber Beretta with a silencer, and Joe had told them to open the trunk and rechloroform their captive if he became loud. Dean and Ben didn't like to go against Joe's instructions, but they were far too scared to take action.

After about an hour the noises from the small trunk stopped. Now the boys worried that Reza's father didn't have enough air. They were still more than three hundred miles from Los Angeles, and having their captive die in transit wasn't part of the plan. Knowing he must act, Dean found a Phillips screwdriver in Ben's bag and worked it through the sturdy trunk again and again until he had made more than a dozen air holes.

Soon the noises started again, this time with fewer words and more gasping. As the truck sped south on Interstate 5 through the flat farmland of California's San Joaquin Valley, the noise from the trunk became so loud that the boys were afraid someone in a nearby car would hear. Still too frightened to open the trunk and confront the man they had abducted, they decided to tape over the holes in the trunk in hopes that their captive would fall unconscious again. The plan seemed to work. The noises stopped and the boys removed the tape.

For the next couple of hours they covered and uncovered the holes to control Eslaminia's noisy pleas.

Around dusk, the truck stopped on a road just off I-5, the main superhighway between Los Angeles and San Francisco. Dean and Ben climbed out into the hot summer evening to inquire about the unscheduled stop. Joe felt they needed to alter their plans a bit. While following behind in his father's pickup, the BBC leader had noticed that the rear lights on the U-Haul truck weren't functioning properly. It would be safer, he thought, to transfer the trunk to the pickup. The last thing the boys needed was to be stopped by the police.

Because the pickup had a window through to the camper, Joe agreed that Dean could ride in front instead of in back with the trunk. The boys had been talking aimlessly for quite a while when they noticed that no noises had come from the trunk for some time. "You'd better check," Joe told Dean.

Kneeling on the seat and leaning through the window, Dean tentatively unlatched the trunk and lifted the lid. He was met with a surge of heat and the overwhelming odor of urine. He slammed the lid back down. Mustering his courage, Dean opened the trunk again, this time fanning the lid for perhaps thirty seconds. Then he took a flashlight and peered inside at Eslaminia, handcuffed and curled up in a fetal position. Dean could see that the man was drooling, and he thought he detected some stomach movement, which he took for breathing. He concluded their captive was alive and sat back down in the cab.

For the next five minutes, the boys traveled in silence down the long dark highway to Los Angeles. Still hearing no sounds from Eslaminia, Karny leaned back through the window, and once again opened the trunk. This time he could detect no breathing. He felt for a pulse, but there was none. "I think he's dead," Dean told Joe.

"Check again," Joe ordered. "See about giving him mouth-to-mouth resuscitation."

But Dean blanched at the suggestion. He had never before seen a dead man and couldn't bear the thought of getting any closer. After checking quickly again from a safe distance, Dean made his final report. "He is dead, Joe. It is not going to do any good."

"Oh shit," Joe said quietly. "I guess we blew it."

Chapter
2

The Gamskys of Chicago were, to all outward appearances, a typical Fifties family. Middle class and midwestern, Larry and Kathy Gamsky lived in a suburban neighborhood filled with others like them. Larry went off to a good job in the city each morning in a brand new company car. His $20,000-a-year salary as a salesman for a pharmaceutical company supported the family well.

In those days Kathy Gamsky felt fortunate. From a poor Wisconsin farming family herself, the thin, round-faced young woman had had the good fortune to fall in love with and marry a good-looking, dynamic man of what she felt to be considerable means. Her handsome husband's father had owned the local dry cleaners in a small Wisconsin town; he had land and other investments as well. But when Larry was very young, both his parents had died, and he had been raised on the family estate by an aunt and a maid.

It seemed to Kathy that Larry had spent a fairly idyllic

childhood, even if he didn't have parents. At the age of nine, he claimed, he had been given a credit card and a boat. Later he had been allowed to purchase a kit and build a car. The way he told it, he had been given unlimited funds to pursue his childhood interests. He had perhaps grown up a bit selfish, with so many people anxious to indulge his every wish, but his bride was used to accommodating others and wanted to please her husband.

During the early years of her marriage, Kathy Gamsky basked in her new position in life. Just out of college, Larry got a job in Chicago as advertising manager for a farm machinery company. He stayed with the firm through 1957, when the couple's first child, Greg, was born. After the baby was born, Larry took the sales job he would still hold two years later on Halloween, 1959, when their second son, Joe, arrived.

At first the aggressive, outgoing young man seemed to thrive in his pharmaceutical job. He had, it turned out, a real aptitude for selling, and he genuinely enjoyed visiting with doctors and telling them about the drugs he handled. But not too long after little Joey was born, Larry Gamsky began to get restless.

One evening, Larry came home with an announcement. He had purchased a franchise to sell stainless steel cookware. Yes, he knew he was already very busy, but he had an idea. Kathy Gamsky would be the one to actually knock on doors and peddle the cookware. At first his wife protested. They were doing just fine without her working, and she really wanted to stay at home with her two young boys. But Larry wouldn't listen. He prodded and needled until his compliant wife agreed to go to work.

The disagreement over Kathy's working and its ultimate resolution set a pattern that would stand for years in the couple's relationship: Larry would make his wishes known, Kathy would resist, Larry would pressure harder, Kathy would give in. Life in the Gamsky household would never be entirely peaceful again, and the children would suffer for it.

Kathy again tried to protest when her husband came up

with a plan to move to California. In many ways, the young mother was still essentially a farm girl. Her family, her friends, and her entire life were in the Midwest. She had never before left the region, and she was afraid of change. But Larry would hear no objections. As a young man, he had spent several vacations on the West Coast and he longed to live there. He hated the Chicago weather, he said, and wanted to move where it was sunny all year round. The cookware business was thriving, as Kathy had turned out to be a natural saleswoman, and Larry argued that they could easily get that going wherever they lived. As usual, his arguments prevailed.

Life in Los Angeles was even worse than Kathy Gamsky had feared. Larry began with a grand plan of establishing the cookware business on a much larger scale than in Chicago. He intended, he said, to hire a sales force to sell the pots and pans while he handled the business end. But the scheme was poorly planned and soon fell apart. The once ambitious Larry never did hire people to work for him. Once again, Kathy Gamsky, very much against her wishes, was going from door to door, selling housewares.

With the whole family depending on her, Kathy could not seem to sell much in her new neighborhood. She didn't know the area well enough to select suitable neighborhoods for her wares; she felt ill-at-ease with the people she met. It seemed to her that Californians just weren't willing to buy. As the family financial situation worsened—they were living almost entirely on savings—Kathy Gamsky kept hoping her husband would look for a job, but he seemed unable to function in Los Angeles. He had lost all ambition.

Soon the Gamskys were out of money. Just two years earlier, Kathy Gamsky's life had seemed so secure; now, with two young children, she was uncertain what to do. While she decided, the young mother packed up her sons and went to stay with a friend in Texas. When her mother died a short time later, Kathy took the boys back to Wisconsin with her for a family visit. There she received some welcome news: Larry Gamsky had landed a job. He had been hired, he happily announced, to be the office manager of something called the American Institute of Hypnosis. Hopeful that the family was back on track, Kathy returned to Los Angeles and her husband.

The picture in California was not quite as rosy as Larry had painted it over the long-distance lines. His job, Kathy learned when she got back, paid only sixty dollars a week, and the family was still extremely precarious financially. Moreover, Kathy learned something that nearly shattered her newly mended and still fragile marriage: without his wife's knowledge, Larry Gamsky, it seemed, had managed to hold on to five thousand dollars from his inheritance. While Kathy and the boys were away, he had spent all the money on two days of therapy at the American Institute of Hypnosis. He had badly needed help, Larry explained. After moving to California, he said, he had felt that he just couldn't function. He had been overwhelmed. The therapy had helped immensely, he told her, hoping for understanding.

Kathy was furious, but her alternatives to life with Larry were few. She decided to stay with him. Her husband was young, she reminded herself. He had suffered some setbacks, but that was natural. He was intelligent; he had a good future. But the five thousand Larry had spent on therapy was to remain forever as a source of bitterness to Kathy.

After the birth of her daughter Kay in 1964, Kathy took one of the few firm stands she would take in her marriage. She wanted to own a house. She was tired of renting. She wanted roots for her growing family. To her surprise, her arguments seemed to fall on receptive ears. One day at lunch, Larry called to tell his wife about a house that was available in Van Nuys, a middle-class San Fernando Valley community of postwar housing tracts.

The three-bedroom bungalow was a far cry from Kathy Gamsky's dream home. The former owners had lost the place in foreclosure and had left it a wreck. The backyard was filled with rubbish and so overgrown with cactus that it was virtually impassable. The swimming pool had nothing in it but a little foul water and a large frog that had taken up residence there. But Larry Gamsky was firm. "This is it," he told his wife in his increasingly autocratic manner. "If you want a house, this is the one. Take it or leave it." Kathy took it.

In Van Nuys, Larry's streaks of selfishness and authoritarianism seemed to grow stronger and stronger. He claimed the garage as his domain, turning it into an expensively furnished workshop for his latest interest, motorcycles. While no expense was spared on Larry's territory, the rest of the house suffered. When the boys needed a desk, Larry banged a piece of plywood and a few four-by-fours together. Clothes for the kids were purchased at thrift shops. When Joey, always the least complaining member of the family, took a paper route at the age of eight, Larry Gamsky began regularly confiscating his son's earnings, explaining that he needed the money.

Larry seemed to show little interest in fatherhood—not in what Kathy considered to be a proper sort of fatherhood. He would not allow his children to call him Dad; he was to be called Larry. "I want you to think of me as your teacher, not your father," he told them. He tried to get the children to call their mother Kathy, but she quickly put a stop to that.

Larry for his part had little patience with his wife's nurturing approach to parenting. When Joe began kindergarten, Larry got mad at his wife for wanting to take the small boy to school. "He'll never grow up if you baby him," Larry insisted. And so the five-year-old learned to cross several busy streets by himself to get to school.

With three small children, Kathy often felt overwhelmingly busy. But if her husband was turning out to be something of a disappointment, her children were everything she could have hoped for. Joey, particularly, seemed to be a model child. From the time he was born, the boy had rarely cried. He never got angry and was able to amuse himself for long periods of time with simple toys. When the children were given IQ tests at school, Kathy Gamsky was pleased but not surprised to learn that they had been classified as "gifted" by the Los Angeles City schools.

Having "a houseful of future Presidents," as she thought of her little brood, was a little intimidating, but Kathy was determined to do right by her children. She read everything she could find about gifted children. In case she was missing something, she joined a local organization called the Gifted Children's Association, where her kids could participate in special advanced courses and where Kathy could get support in dealing with her exceptional youngsters.

When Joe was in sixth grade, Kathy paid a surprise visit to his school one afternoon only to find her middle child in the office instead of the classroom. Officials at the school quickly offered an explanation. Sixth grade was really just a review year, they said. Joe already knew what he needed to know from elementary school. In order to keep him from getting bored, the school had decided he could spend part of each day out of the classroom. Sometimes he tutored first-graders who needed help with reading, and at other times he helped around the office, running errands and performing simple clerical tasks for the staff. Joe seemed happy with the arrangement, but Kathy Gamsky was not. Her son needed new challenges, she felt, to keep his active mind developing.

A year earlier Greg had encountered problems in junior high, and at that time Kathy had seen a small article in the local newspaper that gave her hope. The Harvard School, a rigorous and elite preparatory academy for boys, was offering scholarships to needy junior and senior high-school students with strong intellectual and athletic abilities. Greg had applied for and received the scholarship. He seemed to be thriving at the school. After sizing up Joe's situation, Kathy knew she would have to arrange something for her second son as well. The Harvard School agreed to consider Joe for a scholarship, and the Gamskys were soon notified that he had been accepted and awarded financial aid for the next fall.

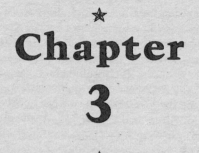

Chapter
3

Switching from a mediocre public school to a rigorous prep school was difficult for both the Gamsky boys, but it was particularly hard on Joe. The Harvard School class of '77, like most Harvard classes, was relentlessly cliquish even by 1971, when Joe joined it. The school boasted among its current crop of pupils the offspring of politicians—Ron Reagan Jr. and H. R. Haldeman's son Peter were in classes just ahead of Joe—of industry captains, and of famous Hollywood personalities. Students judged their peers by how they dressed, who their parents were, where they lived, and what their future prospects were.

In most categories by which Harvard School students judged one another, Joe fell substantially short. While many of the junior high students arrived at school in luxury cars driven by servants, Joe rode the four miles from his home on a very ordinary bicycle. Most of the boys wore expensive clothes; Joe wore Levi's, and, since he was growing rapidly, his pants generally stopped quite a few inches short of his shoes. Moreover, the tall, gangly boy seemed not to care. Joe's round face was basically handsome, with clear skin and a distinctive trail of beauty marks down one side. But the way he carried himself was unattractive, his self-consciousness apparent in every stride. His unruly dark hair was considerably longer than was fashionable, and his classmates assumed that Joe had chosen the style. Even if they had known the truth—that his father refused to spring for haircuts—Joe's classmates wouldn't have been particularly sympathetic. His lack of family wealth was perhaps the biggest stigma of all.

But if Joe's social life was not everything he might have wished, there were nevertheless things about the school he liked. Several summers earlier, Kathy Gamsky had enrolled her children in summer swimming classes. Joe had wanted to take up diving and was disappointed to learn that he was the only person who had signed up for the class. The instructor, a former Olympic diver, had intended to cancel the block of lessons, but when he saw how dismayed Joe was, he agreed to teach the boy one-on-one. By the end of the summer, Joe was diving well, and he particularly loved the high board. That early training stood Joe in good stead at Harvard. Under the terms of his scholarship, he had to participate on an athletic team, and he chose diving.

But Joe did not discover his great passion until after his first year. The Harvard School requires all ninth-graders to take a course in debate. The class is considered by the faculty to be extremely important in shaping the sort of poised, articulate, polished young man Harvard strives to turn out. Students must learn in debate to analyze both sides of an issue, to think quickly, to express ideas articulately.

The Harvard pupils put a lot of emphasis on debate as well, in part because it is taught by one of the school's most popular teachers, Ted Woods. Woods, in his late forties during Joe's years at the school, is passionately devoted to his subject, and his brightest students often respond to his enthusiasm. Each year, dozens of Harvard students give up much of their free time to preparing for and competing in debate tournaments.

It was not surprising that Joe Gamsky was attracted to debate. The internal logic of the discipline appealed to the teenager's organized mind, and the competition gave him an outlet for the none too small ego he was developing in spite of being ostracized by many of his peers. Moreover, debate was the sort of all-encompassing activity at Harvard behind which an unpopular kid could hide. The debate squad provided an instant group of companions who, even if they didn't care to socialize out of the context of debate, could at least be called friends, and Joe was short of friends at Harvard. He was not polished enough to be accepted by the school's leaders, whom he admired, and not rich enough or attractive enough to be accepted by the less academic Harvard playboy set.

Ted Woods quickly recognized that Joe was sharp, articulate, and dedicated. He was the sort of boy Woods thought could make a top-flight debater. He spent all his spare time in Woods's classroom or at home preparing for competition, and although the teacher recognized that part of Joe's dedication stemmed from loneliness, he nevertheless appreciated the boy's diligence. Sometimes Joe agreed to help some of the less proficient debaters prepare their evidence. The boys Joe helped on those occasions were often from groups he would otherwise never have interacted with. Tom May and Steve Taglianetti were two students he coached.

Tom May was one of the more famous kids at the Harvard School. Tall, dark, leading-man types with prominent chins and endearing dimples, Tom and his identical twin Dave were considered very good-looking. And while the May twins weren't among the school's brighter boys, they had a pedigree that made up for it. The sons of Fifties starlet Andra Renn and actor Ty Hardin, who starred in the television series "Bronco," the twins started life with the names Jeff Orson Hardin and John Richard Hardin. But it was the May twins' stepfather who gave them the name that provided their prestige. When the twins were two, their mother, whose relationship with Hardin had long since ended, married David May II, a Beverly Hills powerhouse known equally for his lineage and his eye for pretty women.

May was the grandson of David May, founder of the huge May Company department store chain of the Midwest and West. As a young man, David May II had helped diversify the family holdings by investing heavily in land and helping develop Park La Brea, a massive development of apartment complexes in L.A.'s Miracle Mile district near the county art museum and the La Brea Tar Pits. May's success with marriages, however, was not destined to parallel his business achievements.

Desperately wanting sons of his own, and having none from his previous marriages, May adopted his new wife's two boys and renamed them after May family members. In 1968, when the marriage broke up, May went to court to argue for custody of his two adopted sons, expressing his hope that he would one day "be able to guide the boys to a successful business future." He was awarded joint custody with the boys' mother. Although in subsequent years, as May had other children, he became less interested in the twins, they still clung tightly to their identity as Mays. Most of the students at Harvard thought of them simply as the heirs to the May Company fortune and would have been surprised to know the boys were adopted.

Steve Taglianetti, another of Joe's pupils, was a round, funny-looking boy with a beak-like nose and a receding chin. But like the Mays, he had enough family wealth to get by socially at the Harvard School. Tag was not a particularly dedicated student, preferring boats and cars to books. He and the May twins were considered beneath the notice of the school's most popular kids, who tended to be academically gifted in addition to having money and looks. And if the three boys were ignored by the school's leaders, they in turn had contempt for their tutor, whom they thought to be a nerd.

While Joe was ostracized socially, academically he did very well. All his teachers were impressed with the boy's high degree of motivation. He studied vocabulary on his own at night in preparation for his college boards, setting a goal for himself of ten new words a day.

Woods, like the other teachers, saw Joe's strengths, but he also saw that there were other sides to Joe that could easily become liabilities when it came to actually competing in a debate. The gangly six-foot young man had developed a determination to win that bordered on fanaticism. He was impatient with less proficient debaters and would verbally abuse any partners he felt had not debated well.

Joe could be an excellent debater, Woods felt, but it was unlikely he would ever fulfill his potential. Joe seemed to believe that the point of formal debate was to learn to justify anything. Like many debaters, he became so intent on winning that he seemed to forget the virtues of humor and gentlemanliness that Woods meant to instill. This was definitely not what Woods was trying to teach.

Despite Woods's misgivings, Joe did well in competition, achieving a rating of "distinction" that meant he won more than half the tournaments he competed in. It was not the highest honor conferred on debaters, but it was an achievement nonetheless. By his junior year, though, Joe was confirming Woods's fears. The boy seemed to care more keenly than any other student about winning tournaments. And he just didn't fit in with many of the other squad members. Several times Joe ran for office and lost, each time making a huge fuss. Eventually he ran for team captain, an honor he felt he deserved, but he lost to an amiable and well-liked debater.

Joe did not take the loss lightly. He amassed what support he could from other team members and began to cause trouble. His actions left many team members reeling. Why would a kid care that much about such a minor office? It was the sort of thing that later prompted one of Joe's classmates to conclude, "He desperately wanted to be a leader, but he couldn't find any followers."

Joe's junior year also brought a more serious disappointment. It can be a great temptation to a debater to falsify evidence. In making points, the person arguing quotes authorities he has researched for his evidence, so it is a simple, if highly unethical, trick for a debater to put words in someone's mouth, to make up a quote and attribute it to a recognized authority. At a debate in the spring, Joe did just that. His opponents first made the accusation, and the judges quickly confirmed it. Back at school, Woods investigated independently. There was no doubt: Joe had clearly falsified evidence.

Soon after, Woods called Joe in and informed him that he was no longer on the team. Once a debater had committed such a breach of ethics, Woods felt, there was no going back. Joe was furious. He made several appearances on the closed-circuit television station operated by the school, venting his anger against Woods, the debate program, and the school in general. He put together a thirteen-page petition arguing that Woods, his former mentor, should be fired. Joe's fragile identity at the Harvard School had been dealt a serious blow.

Despite his expulsion from the program, Joe continued to see himself as a debater. At the Harvard School, each senior was allowed a page in the yearbook to do with what he wanted. For his page, Joe chose a picture of himself laughingly pouring the contents of a card file on the head of a fellow debater. Superimposed on the picture is a poem Joe wrote that clearly expresses the isolation he must often have felt at the school:

> My favorite place is a place that is always there.
> For all my life it is my paradise.
> It is the favorite place of mine.

The poem continued, praising the wonders contained in this "favorite place." The final line revealed its location: "This is your mind."

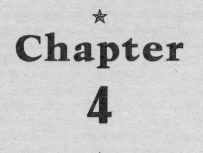

Chapter
4

Greg Gamsky was glad when his brother Joe decided to attend the University of Southern California. The older boy had transferred to the large private college from its crosstown rival, UCLA, a year earlier, and he thought his brother would thrive there. In certain ways, the university, one of the most expensive in the nation, was an odd choice for the Gamsky boys, who could count on virtually no financial support from their family. But USC has an extremely loyal group of alumni, which has endowed it with a large scholarship pool. Both boys easily qualified for aid.

For Greg, his brother's decision meant that the two might again have a chance to get close. During Joe's last year at the Harvard School, his parents finally divorced, and the stresses surrounding the bitter breakup strained the Gamsky boys' relations.

The children were drawn into their parents' bitter struggle when they were asked to decide which parent to live with.

Kay and Greg, both of whom felt deep-seated hostility for Larry Gamsky, remained with their mother. In the end, Joe chose to go with his father.

Joe's decision surprised no one. During the boy's high-school years, Larry Gamsky had begun to show much more of an interest in his younger son. Recognizing Joe's talent and drive, Gamsky had encouraged his son, without his wife's knowledge, to take accelerated accounting courses at UCLA in addition to his full load at Harvard. Gamsky had never put much stock in the fancy prep school his wife had fought so hard to get her kids into. When Joe's scholarship money was partially cut back due to changes in the school's policies, Larry had suggested that perhaps Joe should quit attending Harvard. He was extremely slow to pay the school's bills, responding only to the most threatening letters the school sent. Book learning wasn't what was important, Gamsky thought. He wanted his son to be prepared for the real world, for making the big kill.

Joe later told people that his father, having received training at the American Institute of Hypnosis, often hypnotized him to succeed. The young man seemed to want to please his father, and seeing how willing Joe was, Larry decided his son should become an accountant. He tried to interest Greg in the accelerated program as well, but the older Gamsky boy had shown no interest. His father was nothing better than a Fagin, Greg felt, seeking to exploit his children's economic potential.

At USC, still under his father's guidance, Joe continued taking business and accounting courses, and at nineteen took and passed the California CPA exam. To get ready for the exam, he had taken a preparatory course. After Joe passed, the president of the exam prep company had his photograph taken with Joe and ran it as a newspaper ad, touting Joe as the youngest person he had tutored who'd passed the exam. Later, when he would tell people about his accomplishment, Joe would exaggerate it, proudly describing himself not as the youngest graduate of the prep company to pass the exam, but as the youngest person ever to pass the California test.

If Joe continued to have academic successes at USC, he also began experiencing considerable social success for the first time since enrolling at the Harvard School. At his brother's urging, Joe went through fraternity rush at the heavily Greek-oriented school. In the end he pledged with the Chi Phi, perhaps the least prestigious organization on the school's fraternity row.

During the preceding few years, USC's Chi Phi chapter had been plagued with problems. Many of its members had used drugs and alcohol excessively, bringing the house into conflict with the university administration. During the summer of 1977, the chapter's alumni organization had ordered sweeping changes, and a majority of the members left or were expelled. When Joe went through rush in the fall of 1977, the fraternity was down to just nine people. The house was looking for leaders who could bring back some semblance of order.

The acting president of the fraternity, Said Djabarri, was very impressed with Joe Gamsky, or Joseph Henry Gamsky III, as he listed himself on Chi Phi forms. The young man was serious, articulate, and very bright. He didn't drink much and didn't use drugs. He was, he told the boys, from a very wealthy family, but his father was very strict. He wanted his son to make it without family help. Joe seemed mature far beyond his years. He was just the kind of member the fraternity needed, Djabarri concluded.

Joe impressed most of the house members that fall. It was a little odd, they thought, that his parents could never make it to family functions at the house, but Joe explained that they were very busy. You couldn't hold the busyness of someone's family against him. Everyone realized he was being groomed by Djabarri for a leadership role. In the spring of 1978, when the house was in need of a new president, Joe was named to the post.

Within a few weeks of Joe taking charge, many in the fraternity began to realize they had made a terrible mistake. Denied leadership positions in the past, Joe was now obsessed with power. As the other boys grumbled about him, he became increasingly reclusive, spending most of his time alone in his room. He saw conspiracies everywhere, and began accusing other Chi Phis of plotting against him. The other boys were quick to live up to Gamsky's expectations. They began playing frequent pranks on him, switching off the power to his room, setting his alarm clock back so he missed classes, and generally plaguing the insecure young man. "He went absolutely nuts about the pranks," a fraternity brother remembers. "He screamed and yelled. He really overreacted. He felt the others weren't taking him seriously, and that was the one thing he couldn't tolerate."

After a month or two of the hazing, Djabarri realized the situation couldn't be allowed to continue. He called Joe aside one day and told him that things just weren't working out. It would be best for all concerned if Joe moved out of the house. At first the young man seemed very upset, but when he realized he had no other option, he packed up and left.

After staying one more semester, Joe dropped out of USC. Since passing his CPA exam, he had been working for a large accounting firm in downtown Los Angeles to get in the requisite hours of experience to actually become an accountant. School no longer seemed relevant.

Chapter
5

Westwood Village is unique among the dozens of communities that make up the vast Los Angeles megalopolis. It is part college town, with UCLA taking a huge bite out of the middle of the area, and part affluent chic. Student apartment houses and fraternities sit a half-block from million-dollar homes. Village streets boast the usual college town bookstores, poster shops, and burger joints, but in Westwood such shops are scattered among designer clothing stores and fashionable restaurants. And unlike any other part of Los Angeles, Westwood is a place where people abandon their cars and walk. On weekend nights, the Village becomes almost circus-like as people from all over the city come to see first-run movies, to watch street performers, or to dine in the many chic cafés.

Dean Karny and Arben Dosti spent considerable time in Westwood during 1980. Both students at UCLA, they enjoyed passing spare hours in the nearby Village watching girls, looking at clothes, or grabbing a bite to eat. The two boys did not look much alike. Dean was nearly six feet tall and thin enough that his friends' mothers seemed to feel a need to feed him. His features were delicate, almost pretty. In another time, the blond young man might have been considered effeminate, but in the early 1980s, a certain type of androgynous look was fashionable, and Dean fit right in.

Arben, or Ben as he was called, was an entirely different type. Shorter and more compact, the dark young man had a tendency toward pudginess. His easy grin and relaxed manner softened a face better suited to a middle-aged businessman than to a college student.

But despite the differences in their appearance, the boys shared a style that made them both very attractive to women. Careful in grooming, with well-cut hair and clothes, Dean and Ben could have been picked from a crowd as belonging to the young affluent set who frequented the trendiest Los Angeles clubs and seemed at ease in any social situation.

Neither Ben nor Dean was surprised to run into Joe Gamsky on the streets of Westwood during the spring of 1980. Chance meetings occurred frequently on Village streets. But they were surprised at the change in Joe, whom both boys had known vaguely at the Harvard School. Back then, neither of the others had seen much of interest in the awkward boy. Now he seemed to have grown into his six-foot-four-inch body. Except for his self-conscious, awkward way of moving, a holdover from adolescence, Joe was an attractive young man. His nearly black hair was shorter than in his Harvard days, and he seemed to pay some attention to how he dressed, even if his sense of style wasn't up to Dean and Ben's standards. Much more interesting, Joe seemed to be doing some very ambitious things. After a brief sidewalk chat, Dean impulsively invited Joe and his brother Greg along to dinner and a movie.

Joe was certainly not the sort Ben and Dean usually befriended. He didn't have the casual ease and affluence others in their circle had. But despite his deficiencies, Joe Gamsky now seemed an impressive figure. While Dean still had a year of college to go, even at an accelerated pace made possible by high test scores, Joe had already graduated from USC, or so he said. He had been working for an accounting firm, he told them, where he had essentially served in a consulting capacity. Because of his superior ability, Joe explained, he had never had to do the auditing usually required of junior accountants. But even so, he had found life in a large corporation stifling. Now he was on his own, trading commodities.

Over dinner in an Italian restaurant, Joe told the others about how he had been the youngest person ever to pass the California CPA exam, on which he had received an exceptionally high score. He claimed to have graduated from USC in just a year and a half because of advanced-placement credits and exams he had been allowed to challenge. Joe's tone was matter-of-fact as he recounted his accomplishments. He didn't seem to be bragging, just stating facts. The other two boys were impressed. When Dean left that night, after making plans to meet Joe again, he couldn't help comparing his own life to his former schoolmate's. Joe was clearly on the way up.

In 1980, Dean Karny and Ben Dosti were typical Los Angeles rich kids. Although their families were, by L.A.'s bizarre standards, merely affluent, both boys lived in half-million-dollar homes and had been raised with every advantage. Dean's father was a prominent real-estate developer who had seen early that there was money to be made in California land. Ben's father made a good living in aerospace, but it was his mother, an influential Los Angeles *Times* food writer and critic, who had introduced Ben to life's finer things. Ben had been given his first tuxedo when he was twelve and as a college student knew many of the city's best restaurateurs and maître d's by their first names.

Although Ben's parents lived in Hancock Park, a mid-city community of huge homes and old wealth, while Dean's lived in one of the more rustic canyon developments above Hollywood, the two families had quite a lot in common. Both

Shalom Karny and Luan Dosti were first-generation Americans, and both carried a strong sense of pride from their countries of birth. Luan Dosti was born to a prominent and intellectual family in Albania. During World War II, he and his father journeyed to Italy to see about moving the family there. While they were out of Albania, the government collapsed. It was too late to go back for the rest of the clan. Shalom Karny came to the United States from Israel, where he had been a hero in the war for independence. While Ben and Dean were both all-American in outlook, they shared a respect and appreciation for their heritage.

There was something else the two boys had in common, along with hundreds of other affluent young adults in Los Angeles. As they neared college graduation, the boys felt themselves to be standing on pinnacles. Up to that point, life had been effortlessly good. They lived in grand houses with loving parents who would make any sacrifices for their sons. They had been given cars to drive and nice clothes to wear. They dined in fine restaurants and danced in popular clubs. In short, the boys lived lives that would have been envied by most of the youth in America. Yet it was all beginning to seem quite tenuous. Soon they would be out of the nest, and since their parents were merely well off instead of extremely wealthy, they would have to begin providing for themselves. It would be hard to maintain the life-styles they had always enjoyed, and there was a long way to fall. Getting to know Joe gave the two boys hope.

Dean and Ben saw Joe Gamsky frequently over the months following their chance meeting. In the mornings while the other two were in school, Joe traded commodities at a brokerage house, and by late afternoon they were all free to meet up for a movie, dinner, or the video games Joe loved. Judging by his willingness to pick up the tab at dinner, their former classmate's commodities trading was going well, and the other boys continued to be impressed by him. Within a few months, both Ben and Dean considered Joe among their closest friends.

Joe seemed to enjoy the company of both boys, although his relationship with each was different. In Ben, Joe had found a kindred spirit with regard to business. Ben had always been interested in financial matters—during high school he had invested a little in the stock market—and he enjoyed talking with Joe about his trading. Dean's interest in such things was minimal, and his relationship with Joe was much more personal. Dean had always been a follower, and his new friend was more than willing to lead. Joe in turn thrived on the warm reception he received at the Karny household and began spending increasing amounts of time there. During the summer and fall of 1980, he was sleeping over so much that Danielle Karny, Dean's mother, dubbed the spare bed in Dean's room "Joe's bed."

As the boys' friendship grew, Joe kept coming back to one theme in the long, deep conversations the three often had. He still felt a lot of resentment about his days in the accounting office, and frequently talked about that. The system stifles creative people, Joe told his friends over and over. If you're bright and have initiative, you cannot function well in a corporate hierarchy. "Say you hold a particular position in a company and you have some good ideas," Joe began one evening over dinner, "and you tell them to your direct superior. What does he do? He either tells people above him that he spawned the ideas or he tells you to just do your job and quit making suggestions. There's a real insularism in large American corporations, and petty intrigue is the coin of the realm."

Joe had some ideas for changing all that. During the months after he met up with the other boys in Westwood, he began telling them of his plan for the ideal working environment. He hoped to pull together a group of intelligent, capable, motivated people to work in a nurturing climate they would create for themselves, he explained. It would be a little like the utopian society described by Ayn Rand in one of Joe's favorite books, *Atlas Shrugged*. No one would be bound by external structures laid out by someone else. Each person would perform the functions he was most qualified to perform and most interested in. Moreover, the group would be a social club as well, its members bound in the sort of tight friendships Joe had always hoped to find.

As the months progressed, Joe's plan seemed more and more plausible. The boys knew it would be difficult to recruit others their age to a group that just had good ideas; they needed money as well. But by the fall of 1980, they had a concrete plan for setting up a group. Joe, accompanied by his father, would move to Chicago and trade commodities there. To make the real money, he explained, you had to be there, on the floor, where the trades were actually happening. He was itching to try his hand, and an old friend of his father's had offered to put up the money to lease Joe a seat on the Chicago Mercantile Exchange. Once he had made some real money, he would come back and use it to start the kind of organization they had discussed.

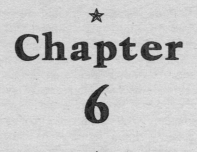

Chapter
6

Chaos reigns unchecked on the floor of the Chicago Mercantile Exchange, where Joe began trading commodities in the fall of 1980. To an outsider, the scene is indecipherable. Three to four thousand people jam the huge high-ceilinged room during working hours, all of them occupied in the arcane business of guessing whether the prices of the basic commodities we consume and currencies we spend will rise or fall. The floor of the room is pockmarked with trading pits, in which red-jacketed traders and brokers do the actual buying and selling of commodities contracts and futures. Around the pits are banks of phones staffed by gold-jacketed phone clerks and runners who take orders from their firms and then communicate them with hand signals to the traders in the pits. The traders and brokers scream to one another constantly about what they want to do, sell or buy, and what price they are looking for. The din is overwhelming. For Joe, it was love at first sight.

Starting with money raised by friends and associates of his father—Larry never dropped a good contact—Joe plunged right into the frenzied trading, quickly gaining a reputation as an up-and-comer. At first he was noticed for his youth and stature, but soon the other traders on the floor were commenting on his style as well. He seemed very confident for someone so young. And although in the intensity of the pits no one could be sure who was making money and who was losing, Joe certainly didn't seem to be hurting. He acted quickly and decisively even during the most tense moments in the pits where he most often traded treasury bills. Moreover, Joe was a real gentleman about money disputes. On one occasion, when a trader who had just become a father made a bad deal in the heat of the moment, Joe agreed to let him off the hook, absorbing the $35,000 loss the other trader would have sustained.

Joe also appeared to have a real knack for raising money. Before he ever left Los Angeles, he spent an evening with Danielle and Shalom Karny, during which they asked him to explain what he was doing. "I've worked out an entirely new system for trading commodities that is quite low-risk in comparison to other trading approaches," Joe told his friend's parents. When pressed for details, Joe told the Karnys that by carefully balancing parallel investments on a particular trade, he could limit any loss to two percent. If an overall investment lost twenty percent, he could get out entirely without further loss.

The Karnys had asked for the explanation primarily because they wanted to know what Joe actually did. They had come to care deeply for their son's friend and felt he was a good influence on Dean, who they sometimes thought had too little initiative. But after hearing Joe's explanation of his trading system, the Karnys began to wonder if they too should invest some money with the bright young man. In January of 1981, after Joe had been in Chicago for a couple of months, Dean invested four thousand dollars with his friend. Dean's parents sent Joe $150,000 to trade. Joe's pitch for money elsewhere was equally low key, but quite successful.

Larry Gamsky was proud of his son. He had always assumed that with a little guidance from his dad, Joe would go far. Now it looked as if he was really on the way. Shortly after their arrival in Chicago, the father and son moved into a nice house in the upscale Lake Forest suburb. In honor of his new life, Larry Gamsky, who had never really liked his ethnic-sounding name, decided to file for a legal change. After considering dozens of possibilities, he settled on Ryan Hunt. Joe soon decided to follow his father's lead, and in 1981 Joe Gamsky became Joe Hunt.

Despite his move to Chicago, Joe's relationship with Ben Dosti and Dean Karny remained close. Joe returned to L.A. frequently for weekends, impressing his friends with the thousands of dollars he carried in his pockets. If Joe had been generous before about picking up tabs for movies or dinner, after he moved to Chicago he became much more so. Over dinner at expensive restaurants he regaled his friends, who were both still in college, about his successes in Chicago. During the winter of 1981, Joe invited Dean and Ben and a friend of theirs, Ronald Pardovich, to go to New York City, where the four boys stayed at the posh Plaza Hotel and took in the sights.

Because Joe seemed to be doing so well, Ben and Dean approached him with a plan of their own. Was he earning enough, they wondered, to advance Dean some of the profits from his investments so that Ben and Dean could afford to move out of their parents' homes? The two boys had found an apartment they liked a lot in Beverly Hills, and Joe assured them they should snap it up. Ben had recently sold his car, so he put down the advance money to secure the apartment, and Joe assured him he would send funds to replace Ben's deposit.

By March, Joe had still not sent the apartment money. More alarming, he had grown impossible to reach by phone. For several weeks, Dean left frequent messages, but his calls were not returned. On the few occasions when Joe answered the phone himself, he always insisted he was on his way out and hung up immediately.

At the end of April, Joe finally fessed up to what was happening. He had worked his account up to about fourteen million, he told the Karnys, when he was virtually cleaned out. Joe had a ready if implausible explanation for what had happened: when a person made money on a trade, Joe told the Karnys, somebody else lost. Joe had been such a shrewd trader that he had gotten a lot of people angry. A large brokerage house had conspired to squeeze him out of a big position he was holding, and he had lost big as a result. But Joe, always optimistic, assured the Karnys that he had a little capital left and that he would soon be able to make the money back and repay them.

No records are available to show how Joe did after his initial losses, but shortly thereafter he was again displaying many of the trappings of success. Some of the other traders were now so impressed with the young man that they wondered if he was related to the Texas Hunt brothers. After several months of trading, Joe hired Leslie Eto, a young clerk for a commodities house where he had been trading, to handle his outtakes. All day every day the traders in the pits scream buy and sell orders at one another. In the intensity of the moment, tempers often flare, and at the end of the day disputes frequently rage about who exactly agreed to what. An outtake clerk settles accounts at the end of the day, negotiating exactly what is to be paid and received.

Eto, a pretty, bright young woman, was impressed by Joe. While many of the traders had hair-trigger tempers, Joe always seemed on an even keel. If a dispute arose over what had been agreed to in a trade, Joe usually gave the benefit of the doubt to the other person. The only thing Eto didn't love about working for Joe was his father, for whom Joe had gotten a gold runner's jacket so that he could have free access to the floor. Ryan Hunt, Eto felt, viewed her as a luxury, and he didn't bother to hide his feelings in front of her. He rarely spoke to the young outtake clerk and pulled Joe away out of earshot if he had something to say to him.

After hours, Joe sometimes socialized with several of the other young men on the floor, stopping in at a favorite bar of many of the traders, the Bombay Bicycle Club, or BBC, to play video games before heading home. "In retrospect, if there was anything odd about Joe," one trader who observed him recalled, "it was the way he played those video games. It was with such intensity, as if this was life or death."

While Joe's relationship with his father was good during the two years he lived in Chicago, his relationship with the rest of his family deteriorated. After their parents' divorce, Greg and Kay had tried to remain close to Joe, despite their difficulty understanding his preference for his father. But their relationship with Larry, now Ryan Hunt, continued to crumble. Soon after he moved to Chicago, the other Gamsky kids decided they no longer wanted any contact with their father.

At first, his mother, brother, and sister continued to keep in touch with Joe. When Greg read a newspaper article about dental bonding and how it could result in whitened teeth, he clipped it and sent it to his brother in Chicago. As a child, Joe had once been given an excessive dose of fluoride, which had turned his teeth brown. Greg thought his brother might be interested in correcting the problem. But soon after he sent his brotherly advice to Chicago, Greg received a note from Ryan, who had spied his older son's address on the letter to Joe. That was it, Greg had decided. If he couldn't write to his brother without his father intercepting the letter, then he simply wouldn't write. Kathy and Kay had similar feelings about Ryan, and soon after Joe and his father moved to Chicago, the rest of the family lost touch with both father and son.

* * *

As Joe grew more distant from most of his family, he continued to grow closer to his Los Angeles friends, who firmly believed Joe would make good on his losses. Each time Joe saw them, he made it clear that he had not abandoned his goal of starting a business and social group with them. It was just a matter of time, he assured them, until he had raised enough money to be able to get things going.

In December of 1981, Joe went with Dean, Ben, and a couple of other boys on a four-day skiing vacation to Mammoth Lakes in California's Sierra Nevada mountain range. Since Joe didn't ski, he spent his time at the lodge playing video games and talking to whichever of the boys wasn't on the slopes.

Dean Karny was grateful for Joe's friendly ear on the ski trip. He had recently broken up with a girl he had hoped to marry. The highly emotional young man was devastated. Every time he thought of the girl or saw her, he told Joe, he got so upset he threw up. Joe proved to be a true friend. Not only was he always available to listen to Dean's troubles; he also tried to get his friend to look at the situation differently. "He told me that because of my personality I had built up a feeling that I needed this girl's acceptance and admiration in order to feel like a complete person," Dean later recalled. "Then he explained to me all of the problems that she had, and he critically dissected her. After that, I didn't feel that I needed her anymore."

Shortly after the ski trip, Joe accompanied Dean to Florida to meet with a Canadian doctor friend of the Karnys who had, with a group of his associates, raised an additional $250,000 for Joe to trade in Chicago. Before and after their meetings with the new investor, the boys continued to discuss Dean's girl troubles. The way Joe saw it, the time had come for Dean to think not about his specific problems but about the larger picture.

"We were talking some more about my relationship with this girlfriend," Karny later recalled, "and I was still hurting over that situation, and what he did was, he got me to step back and look at the relationships between males and females from a much different and larger perspective. He explained what appeared to be scientific theories about the evolution of the species and genetic programming, and he explained some of the things that have gone on in my personal relationships from this larger perspective, so I felt that I understood them from a more human aspect, and my particular problems felt and seemed minuscule, more just part of everything else that was going on."

When Dean tried to tell Joe how much his philosophical advice had helped, Joe responded cryptically. "It's a little like turning black into white, Dean. That sounds like a paradox, but it really isn't. By reorienting your perspective, the way you did with your girlfriend, you can see almost anything in a completely different way." Joe was working on a unified theory based on these confusing principles, he told Dean. He would call it Paradox Philosophy.

The Florida and Mammoth Lakes discussions were a turning point in the relationship between Joe and Dean. Years later, Dean would see the seemingly helpful advice Joe had offered as insidious. Although he got over his disappointment about his girlfriend, he later conceded, he didn't become independent as a result of his counseling sessions with Joe. "As I look back on it now," Karny would later testify in court, "it seems pretty clear to me that the acceptance and admiration I needed was supplied by Joe after that." Joe had acquired his first blind follower.

John Troelstrup was at first inclined to write off the irate woman who called him in December of 1982 as a chronic complainer. As an attorney in the Chicago Mercantile Exchange's regulatory office, Troelstrup often received complaints from people who were annoyed they had lost money and now wanted revenge on the trader who had lost it. But as he listened to the woman's story, he realized she might really have something.

The woman represented a number of wealthy investors who had come to Joe Hunt through his father and had put up a large sum for Joe to invest. But now the investors were alarmed, because as far as they could tell, Joe maintained no records in their names. He seemed unwilling to supply any documentation of the trades he was making. She had demanded her investors' money back, but Joe had just stalled.

Finally, the woman had gotten Joe to meet her in the vault of her bank, where he promised to return her money if she in return agreed to turn over to him certain documents and a letter of complaint she had composed to the Merc. The woman arrived at the bank first and alerted the guards in the safety deposit section to be watchful. She didn't trust Joe. When he arrived, he opened a briefcase to show her the money he had brought. It was only two thousand dollars, far less than the amount they had agreed on. After a brief discussion, the woman agreed to take the cash and turn over her document. But after getting the paper, Joe tried to grab back his briefcase and run, hurting the woman in the scuffle. A bank guard called the police, and Joe was arrested for assault. Still panicked about the money, the woman had called Troelstrup.

Troelstrup was very familiar with the legal problems of the Texas Hunt brothers, and he was quite intrigued by this young man with the same last name. One thing was immediately clear: Joe was trading other people's money. By law, a floor trader like Joe was allowed to trade only his own money except in certain well-defined situations. On instinct, Troelstrup had his investigators check for a name change, and found that indeed Joe Hunt had changed his name. What's more, Joe's name change was illegal, unlike his father's legal change, as Joe hadn't been residing in Illinois long enough at the time he made the application.

Following Merc policy, the exchange's investigators called Joe in to be interviewed. They tried always to begin by assuming that a trader simply didn't understand the rules before accusing him of deliberately violating them. But after their initial conversation with Joe, Troelstrup and his staff were convinced they were dealing with a very twisted personality. "Joe seemed to feel a compulsion to sell himself to me," Troelstrup recalled of his first meeting with Joe. "He really thought and believed to the last moment that he could talk his way out of it. It was as if he needed approval so badly and had never grown out of that stage of childhood. He could be truculent, insulting, and demeaning all in the same conversation, and he could shift from one demeanor to another and not be conscious of it." During their conversations, Hunt hinted, without evidence, that his accusers had mob connections, something Troelstrup dismissed.

In the winter of 1982, when Hunt refused to formally answer the pending complaint against him, he was suspended from trading for ten days. Shortly thereafter he was formally taken before the board for disciplinary action. The day of his hearing was bitterly cold, even by Chicago standards, and the members of the committee hoped the matter could be resolved quickly. But Joe's speech went on and on. By the end, the Merc investigators were flabbergasted. Joe had spoken for several hours, using big words and rhetorical tricks. But in the end he had really said nothing.

In a quick and easy decision, the board suspended Joe from trading for ten years. They had imposed the maximum sentence on the young trader.

His friends in Los Angeles heard a highly edited version of what had happened. The way Joe told it, he had so shown up the Merc investigators that they had meted out a severe punishment only because they were furious that he had embarrassed them. "The way that he described his suspension," Dean would testify later, "was an example of how Paradox Philosophy would be used to manipulate someone's focus. Something that appeared bad—a suspension for ten years— the way he described it . . . was more of a testimonial to what a powerful personality he was that he had gotten all of these people so bent out of shape that they had thrown him off the exchange for the longest time ever. The shift of perspective on something like that—turning it from a negative thing to a positive thing . . . was the way I understood the Paradox Philosophy could be used to shift someone's perspective on any matter."

In the end, Joe's problems with the Merc didn't keep him from trading for long. He invited Ben to move to Chicago to carry out the actual buying and selling on the floor while Joe called the shots from behind the scenes. Dean's parents, who still believed in Joe despite his setbacks, put up another thirty thousand dollars for the boys to trade. Some Canadian friends of the Karnys kicked in another fifty thousand dollars. But even the new infusion of cash didn't help in the end. By fall, the boys had lost all the money and decided to move back to California. When Joe returned to Los Angeles in the winter of 1982, he had four dollars in his pocket.

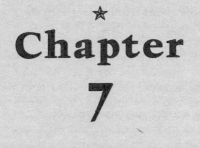

Chapter
7

Joe seemed nonchalant about his failures in Chicago. It was true he hadn't raised the money to start his group, but he had returned from Chicago with something else for the organization: a name. They would call themselves the BBC as a tribute to Joe's favorite Chicago bar, the Bombay Bicycle Club. The name was a strange choice for a teetotaler, but Joe liked the sound of the letters. They would worry later about raising money. What the club needed now, Joe said, was members.

Dean Karny and Ben Dosti had remained equally enthusiastic about starting the BBC and were glad that Joe was ready to get things rolling. For all three boys, the club concept had grown in importance. Within its structure, they hoped, they would make vast sums of money; they would gain power; they would feel purpose. Dean invited Joe to share a San Fernando Valley condominium Dean's parents had built and were letting their son live in, and he supported his friend with the money he made giving tennis lessons. In their spare time, the boys carefully planned the BBC's start-up.

During the time he was in Chicago, Joe had crystallized the tenets of his Paradox Philosophy, which he hoped would stand as the guiding principle of the BBC. Reduced to its simplest terms, the philosophy held simply that ends justified means, that anything could be justified if it benefited the person acting. But as Joe explained his thinking to Dean and Ben, it sounded much more sophisticated. They should analyze all situations, Joe said, in terms of the ultimate effect on themselves, not on others. "One of the things Joe used to say," Karny would later recall, "was that Paradox Philosophy enabled you to find a center of focus for yourself so that you could . . . become reconciled completely to what you wanted to do, and all of the impediments to your progress would be outside of yourself. In other words, you wouldn't cause yourself to fail." But the boys didn't realize then just how far Joe would carry his philosophy.

As the boys began planning a BBC recruitment drive, Joe schooled his two friends well in how to approach potential members and bring them around by using Paradox Philosophy. "It became easier to convince our parents of things," Dean recalled. "It became easier to win the affection of girls, because we were identifying the central premises of their lives, juxtaposing them, turning them around so that, just as Joe became the answer to us, we became the answer to them. Basically, Joe provided the answers to all of our difficulties and coached us in manipulating other people."

In turn, Dean and Ben attempted to teach Joe some of the social skills they felt he was still lacking. "Joe came back from Chicago wearing suits that were too small for him," Dean later said. "His hair was too long. Ben and I knew all about style and social graces, and Joe learned a lot from us." Once Joe was able to present himself to their satisfaction, the three boys went out to sign up members for their organization.

Dean and Ben proved to be excellent recruiters. Ben was smooth and affable with an ability to make friends easily. People liked Ben. And Dean was someone without enemies. While not nearly so outgoing as Ben, Dean was thoroughly inoffensive. What's more, he knew how to behave; he was an asset at any party. An excellent tennis player, Dean was the preferred tennis teacher for several of L.A.'s affluent families. Not only was he a good instructor, he was so charming about it all. When Dean and Ben began spreading news of their idea for a fraternal and investment group in the winter and early spring of 1983, many of L.A.'s socially important progeny fell into line.

Evan Dicker, the son of a prominent Los Angeles property attorney, was among the first of the BBC boys to be recruited for the organization, and he was typical in many ways of the boys who were drawn in. Evan had known from the time he was very young that he would be a lawyer one day: that's what the Dicker men did. But at twenty-one he seemed far more interested in searching out the best clubs and trying to anticipate the next fashion trend. Despite his certainty that he would one day be a lawyer, he was far from sure just how he would get there.

Tall and lanky, exceptionally stylish, Dicker was like the rake in a Forties comedy. He had a tendency to drink too much on occasion. He had a quick, often razor-sharp wit. He was very bright, but equally lazy, and he desperately wanted to belong. "Evan was wearing a big sign around his neck that said 'Mold Me,'" a friend said. "He was the sort of guy who always helped the hero get the girl, but rarely got her himself."

Evan had not really taken to Joe on the ski trip the preceding winter. In Evan's mind, there was one purpose for the trip—having fun. Joe had seemed too serious, even antisocial. But after the trip, Evan had remained close to Dean and Ben. Evan knew Ben from "Beverly," as Beverly Hills High School is known to its alumni. Ben had gone there after junior high at the Harvard School. Dean gave Evan tennis lessons; Evan helped Dean land a file clerk job with his father's law firm.

One evening after Joe returned from Chicago, Dean took him to Evan's Beverly Hills apartment. By the end of the night, Evan had a very different sense of Joe Hunt. Joe had immediately keyed in on Evan's serious side, on his keen mind and interest in intellectual thought. Sprawled out on chairs in Evan's bedroom, the boys began by discussing history and the notion of studying history to prevent repeating the same mistakes. From there, they branched out into philosophy, particularly Aristotle and Plato.

Joe then began talking to Evan about the importance of a philosophy based on reality, on actual events and needs, as opposed to a philosophy based on abstract laws and rules. It was heady stuff to a bright but lazy college student desperate to be led by someone. By the end of the discussion, Evan was very impressed. Joe seemed to have an excellent grasp of history and philosophy. He had thought about so many of the issues that Evan liked to ponder, and he had come up with answers. He was a very convincing fellow.

Dean and Joe also told Evan about the group they were forming. At first it would be a social group, for people who shared common philosophical beliefs. Later it would grow into a business venture as well. Joe would trade commodities, he told Evan. "I had a great deal of success in commodities," he claimed, "before I was railroaded off the Chicago Mercantile Exchange." Other members would pursue other businesses. Before the boys left that evening, they asked Evan if he wanted to join their group. He said yes immediately.

During the months that followed Evan's recruitment, Dean and Ben scoured their address books for other potential BBC members. The boys needed young men with style, a willingness to be led, and most important, money. At Dean's and Ben's insistence, the boys began making a point of being seen in the right places as they tried to step up recruitment. "We tried to project this image of the BBC as being a cool group of people who really had our heads screwed on straight, who were making money and having pretty girlfriends and that sort of thing," Karny recalls. It was all essential for attracting the right sort to the group.

One of the boys' favorite night spots as they began their BBC recruitment drive was a trendy Hollywood nightclub called At Sunset. Perched just above Sunset Boulevard at the east end of the Strip, the club was a favorite spot of affluent West Side youths to go and drink, dance and be seen. Joe didn't drink alcohol, because, as he once explained to a BBC member, "he didn't want to harm the temple," and he rarely danced, but nevertheless, Joe liked the nightclub. He would sit for hours at a table holding court and talking up his new group.

One night at Joe's At Sunset table, an unattached girl sat down with her two brothers to chat. Her brothers were friends of Evan Dicker, who was also at the table. But the pretty petite blonde, Brooke Roberts, was clearly more interested in Joe.

Brooke's attraction to Joe was a clear-cut sign that he had moved far beyond his high-school misfit-nerd image. Brooke came from a world very different from Joe's. The eighteen-year-old daughter of movie and record producer Bobby Roberts, she had been raised in the gated community of Bel Air, one of the city's most exclusive enclaves. Her father had built his fortune during the Sixties by managing such performers as Ann-Margret, Richard Pryor, Paul Anka, the Mamas and the Papas, and Barry Mann. In 1965 he founded Dunhill Records. From there, he had gone on to produce several movies, including *The Hot Rock*, *Death Wish*, and *Death Wish II*. Brooke attended private schools and had been given the best of everything.

Even in her own highly rarefied world, the Roberts girl stood out. Her self-confidence bordered on haughtiness. She was known to have an acid tongue with which she quickly dismissed anyone she felt didn't live up to her standards. Pretty and petite with pale naturally blond hair, she had the classic California Girl looks. And she knew what to do with them. As one friend later put it, "Brooke was a groover. She was trendy. Very, very trendy. If you're good at being trendy, you're doing things before they become fashionable. Brooke was." It was no wonder Joe was intrigued by her attentions.

One evening shortly after Brooke and Joe met, a group of people including Brooke had gathered at Evan Dicker's house to go to a movie. Joe stopped in for a few minutes, and when he left Brooke left with him. By winter, the two were inseparable, and in April of 1983, Brooke, much to her parents' dismay, went to live with Joc in the condominium he shared with Dean Karny.

The fledgling BBC had developed a high profile, which was also having a positive effect on recruitment. During the fall and winter of 1982 and 1983, the boys successfully recruited a handful of boys from among the most affluent Los Angeles families. Among their ranks they now counted Alex Gaon, the son of a prominent manufacturer of designer blue jeans. A membership list made up by Joe and Dean also included Cary Bren, whose father heads the huge Irvine Company development firm and is one of America's wealthiest men. But Bren's name on the rolls was more wishful thinking than fact. Although Joe was very interested in recruiting Cary, the boy had no real use for the BBC. His future was assured with his father's business. Much of the contact between the BBC and Bren consisted of the BBC boys making trips out to watch him race formula cars at local tracks. The group's biggest actual membership score came about by accident in the spring of 1983 at the Hard Rock Cafe.

The Hard Rock is something of a mecca for American teens. On the ground floor of the Beverly Center, Los Angeles's most sophisticated and upscale shopping mall, the Hard Rock, since the day it opened, has been a place to be seen. At almost any time of day a line of would-be customers stretches around the corner outside. But the truly hip don't have to wait. Anyone recognized by the guard at the door as being especially desirable is automatically admitted. The boys in the BBC didn't wait in line.

In the early spring of 1983, when Dean spotted his former

Harvard School classmates Dave and Tom May at the Hard Rock bar, he knew immediately they were just what the group needed. Joe was determined to attract names that would convince the world that the BBC had clout and money behind it. The May twins had the kind of name Joe was looking for

Tom and Dave May were perfect BBC recruits. Although their names suggested a perfect pedigree, in fact the twins' futures were far from certain. Over the years since their mother and adopted father had divorced, the boys' contact with David May II had tapered off. By April of 1983 when Dean Karny and Joe Hunt came around, the twins were not at all sure what they would do with their lives. Neither boy had excelled academically, although Tom had graduated from USC with a business major. The preceding year, hoping to carve out a niche for themselves, they had bought into a nightclub in the Southern California beach community of Dana Point, south of Los Angeles near Newport Beach. But the nightclub was failing, and the boys had no idea what they would do next.

Dean Karny was careful not to push too hard that first night. When Dave and Tom asked what he was doing, he simply said that he had hooked up with Joe Hunt, whom they might remember as Joe Gamsky. Hunt, he told them, had just returned from Chicago, where he had been successfully trading commodities. The boys had a hard time imagining that Joe had grown beyond the nerd they remembered from high school, but Dean assured them he had. They were starting some pretty exciting things, Dean said; perhaps the twins would like to meet with Joe and hear about them. Yes, the boys said, they would like that.

A couple of weeks later, Joe and Dean paid the May boys a visit at their Dana Point nightclub. After receiving a tour, Joe was lavish with his praise for the failing endeavor. He was impressed with what he saw, he told the boys. He then explained a little about the BBC concept. "You guys have worked hard to put together a successful club," Joe told them. "You've got exactly the kind of initiative and drive I'd like to see in the BBC." After discussing commodities trading with the boys and encouraging them to consider investing with him, Joe invited the twins to an organizing meeting of the BBC to be held soon.

If the BBC was excited about having the Mays, the Mays were equally excited about having the BBC. Like many of the other boys, the twins were eager to find prestigious work that they could step into without further experience or training. Joe Hunt's BBC seemed just the ticket. As Dave May later put it, "He was saying that young people could be in control of their destinies, and that was very appealing to me at the time. I didn't want to start at the bottom. I wanted to impress my family very much." Moreover, Dave recalls, the concept sounded very possible the way Joe presented it. "He had a fantastic, dramatic way of presenting things. He made it sound like you were idiotic not to become involved."

Chapter
8

The BBC recruitment drive had been so successful that some thirty young men showed up for the first official BBC meeting, which was held at Joe and Dean's condominium in early March of 1983. The two hosts had worked long hours preparing for the event. The boys they'd invited were sophisticated fellows, and it was important that they not think the BBC was a bubble-gum operation. By the time of the meeting they were ready. Not only did Joe have a well-planned presentation to make, they had prepared a manual of BBC operations, which would be passed out to each boy.

Joe was at his best that night. Dressed in clothes Dean had helped him shop for and drawing on the rhetorical skills he had learned in debating, Joe began slowly, explaining to the boys that the BBC might or might not be the thing for them. "We can really only use the very best," he told them. "The organization will rise or fall on the dedication and skill of its members."

The group's method of operation would be simple, Joe explained. Any member with a good idea would put it up before the group. If they all agreed the concept was sound, the BBC would supply funding and manpower. Joe was going to trade commodities, he told them. He would take investors' money and use it to make profits both for the investors and the BBC. The group was looking for people with capital, Joe said, and he encouraged them to bring in their friends and family. But equally important, they were looking for ideas, and for bright, motivated people who could implement them.

It was a stirring speech. Just to be included at such a meeting made the young men, some of whom were far from motivated, feel important. And Joe seemed so together. The members of his audience could only follow part of what he said. To those who didn't know he studied *Word Power* books, Joe's vocabulary seemed almost unbelievable.

One of the key points addressed in Joe's speech was how the BBC would offer an alternative to the traditional corporate path, which Joe felt set up impediments to bright young people. In the handbook he passed out, Joe had set out the objectives of the group, including its commitment to Paradox Philosophy, which he had explained to each of the group's new members. "The overall objective of the BBC," the manual said, "is to broaden the extent and type of choices available to its members. To this end, the BBC's ancillary objectives are:

1. To provide a social context; to create a network of individuals bound together by a common goal and an understanding of Paradox Philosophy.
2. To provide an environment and the machinery necessary to translate the ideas of its members into reality, so that the substantial barrier to enterprises of great pitch and moment is their conception, and not the acquisition of the means of implementation."

The third of the group's ancillary objectives as laid out in the manual was a clear reflection of Joe's frustration with the people who had exerted control over him in his past business enterprises. The BBC would "provide a means (effective and speedy) of redress for its members so that they may argue a point on its merits rather than be forced to bow to intrigue, rank, prejudice or insularism."

At the bottom of the handbook's first page was a quote from *Hamlet:*

> For who would bear the whips and scorns of time,
> The oppressor's wrong, the proud man's contumely,
> The pangs of despised love, the law's delay,
> The insolence of office and the spurns
> That patient merit of the unworthy takes . . .

While some of the manual seemed to outline tenets being explored by progressive companies across the nation, other parts of the book would have raised more than a few eyebrows in the business community. In describing the actual structure of the BBC, Joe had borrowed terms from science-fiction books that lent an almost eerie feeling to the manual. "The basic unit in the BBC will be the cell," Joe's pamphlet spelled out. "A cell will consist of four to nine members. If a cell shrinks, for any reason, to less than four members, it will be joined to another cell. If a cell expands to ten members, it will divide (mitosis?) into two cells of five." Each cell was to have a "nexus" through which information could be passed to others in the cell. The nexuses from four to nine cells would meet together at the "section level" headed by an "axis." The axes would get together in groups of four to nine under the leadership of a "thrax." "This structure can be expanded infinitely," the manual pointed out hopefully. "The structure as diagrammed can encompass up to 2,187 individuals, before requiring a level over that of thrax, and will suffice for now."

The BBC's businesses, according to the manual, would have their own, equally bizarre terminology. Each BBC enterprise would be called a "shape." To start a shape, a BBC member would make a proposal to the core membership. If it was approved, then anyone who wanted to become involved in a particular operation would be part of the shape. A shape would be run, in essence, by one or more "factors," selected to lead the shape by the core membership of the BBC.

By way of demonstrating just what a shape was, the manual contained a couple of reports from different shapes within the BBC. The commodities shape, for example, had as its factors Joe Hunt, Alex Gaon, and Ben Dosti. They were looking, the report said, for several "inputs" into the shape, including:

1. Money.
2. Intellectual curiosity. Room exists for people to conduct a study of applications for our spread approach to commodities other than T-bills.
3. Accounting skills. A vast number of transactions (ours) have to be tracked and accumulated.

The expected "output" of the Commodities Shape was also described: "As the output of this Shape, we plan to realize more money than we put in."

A final oddity in the BBC manual was a discussion of what Joe and Dean had decided to call "Shadings," the leaders of the BBC. The nature of a Shading was described as follows: "A Shading must understand Paradox Philosophy. Such an understanding must go beyond mere deference and entail implementation. A Shading must be the embodiment of Paradox Philosophy." The Shadings would, in addition to serving as examples and leaders for the rest of the group, sit on something called Paradox Court, the body through which differences among members were to be resolved. Paradox Court was defined in the manual as being "composed entirely of Shadings." In resolving disputes, the manual said, "the Paradox Court is exclusively interested in issues advanced in philosophy and will decide all such issues in the Paradox approach."

If any of the group's new members had questions about

such things as why Joe, Dean, and Ben were the only Shadings, or about who had appointed them, no one asked them. Instead the group seemed quite enthusiastic. The force of Joe Hunt's personality that evening seemed to have been enough to convince the assembled boys that the BBC was for them. In spite of the somewhat bizarre philosophical constructs on which the BBC was to be based, its new members couldn't wait to get going.

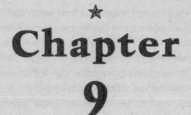

Chapter
9

Joe Hunt was antsy. A couple of the BBC members had begun letting him trade their small commodities accounts during the winter and spring of 1983, but he was itching for some bigger sums to play with. So he began urging all the BBC members to bring him people who wanted to invest. Joe himself decided to lean on Dave and Tom May in hopes of getting them to put up some cash.

Joe's timing was fortuitous. The twins had recently inherited about $100,000 each from a May uncle, and they hoped to prove themselves with the money. Joe approached the boys individually about investing, promising them returns of at least thirty percent per year. Joe would make an equal amount as his commission. Moreover, he told them, the investments would be virtually risk-free. It was a pitch similar to the one he had given the Karnys and their friends. But those previous investors weren't around to dispute Joe's assessment of the risks.

Tom May didn't like the idea of putting money into something he didn't really understand, so he asked Joe for an explanation of just what was involved in trading commodities. Over lunch in a Westwood Village café, Joe explained the strategies involved in a soft, patient voice, but in what would become a pattern in Joe's dealings with Tom, he phrased his answers so they were deliberately above the other boy's head. When Tom asked for clarification, Joe again gave complicated answers, until Tom, who greatly feared appearing stupid, quit asking.

After a couple of meetings, Tom was convinced of three things: that he could make substantial profits on his money, that his investment would be risk-free, and that Joe Hunt was a genius. But it was Dave May who put money in first.

At the end of May, Dave put in ten thousand dollars. A month later, Joe gave him back a check for five thousand, saying the money represented profit on his account. Dave responded by investing an additional seventy thousand. Tom, wanting in on the action, kicked in eighty thousand dollars of his own. But if part of the twins' hope was to impress their adoptive father, they would have to wait. After putting in their own cash, the boys approached David May II about investing with Joe. In a brief letter to the boys he declined, saying Joe sounded like a fraud. The boys couldn't wait for the day they could triumphantly return to their father with news of the profits they so confidently anticipated.

Nets spread by the other BBC members were also beginning to yield catches during the late spring of 1983. In early May, Joe met with Steve Weiss, the father of a BBC member's friend, about investing in commodities. Weiss was a Hollywood videotape editor who, in the spirit of California-style self-fulfillment, was making a transition to becoming a psychotherapist. Despite his graying hair and age-sharpened features, Weiss was young in spirit and outlook. He was interested in his daughter and her friends and was pleased to hear about young people who were doing well. When his daughter urged him to consider investing with Joe Hunt, he was receptive. Over the course of his lifetime, Weiss, then fifty-eight, had saved up a small nest egg. Cautious by nature, he had never invested in anything so exotic-sounding as commodities, but he told his daughter he would be happy to talk to Joe about making his savings grow.

Weiss found his initial meeting with Joe strange. At Joe's insistence, they met on the sidewalk outside the Beverly Hills commodities firm of Cantor Fitzgerald, one of the brokerage houses where Joe traded. Joe seemed rushed, but very professional. Weiss explained that he had a little discretionary money, around five thousand dollars, that he would be interested in investing in hopes of turning it into enough for a vacation the next year. Joe told Weiss that would be no problem, but that they should meet again.

A few weeks later, Weiss returned to Cantor Fitzgerald. This time, Joe met with him in the vestibule. Again the meeting was brief. "Just what are you investing in?" the older man asked. "The money is invested in commodities," Joe said, keeping his answer simple. "Specifically, I'm investing in government instruments." He had a system that guaranteed success, he assured Weiss, but his methods were absolutely secret. Weiss would have to take Joe's word. If he invested, he could expect approximately an eighteen-percent return on his investment. The tall attractive young man was very impressive, Weiss thought. He spoke directly and well. He never pressured his potential investor. He seemed anything but a fly-by-night wheeler-dealer. At the end of the second meeting, in a move that would soon have a profound impact on the BBC, Weiss gave Joe a check for five thousand dollars.

Less than two weeks after receiving the investments from the Mays and Steve Weiss, Joe claimed he had made significant profits in the commodities market, which would enable the BBC to rent offices. There would be no more investor meetings on sidewalks. Joe had learned well by this time the importance of appearances. "He was using any name, any innuendo that he could, to convince the world that the BBC had power, big clout, big money behind it, and everyone else did everything they could to back him up on this," Karny later said. "Everything wound up being used as some sort of prop for the image that he was trying to project." The right headquarters, Joe realized, would be the most effective prop of all.

The office suite the boys selected was on Third Street in a good section of Los Angeles, adjacent to Beverly Hills. When Joe realized he probably didn't have the credit on his own to secure the lease, he trotted out one of his best props, Tom May, whose name helped convince the landlord to lease to the young men. The suite, with several offices, a conference room, and secretarial and storage areas, was far more space than the boys needed, but Joe wanted something impressive. In addition, he expected the organization to grow rapidly, so why not plan ahead. Dean selected tasteful Scandinavian-style furniture for the offices. In the conference room, a complete audiovisual system was installed. On the wall Joe hung what was perhaps the most striking symbol of his ambition, an eight-foot-by-twelve-foot map of the world.

During the spring, Joe sent out statements to his investors announcing his profit for the previous quarter. Steve Weiss was sent a check for four thousand dollars, which Joe said represented the one-month profit on Weiss's five-thousand dollar investment. It is unclear from existing records whether Joe had really made any profit at all during the period, but one thing was certain: doling out checks and telling investors they represented profit was a wonderful way of generating more investments.

By the end of June, Steve Weiss had invested another fifteen thousand dollars. And, much more significantly for the BBC's future, he had begun talking up Joe's skills to his friends and family. "I would get together with my relatives and some of my close friends to tell them about Joe," Weiss later testified in court. "I like to share good fortune with people who are near and dear to me." During the rest of the summer, more than thirty investors brought in by Weiss handed over money to Joe, most of them investing small amounts at first and later, after receiving statements showing huge profits, investing sums of up to $200,000.

As Joe's skills in attracting investors grew, so did his ability to manipulate people. As he had with the BBC members, Joe tried to gauge the motivations of each investor and play on them. Since Steve Weiss was bringing in most of the BBC's biggest investors, he was a key figure for Joe to keep happy. After picking up that Weiss was actively concerned about social and humanitarian issues, and that he believed strongly in charity, Joe engaged the older man in a discussion of what they could do for others with the money they were generating. Joe suggested that perhaps they could set up a fund with some of their profits to benefit people in need. He made no firm promises, saying that the fund would only receive monies when Joe felt profits were high enough to justify them. But at the end of their discussion, Weiss was deeply impressed with the young businessman's principles. It was the sort of thing that justified his faith in the younger generation. Who said kids today were completely materialistic?

The BBC boys seemed to thrive on their new roles as businessmen. Each morning, Ben and Joe got to the office early to study the commodities quotation machines that had been installed there. The others wandered in later in the day, and although there was little work going on, they seemed to enjoy the sense of purpose provided by having an office to go to. As BBC secretary Joanne Meltzer put it, "They were like little boys who'd dressed up in Daddy's business suit and gone to Daddy's office to play businessman." And although they were all, in chronological terms, old enough to be called men, the BBC members were happy to continue to think of themselves as boys. A few years later, when Dean Karny was questioned on the witness stand about why he referred to himself and the others as boys, he looked surprised. "We certainly didn't think of ourselves as men," he said.

The boys were ostensibly looking into new business opportunities, and in fact, despite late arrivals, long lunches, and early departures, some of them actually did put together plans. Steve Taglianetti, Joe's Harvard School classmate whom the Mays brought into the BBC, became the driving force behind a company called Westcars of North America. The business was set up to import "gray market" cars—luxury automobiles from Europe that were to be upgraded to meet American emissions standards and then sold at a profit.

The boys had such high hopes that their business endeavors would pay off that Tom May and several of the other boys decided in jest that they should change what the initials BBC stood for. Instead of Bombay Bicycle Club, they joked, the letters BBC could stand for Billionaire Boys Club. The name was never officially adopted, but they often chuckled over it.

Although Joe hadn't seen his mother or siblings in more than a year, he continued to remain loyal to his father. When Ryan Hunt came to him with plans for a marketing company called Fire Safety, which would distribute fire retardant chemicals, Joe was receptive. Soon Joe's father was working on his project under the umbrella of the BBC.

In addition to his "commodities shape," Joe also began working on a deal for which he had high hopes. Joe had heard about a man named Gene Browning, an Orange County biochemist who had developed a huge grinding machine he called a Cyclotron, which could be used to crush rocks for mining purposes. Browning had spent years developing the attrition mill and invested hundreds of thousands of dollars of his own. Now, somewhat discouraged and out of money, he was looking for working capital to perfect his Cyclotron. After hearing about the technology, Joe wanted to negotiate a deal. The BBC would provide financing in exchange for a substantial share in the company.

Joe's initial meeting with Browning at his home in Orange County went very well. The middle-aged man was impressed enough to invite the boys out to the desert location where he had built a prototype of his machine. Joe told his followers that he was not about to blow the opportunity. They needed to show Browning their mettle; he had to believe they could deliver the kind of financial support he needed. Joe wanted a group of BBC members to accompany him to the site, and he wanted them to look good. They were to drive the best cars they could come up with, Joe said, and if that meant borrowing their parents' cars, then that's what they would do.

On the morning of the trip out to Browning's, the boys, all wearing business suits, gathered at a coffee shop in the San Fernando Valley. Over breakfast, Joe lectured the boys. "Act professional," he told them. "We want to demonstrate to Dr. Browning that we are not just a bunch of kids, that we are serious, responsible businessmen." After delivering his lecture, Joe paid the check, and they went out to the parking lot, where an impressive collection of cars had been assembled. Alex Gaon had brought his father's Rolls-Royce. Evan Dicker drove his Porsche. The convoy also included a BMW and another Porsche. The boys piled into the cars and began their two-hour drive to the desert.

If Joe Hunt was convinced he could benefit from Gene Browning, the older man was equally hopeful that Joe would be the solution to his problems. The caravan of imported luxury cars made quite an impression on the scientist as it pulled into his site near Hesperia, California. He intended to proceed cautiously, but it really looked as if this group was prosperous. Maybe at last he would get the kind of financing he needed for his invention. The boys seemed interested in his machine and interested in doing business, and by the end of their visit Browning was getting very excited. Some of the boys seemed young and silly, but Hunt was impressive.

Browning knew he should be cautious. In the fifteen years

since he had begun developing his attrition mill, Browning had, he felt, been ripped off several times by fly-by-night investors who made big promises but only left him deeper in debt. Joe Hunt seemed different. The group might be young, but with the family money these boys clearly had and the guiding hand of Hunt, perhaps an alliance with the BBC would at last mean the realization of Browning's dreams.

Shortly after the first meeting, Gene Browning signed an agreement with the BBC. The group was to have full rights to developing and marketing the machine. Browning for his part would draw an adequate salary, and he would be given a house, a BMW, and a percentage of the profits. As soon as the contract was signed, Browning was handed the keys to one of Westcars' dark gray BMWs. As he headed home, he was deeply satisfied.

Chapter
10

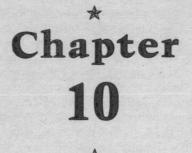

Despite his quick success at raising money, Joe was not content. In Chicago he had gotten used to playing with large sums, and he liked that. Investments of five or ten thousand dollars were fine, but Joe, in his understated, softspoken way, was looking for the big kill. He continued to urge the BBC's members to bring in investors and frequently asked if anyone had names of people he should approach. At one early meeting, Joe's request was answered.

"I know a guy with a lot of money," volunteered a South African boy who briefly belonged to the BBC during its early days. "You'd really have to watch out for him, though," he continued tentatively. "He has a reputation for being a con artist." Joe wasn't daunted by the warning, and pressed for details. The man's name was Ron Levin, and he was a forty-year-old homosexual who liked to take young men under his wing. Joe was intrigued.

Ron Levin and Joe Hunt were in many ways very much

alike. Both were keenly intelligent, and both had trouble operating in many types of traditional institutions. Neither felt he had to play by the rules and each put himself above all others. But however alike the two men were in the spring of 1983, they had developed their personalities by very different routes.

Ron Levin was born in Cleveland, Ohio, to Carol and Roy Glick, on February 16, 1942. A year and a half after Ron was born, his father joined the service and was eventually sent to fight in the European theater of the war. Very soon after arriving in France, Glick was killed, leaving his widow and small child to fend for themselves. Shortly after her husband's death, Carol Glick moved with her mother and son to California.

By the time Ronnie started school at the age of six, he had clear-cut problems. Despite the sharp intelligence his devoted mother noticed, Ronnie wasn't cut out for school. He was seriously hyperactive and couldn't function in a structured setting. Between the ages of six and nine, the boy attended half a dozen different schools and was asked to leave each one because of behavior problems. "He would sharpen his pencil six or seven times, and he just couldn't contain himself," Levin's mother recalls. "He was constantly moving."

In 1951, when Ronnie was nine, his mother married Martin Levin, a decent, hardworking garment retailer who adopted Carol's young son and raised him as his own. That same year, the Levins decided that their son's academic problems needed serious attention. At nine Ronnie could barely read, and so the Levins enrolled him in a remedial program at UCLA. Soon the boy had not only learned to read but had become an insatiable bookworm.

But becoming literate didn't solve Ronnie's problems with school. His hyperactivity didn't recede, even when he hit adolescence, and he eventually dropped out of high school. A couple of stabs at junior college yielded no better results, and by the time Ron reached his twenties, the young man had given up on formal education, although he continued throughout his life to study voraciously subjects that interested him. "He utilized something like an immersion technique," Levin's friend Mark Geller would later recall. "It might last only for a month or two months or three months, but he would read every book on the subject. He would find every consultant that he could find. He would immerse himself in [the subject], so that he knew it extremely well, and then he would go on to something else."

With a fierce loyalty forged by her constant battles for her troubled son, Carol Levin refused to give up on Ronnie. With the full support of her doting husband, who by this time had become quite successful in the clothing business, Carol Levin provided her son with money for rent and food. She continued to lavish love on him, calling several times a week and turning a blind eye to her son's considerable idiosyncrasies. All that Carol Levin knew was that she loved Ronnie and he loved her. Year after year, she photographed the floral arrangements he gave her on special occasions and tucked the snapshots carefully away with the cards he sent along with them. Even as the two much younger sons she had with Martin Levin grew up and became independent, Carol Levin didn't judge Ronnie harshly. For his part he protected his mother from knowing about many aspects of his life, telling her only about his successes.

From the time Ronnie became an adult, his overwhelming ambition was to become a real part of Beverly Hills. Having been raised on the outskirts of the wealthy enclave, Levin had seen from an early age the power and status that being part of the Beverly Hills elite afforded. By the time he was ready to enter adulthood, Levin, like Joe Hunt, was determined to quit pressing his nose up against the window. He wanted in.

With little formal education and no patience, Levin, now a hyperactive adult, was ill-equipped to gain entry to Beverly Hills in a conventional fashion. And so he joined the dozens of hucksters and con men who prefer to pluck their pigeons where the prey is fat. During his twenties and early thirties, Levin founded dozens of companies. He opened advertising agencies, a legal research organization, a firm that sold silver paperweights, import-export firms, a record company, and a business that marketed a "Super Sex Catalog" which sold mail order for two dollars and claimed to be "the most complete illustrated catalogue of sexual devices and products in the world."

"Ron always had a million ideas," a friend from the period recalls. "When he first came up with an idea for a new business, I think he wasn't setting out to rip people off. He intended to run the company well and make a lot of money. But then, well, I think he realized that he could make a lot more money if he didn't worry too much about those promises he'd made." A trail of lawsuits left in the wake of these enterprises would indicate that, whatever his intentions, Levin was not big on follow-through. Generally, the lawsuits involved things Levin had ordered and received but never paid for, or things Levin had been paid to do but had never done.

In March of 1975, Levin, who was then starting an international trading firm, sent out through Western Union 838 telegrams to businesses in Yemen and Qatar. "We represent hundreds of American companies who desire to sell their products throughout the Middle East," the message read. "We note that you have needs for certain products. Please advise us how to receive orders for these items so that we may bid to supply them." The telegrams then contained a list of types of products the firm supposedly handled, including aircraft and airport equipment, food products, automotive equipment, computer hardware and software, and jewelry. None of Levin's friends recalls the company ever getting off the ground, but Western Union later sued for thirty thousand dollars, which was owed for the telegrams, and by a jewelry company that provided Levin's company with nearly twenty thousand dollar's worth of jewelry.

Legitimate or not, by the late Seventies, Ron Levin's scams had brought in enough money to enable him to move into a large old duplex on a shady Beverly Hills street around the corner from Saks Fifth Avenue. For the first time in his life, his parents weren't paying the rent, and for the first time he was a part of the society he craved.

Levin's newfound status convinced him that no one cared what rules he played by. In a town that cherishes eccentricities, and in which half the shoppers on Rodeo Drive are living on credit, Levin's increasingly oddball manners were not only tolerated but encouraged. His charming side made him a popular guest at the most important parties. Now when he called his mother he could brag about his friendships with Muhammad Ali, Bianca Jagger, and Andy Warhol.

Far from trying to hide his crooked side from his new friends, Levin boasted openly about his dishonest schemes. He was fond of telling people that if he had to give back everything he had "scammed up," he would have no furniture, no clothing, and no money. On the wall of his home office, next to an autographed poster of Muhammad Ali, Levin proudly displayed a picture somebody had given him of the Pope addressing a large crowd. The caption on the picture read: "Ron Levin addressing his creditors." Tere Tereba, a fashion designer who met Levin at a 1971 dinner hosted by Andy Warhol, recalls her first meeting with him. "I remember vividly having a discussion with him. I asked him what he did. He told me he was a thief."

Occasionally, Levin's scamming got him into trouble, but he never seemed too worried. Tereba remembers standing with Levin and film director Paul Morrisey one day in front of Nate 'N' Al's, a popular Beverly Hills delicatessen. An angry man approached Levin and began screaming, "You owe me money, Ronnie, and if I don't get it, you're dead!" But as Tereba and Morrisey watched in horror, Levin reacted coolly. After shoving the man away, he hustled his friends into his car and drove off quickly, highly amused by the scene.

Dean Factor, the college-age son of one of Levin's friends and a big admirer of the older man, recalls once entering Cartier in Beverly Hills with Levin. "The man behind the counter said, 'Aren't you Ron Levin? You owe me money.' Ron said, 'No, I'm George Levin, Ron's brother, and good luck collecting. He owes me money too.' " During the late Seventies, Levin served a several-month jail term after he was convicted of theft for one of his frauds. But the experience didn't seem to faze him, and he later regaled his friends with stories about life in jail.

Despite his obvious eccentricities, Levin developed dozens of seemingly close friends. He was generous—some say to a fault—loyal, and lots of fun. Standing six foot one and sporting a grand head of prematurely silver hair and an impeccable beard, he cut a striking figure. Frequently, on weeks when he wasn't dieting to maintain his slim figure, Levin would go to restaurants and order several complete meals brought to his table which he ate with gusto. He loved to entertain, and would often rent a room at the Beverly Hills Hotel in order to get a cabana by the hotel pool, which is widely acknowledged as one of the best places to be seen on the West Side.

But if Levin could be fun, he could also be volatile. Rarely attempting to curb his irrational temper, he would often bark nastily at waiters, shopkeepers, and friends. "When I went to Ron's house," a friend recalls, "I was always shocked at how much time he spent on the phone screaming at people."

Although Ron eventually became happy with where he had arrived, he was nevertheless always somewhat ashamed of his roots. His parents, while thoroughly respectable, were not glamorous. Not content to be the son of a middle-class clothes dealer, even a successful one, Levin invented various stories about his origins, including one that had him actually a Rothschild and the heir to various fortunes. On occasion, he used the name Ron Rothschild.

Like Joe Hunt, Levin also relied on props to impress people, spending thousands of dollars a month on clothes, always leasing the right cars, and maintaining a daily housekeeper, who stayed on with Levin even after he stung her for nearly twenty-five thousand dollars in a Rolls-Royce deal that went awry. Embarrassed about his lack of education, Levin sometimes claimed to have graduated from Harvard University or to have gotten a law degree. He frequently talked about going to medical school, and in fact maintained comprehensive legal and medical libraries in his house.

In his tales, his mother took on almost mythic proportions as a grand and beautiful woman who delighted in bestowing her wealth on those less fortunate. Each year, he told people, she gave large sums for scholarships to medical school.

Levin's friends seldom pointed out the obvious contradictions in the various stories he told. In the Beverly Hills circles in which Levin was now running, interesting fictional origins were considered far superior to boring factual ones. People chose to believe Levin because it was fun to believe him.

Despite his opulent life and glamorous friends, Levin was a very lonely man. "He needed people around him constantly," recalls a close friend. "He pretended he was happy, but in fact he was desperately lonely." Frequently, Levin employed handsome young men to run errands, hang around the house, and do odd jobs for him. Although Levin was certainly more inclined to homosexuality than to heterosexuality, some of his closest friends thought he was actually somewhat asexual. Most of the young men he loved having around were not themselves gay, and he rarely approached them sexually. As with other parts of his life, the show seemed to be enough. As one acquaintance put it, "Ron Levin was the kind of guy who, given the choice, would rather that you see him with a bunch of young men and *not* have them sexually than to actually have them without you knowing about it." Some of the boys Ronnie gathered around him were the sons of his friends. He acted like their indulgent uncle, slipping them money, buying lavish gifts, and footing the bill for pleasure trips he took with them to Palm Springs or New York.

Over the years, several of Levin's businesses actually did quite well. During the late Seventies, he established a legal research firm that employed law students and lawyers, including a couple who were practicing with suspended licenses, to answer legal questions for lawyers and lay people. With offices on Wilshire Boulevard in Beverly Hills, the company caught on quickly and actually generated a fair amount of money for a time. But as with most of his pursuits, Levin soon lost interest in the operation, and lawsuits began piling up against the company as clients alleged that suits had been handled poorly, if at all, and that Levin had been posing as a lawyer.

During his time in the legal research business, Levin had become an avid lawsuit enthusiast. Often representing himself, he pursued legal actions against a variety of individuals and companies with gusto. In one case, Levin sued a cleaning company for eleven million dollars, claiming that when the company had cleaned his office, workers had thrown away things essential to his business. On several occasions he sued insurance companies for their failure to pay him for losses he claimed to have sustained. He once sued an apartment owner for damages after he "tripped and fell violently" when an elevator stopped two inches below floor level.

Perhaps Levin's most successful business venture was in the arena every Southern California con man eventually enters—the media. Levin had long been interested in media, having run a couple of advertising agencies during the early Seventies. But it wasn't until 1981 that he got an idea for entering the business in a way that would make him some money. Levin had heard that local television news crews didn't cover events that happened late at night, and he thought there might be a market in providing videotape of late-night events.

In his usual fashion, Levin found a way to get equipment without paying for it. He approached the Panasonic Company and the RCA Corporation with requests to borrow state-of-the-art video recording equipment worth more than $130,000, telling them the cameras would be used as props for a TV pilot called "The Reporters" about a group of television reporters who gathered late-night footage. After somehow persuading people at both companies to lend him what he needed, Levin began using it for his new company, Network News, and continued using it until the two companies filed suit months later to get their equipment back.

For a while, Levin thrived on the excitement of running Network News. He successfully sued the Los Angeles Police Department to get press credentials, and he spent his nights sitting in the downtown police station press office monitoring emergency radio calls. If a fire broke out or a big accident occurred, he dispatched a crew to catch the action with the recording equipment he had "borrowed." Levin's Peck Drive duplex was often filled during this period with young film students and would-be journalists willing to shoot footage and edit it together for low wages. Levin had big plans for the operation and hoped eventually to sell investigative news stories to the big network shows.

When Joe Hunt met Ron Levin in May of 1983, Network News was going strong. Levin had a lot of cash and gave every appearance of being highly successful. But what impressed Joe Hunt most was that Levin was proud about having made his money outside the system. Here was a man cast in Joe's own mold.

Chapter
11

Joe Hunt went alone to his first meeting with Ron Levin. From the moment the BBC member had issued his warning about Levin, Joe had been looking forward to the challenge of matching wits with an accomplished con man. But he was less certain about the other BBC members. "Originally, Joe wanted to keep his relationship with Ron Levin private," Dean Karny later recalled, "because he didn't know how some of us less sophisticated boys would be when we were in conversation with a guy as slick as Ron Levin." But Joe soon realized that his attractive young followers might be his trump card in dealing with Levin.

Very soon, Hunt introduced Levin to Dean Karny, and later, trotting out his favorite symbols of BBC prosperity, to the May twins. Levin seemed to love having the BBC boys around, perhaps seeing in the smooth faces of the boys much that he used to possess but was now losing: looks, youth, ambition. He would hold court, generally not bothering to change from his bathrobe, which he liked to wear all day. Several of the BBC boys seemed to enjoy the scene at Levin's, too, and began dropping by frequently to chat or to borrow items from his many closets of exquisite clothes.

The most electric attraction, however, was between Ron Levin and Joe himself. Each recognized instantly how very like the other he was, and each vied to prove himself superior. From the beginning, there was a wariness between the two. "Joe always looked at Ron as a potential target, and I believe that Ron looked at Joe as a sort of plaything," Karny said. Never entirely at ease around each other, the two men argued constantly, always taking contrary positions and then running to books to verify their points. Joe worked hard to convince Ron of his superiority, but the older man refused to be impressed. When Joe got an investor to put up $150,000 in option money for Browning's grinding machine, he bragged to Ron about his business competence. But far from being impressed, Levin laughed. "You've got to give me the name of this guy. If you could convince him to put money into that thing, I could sell him the Brooklyn Bridge."

After a month or so of trying to get Levin to invest with the BBC, Joe began to get frustrated. The older man seemed to be stringing him along. He never said he wouldn't invest in commodities with the BBC, but he also didn't come through with any cash. Joe was certain Ron had money, and he probably wanted to increase what he had. Joe concluded that Levin did not take him seriously as a businessman.

Finally, at the end of June, Levin seemed to yield to Joe's pressure. He would, he told Hunt, put up five million dollars for Hunt to trade in the commodities market. They would split the profits evenly. The investment was far larger than Joe had even dared hope for. He was ecstatic.

Chapter
12

Joe Hunt was as busy as he had ever been during the summer of 1983. With Ron Levin's money now added to the Mays', Hunt was playing with very large sums in the market, and he loved it. In addition, Steve Weiss was now steadily bringing in other investors, and it looked as if there would continue to be assets to invest.

Joe thrived on the intensity of high-stakes trading, which he hadn't experienced since leaving Chicago. He spent long hours at the Beverly Hills offices of Cantor Fitzgerald, the trading firm at which he had invested the Mays' money, and spoke often to the broker at Clayton Brokerage, where Ron Levin had insisted his funds be invested.

During the early part of the summer, things didn't go as well with the Levin account as Joe had hoped. From a beginning balance of more than five million dollars, the account plummeted to under one million by the end of July. But at

Clayton Brokerage, Joe was dealing with a broker named Jack Friedman, whom he found to be very helpful.

Friedman was typical of the sort attracted to commodities trading. Brash and irreverent with a sharp sense of humor, the plump young broker was something of a maverick. When he had something to say, he said it, regardless of whom he might offend. After watching Joe's trading decisions for a short time, Friedman was unimpressed.

Joe had no real concept of how to manage an account, Friedman felt. Frequently, the young investor put too much of his capital into one commodity. Even more potentially dangerous, his account was tremendously overmargined. In the commodities market, traders can purchase options on huge numbers of shares with very little money down. If the commodity price goes up, the trader reaps the profit on all the shares. But if the price goes down, a "margin call" is issued, and the purchaser must make good on the difference between the old price and the new for all the shares. The way Friedman saw it, Joe was overleveraged. One big margin call would have broken him. The broker didn't try to save Joe's feelings. He told him exactly what the problems were, and Joe listened. By early August, following Friedman's advice, Joe had turned the Levin account around, and it began rising rapidly.

With the Mays' account and accounts he was trading for Dean Karny and Alex Gaon at Cantor Fitzgerald, Joe didn't have the benefit of his new mentor's expertise, but he had plenty of self-confidence. In early August, when he felt the market was in a great place, Joe made bigger purchases than he ever had before, acquiring a number of positions in the accounts for Treasury bills and Ginnie Mae mortgages. But shortly thereafter, during a market reversal on the positions, Cantor Fitzgerald got nervous.

After the market closed one afternoon during the second week of August, a Cantor Fitzgerald employee approached Joe as he was preparing to leave and warned him that he would have to come up with an additional one and a half million dollars for a margin account to cover what was beginning to look like a potential disaster. Otherwise Cantor Fitzgerald would liquidate the positions immediately to prevent further loss. After Joe failed to come up with the additional cash, the contracts held in the names of Dean Karny and Tom May were sold. Not only was there no money left in the accounts, but Cantor Fitzgerald was demanding nearly half a million dollars it said the accounts had lost.

August 9 was, in Dave May's words, "a black-letter day." That morning, Tom got a call at the office from a Cantor Fitzgerald employee who informed him there were serious problems with his account. When the twins demanded an explanation, Joe called them into his large office and asked them to be seated in chairs facing the desk. "I've got some good news and some bad news," he told them, looking unruffled and speaking in even tones. "The bad news is I've lost all your money. The good news is that if you just hang in, I'll pay you back three hundred thousand dollars."

The losses weren't Joe's fault, he explained calmly to the twins. It was a ridiculous policy of Cantor Fitzgerald's that had caused the problems. Joe then gave the brothers a pep talk about how the BBC was a golden opportunity and they shouldn't blow it. Besides, Joe reminded them, they had nothing left to lose. After some long pauses, the brothers agreed to ride things out with the organization. For two boys playing at being businessmen, the dose of reality was unpleasant. As Tom later said, "We sort of figured that if we kept quiet, the dust would just get kind of brushed under the carpet, and we wouldn't have to deal with the loss. I wouldn't have to go back to my dad and say, 'Dad, I know you have a bet with your accountants that we'd blow our inheritance in a year, but it only took us two months.' "

Despite his decision to continue with the BBC, it was nevertheless a nasty shock for Tom May when he got a call from a businesslike Cantor Fitzgerald lawyer a few days later asking him how he was going to make good on his debt. "What debt?" Tom asked. The lawyer then informed him that he had authorized Joe Hunt to make trades and that part of that authorization, they maintained, obligated him to cover the margin calls. They wanted more than $200,000 from the stunned young man. But again, Tom decided to cast his fortunes with Joe Hunt. He saw no alternative.

Shortly after the losses, Joe took Dave and Tom aside. Worried that they had good reason to feel disillusioned with the BBC, Joe felt he needed to do something quickly to assure their continued loyalty. "I was very impressed with your reaction to the bad news about your accounts," he told them. "I felt you displayed a maturity unusual in people your age. I definitely think you are both Shading material." The twins were flattered. But as the weeks passed, nothing more was ever said about the proposition, and Dean, Ben, and Joe remained the only Shadings in the BBC.

Not everybody in the BBC was fully aware of what had happened at Cantor Fitzgerald. Most of the boys knew that Alex Gaon was drifting away from the group, and that Tom and Dave had lost some money, but they were still willing to believe in Joe. And very soon Joe proved himself worthy of their confidence.

With Jack Friedman advising him, Joe seemed to have developed the magic touch of which every commodities trader dreams; each decision he made with Ron Levin's investments resulted in profits. The continuing problems at Cantor Fitzgerald seemed almost irrelevant as the Levin account swelled. On August 17, when Ron ordered that all positions be liquidated, the account balance was $13,997,448.86. In just over two weeks, from the account's low point of about one million dollars, Joe had made thirteen million dollars. Under the terms of his agreement with Levin, Joe was to receive half of all profits, or more than four million dollars.

After receiving the final statements on the Levin account, Joe called a meeting of the BBC's inner circle. "Despite our losses in certain other areas," Joe began when they had assembled around the table in the BBC conference room, "I have made substantial amounts of money trading commodities for Ron Levin."

The boys were at first a little skeptical. Most of them admired Joe greatly, but they had heard this before. Despite his measured tones and understated manner, Joe was often overly optimistic about the BBC's financial position. But this time he had proof. To punctuate his words, Joe passed around statements from Clayton Brokerage for the others to examine. The figures seemed indisputable. "Some of the money will provide working capital for other BBC operations," Joe continued, "and some of it will go to those of you who have really given your all to the organization." Dave and Tom, who were still feeling the sting of their losses, were to get $300,000 apiece. The others were to get lesser but not insubstantial sums.

On the strength of the profits he was expecting from Levin, Joe decided the time had come to move from the condominium owned by Karny's parents. There still weren't funds for the kind of BBC living quarters Joe envisioned, in which all the BBC members would live in the same vast compound. But Joe felt the group now had enough to begin moving in that direction. As a first step, the boys rented a spacious three-bedroom condominium in a Wilshire Boulevard luxury high-rise between Westwood Village and Beverly Hills. Joe, Dean, Ben, Brooke, and another BBC member moved into apartment 1505 at the Wilshire Manning. From his new bedroom, Joe had a commanding view of the city of Los Angeles.

Chapter
13

Joe Hunt was deeply contented during the fall of 1983. He had never before in his life had the kind of security he now enjoyed. He had close friends, a devoted girlfriend, and as soon as Levin paid him he would have more money than he could have hoped for.

On the business side things were thriving as well. With Gene Browning the BBC was making plans to rent warehouse space and begin constructing the first Cyclotron. Dean Karny was preparing for a trip to Europe to purchase automobiles for Westcars. Many of the boys had agreed to hand over the pink slips of their own cars in order to make Westcars look like it already had substantial assets, so, on paper at least, that company was off and running. Joe was optimistic that real success for it would soon follow.

Early that fall, the BBC also initiated its first takeover attempt. Joe Hunt had been told about an Orange County company called Cogenco, whose president, Bruce Swartout, claimed to hold the patent on a device for converting thermal energy from smokestacks into electricity. The man was looking for capital to market the device.

From the moment he heard about Cogenco, Joe coveted the company. With Microgenesis and Cogenco, the BBC could really become powerful in the energy field. After complicated negotiations, during which Joe again trotted out all the props that had so impressed Gene Browning, a deal was struck. Joe would give Swartout all outstanding shares in a BBC company called Cyclotronics of North America, which Swartout believed held the rights to Browning's attrition mill. In exchange, the BBC would receive a substantial share of Cogenco. What Joe neglected to tell Swartout was that rights to the milling machine were actually held by a different company, Microgenesis of North America. The stock the BBC was putting up was virtually worthless.

If Joe was unhappy that fall with any aspect of the BBC's business, it was his own "Commodities Shape." He had thrived on the excitement of playing with the huge sums he had traded during the summer, and he missed having that kind of money. Steve Weiss's investors were providing a steady flow of capital, but Joe was looking for another big investor. In early October, he heard about Steve Lopez.

The closely packed tables at the Bistro Gardens restaurant in Beverly Hills are generally filled with people trying to impress one another, and at nine o'clock one evening in early October, Joe Hunt and Ben Dosti were among them. The boys had gone to the popular café to meet with Steve Lopez, a wealthy young Indian man whose parents had moved from India to Singapore. The Lopez family had recently decided to sock away some money in the United States, and they had dispatched their only son to scout out good investments. Unfamiliar with American business and culture, Lopez desperately needed someone to guide him. He hoped Joe Hunt would be that person.

Over dinner, Steve explained his needs. A dark-skinned, intensely nervous young man with a pronounced facial tic, Lopez was definitely not in the mold of the typical, self-confident BBC boy. But there was one thing that made him very attractive to Joe: he was, he explained over dinner, looking for an investment to increase his parents' capital. For now, he had a couple hundred thousand dollars to invest; if things went well with that, he should be able to raise several million more from family and friends in Singapore and elsewhere in Asia.

Joe then began his pitch. He had, he told Lopez, developed a commodities trading system capable of generating significant profits. If Steve invested with him, he could expect very substantial returns, perhaps as much as two to three hundred percent.

"But isn't the commodities market pretty shaky?" the Indian boy asked.

"Not the way we do it," Joe assured him, his intense eyes looking straight into Lopez's. "I have developed a system that has virtually eliminated the risk." It was Joe's usual pitch, and he was by now very good at delivering it. Steve pressed for details about the system, and the BBC leader offered explanations, but by the end of the evening Lopez still had little idea what was involved.

He did know one thing, however: he instinctively liked Joe Hunt. He seemed very mature, and Lopez, a teetotaler himself, liked the fact that Joe didn't drink. It was impressive, Steve thought, that someone his own age had come so far. He wanted to invest with Joe, but he was reluctant to put his parents' money into something he didn't entirely understand. So before leaving he made a final request. "This all still seems like Greek to me. Could you give me something in writing, so I could study it all?"

Joe readily agreed.

At his next meeting with Joe Hunt, Steve was still not provided with a written explanation of the trading. But Joe had something better. "I think you should take a look at these," he told the Indian boy, handing him a stack of Clayton Brokerage statements from his trading for Ron Levin. It was all there in black and white. Joe Hunt seemed to be a trading whiz. The lavish offices on Third Street were a testament to his success. Very shortly thereafter, Lopez put his parents' money in Joe's hands, setting up an account called International Marketing Operations. He would also, he promised, recruit other investors in Asia. The BBC was now going so strong that Joe felt the group could afford to lease another condominium at the Wilshire Manning. Ben Dosti and Steve Lopez, who was made a full BBC member, shared the new rental.

In late October, Joe heard about a young man just out of law school named Jerry Eisenberg. He would be perfect for the BBC, someone suggested. Joe liked the idea. He had thought for some time that it would be nice to have corporate counsel for the group. Eisenberg sounded perfect. He was young, eager, and very ambitious. Always aware of projecting the proper image, Joe invited Eisenberg to meet with the group at the Hard Rock Cafe, where the BBC was having dinner to celebrate the Cogenco deal. To Eisenberg, then on the outside looking in, the group was very impressive. There they were, just a bunch of kids really, dressed impeccably at a huge table in the hippest restaurant in Los Angeles. Everyone was drinking and eating and nobody seemed a bit concerned about money. "I had a vision that that's where I could be," Eisenberg recalls. "There they were, celebrating the closing of a big deal. They were an impressive bunch of guys—all young, all bright, all with money and pretty girlfriends, all successful." Eisenberg joined up on the spot.

Chapter 14

With the addition of the second Manning apartment, the BBC now had enough room for half a dozen members to live in the same location. The move helped to consolidate the group emotionally as well as physically. Increasingly, the boys were socializing together instead of with friends from outside the organization—or "normies," as Joe called them. A couple of the boys had drifted away with Alex Gaon after Hunt's commodities debacle during the summer, but in many ways that left the rest of the group more cohesive.

Since few of the boys drew any salary from the BBC, Joe was left to decide who got what. He usually carried several thousand dollars with him in hundred-dollar bills, and he doled out money as he saw fit. Some days he would take one or more boys shopping for clothes, buying Italian designer suits, silk ties, or leather jackets for them with BBC monies. Other times he would hand out cash bonuses, or pick up the tab for pricey dinners. Since most of the members were receiving monthly checks from their parents, the money Joe gave out was not absolutely necessary, but it was certainly nice. And without question, it gave Joe an added measure of control over the boys' lives.

Joe also made a point of having fun with his followers, occasionally singling out one boy or another for special attention. During the early winter, Joe invited Tom May to go on a shooting trip, a sort of male bonding experience. The two boys traveled in Joe's black Jeep to Soledad Canyon, a wilderness area about an hour away from downtown Los Angeles. It was a favorite place of his, Joe told Tom as they headed north on the freeway. He had gone there with his father when he was a kid, and he knew the area very well.

The day was lovely, and as he maneuvered his Jeep along the narrow two-lane highway at the base of the canyon, Joe seemed much more relaxed than he did in the office. After turning onto a winding dirt road that led up into the dry California foothills, Joe spotted the place he was looking for. He parked the car, and the boys unloaded two .22 rifles and a shotgun and began shooting tin cans like a couple of kids. It was fun being with Joe like this, Tom thought.

When they had both tired of target practice, Joe suggested a hike. "I know an incredible place," he said. "It's near here, but it's rough going." The boys battled their way through dense brush, finally arriving at a streambed. Then they walked upstream until they came to a waterfall. It was a surprise to find such a place in the otherwise parched canyon. "You could hide anything up in these hills," Joe Hunt said seriously, "and no one would ever find it."

Brooke Roberts had turned out to be the perfect girl for Joe. When he wanted her, she was right by his side. When he had important business, she was content to tend the home fires. The petite Brooke was dwarfed by six-foot-four-inch Joe and she seemed overshadowed emotionally as well; many of Brooke's friends were shocked by her devotion to her lover.

This was a girl, they thought, who used to think about nothing but the latest trend. Now she sat at home making cute cards for Joe—or Joseph, as she called him. The prickles in her personality seemed reserved now for people she felt were threatening her boyfriend. With Joe she seemed utterly tamed. When Joseph hurt his leg riding a motorcycle, Brooke called the BBC's secretary and told her to remind Joe to take his medication. When she was in the vicinity of the BBC office, she often stopped in with fruit she had picked up for him at a nearby market.

Privately, many of the BBC boys felt Joe was sometimes more than a little cold to his adoring mate. She was clearly in love. But when he talked about her, it was very distantly. "I'm very fond of Brooke," he would say. "She's really a very nice girl."

When it came to Brooke's parents, however, Joe was less reserved. He couldn't stand the way they were trying to control her life and, by extension, his. They had never adjusted to their young daughter's moving in with Hunt. They thought she was far too young to be living with anyone, and there was something they just didn't like about Joe. When Brooke defied their wishes and went off with him, they had basically cut off communication. When one of her brothers discovered where Brooke was living, he took back the car she drove and returned it to his father, the car's rightful owner. Joe occasionally erupted angrily about her family, unable to stand the thought of people who didn't immediately recognize his superiority.

If Joe was quite pleased with his own girlfriend, he was sometimes less than happy with those of his followers. When Dean Karny began seeing a spirited, fun-loving young woman whom Joe considered entirely too frivolous, he made his views known. One Saturday night when Joe was sitting with the couple in a booth at the noisy, popular club At Sunset, he and Dean's girlfriend began arguing. Each tried to pull Dean into the fray, until, the young woman recalls, "Joe had one arm and I had the other. It was like we were both saying, 'Pick me. Pick me.' " Dean had little to do with the girl after that. "One by one people would break up with their old girlfriends, would tell their dads to go fly a kite, and would become more isolated from society and 'normies,' " Dean later recalled.

Ben Dosti was an exception. During the same period, Ben was seeing a pretty, bright, self-confident young woman who will be called Kate Johnston in this book. At a glance, Kate seemed a perfect companion for a BBC boy. From a wealthy family herself, she was always perfectly groomed and fashionably dressed. She was articulate and interesting. Because of her belief in Ben, Kate invested some money with the BBC. But from the beginning, Kate and Joe were like oil and water.

She couldn't stand the way all the BBC boys let Joe control their lives, and so she challenged him constantly. He couldn't abide the way she stood up to him. Joe viewed his vocabulary as his strongest weapon, and regularly whipped out obscure, four-syllable words to dazzle his audience. On several occasions, Kate challenged Joe's use of words, pointing out that he had used a word incorrectly. Each time he was furious.

Kate also didn't believe many of the stories with which Joe had so impressed his followers. After he bragged to her that he had gotten his degree from USC in only a year and a half, she called the school and discovered that he had never graduated at all. Similarly, she learned he was not a certified public accountant, as he sometimes claimed to be; he had never completed the required apprenticeship for licensing. Kate's flare-ups at Joe were causing difficulties in her relationship with Ben. Ultimately, although Ben wouldn't break up with Kate, as Dean had with his girlfriend, he simply quit taking her along on BBC outings, keeping his relationship with her separate from his activities with the BBC. Joe wasn't crazy about the arrangement, but it was tolerable.

The BBC's only other social problem in Joe's mind was Dave May. Since Joe had lost Dave's money, Dave had started acting more aggressively toward the BBC leader, challenging his statements and mocking him before the other boys. Once on a trip to New York, Joe was describing his vision of a BBC compound in which all the BBC boys would live communally. They would, Joe said, have a garage full of fancy cars they could all use whenever they pleased. But Dave refused to see the beauty of the possibility. "Yeah," he said, "but what if my brother wanted to use the Ferrari the same night I did?"

There was only one solution as far as Joe was concerned: Dave must be isolated from the rest of the group. As soon as the warehouse was ready, Dave would be sent off to work on the attrition mill, Gene Browning's Cyclotron. In the meantime, Joe missed no opportunity to publicly ridicule Dave for his challenging statements, questioning whether he had the mind to comprehend the larger issues of Paradox Philosophy.

But Joe was careful. He knew that the Mays were among his strongest assets, and he couldn't afford to lose them. So while he derided Dave, Joe was careful to praise Tom lavishly. "You're not like your brother," Joe would tell Tom frequently. "You've got a good head on your shoulders. I really think you're Shading material." Tom was unaware that Joe ridiculed him, too, when he wasn't around.

Now that the BBC was down to a core of serious participants, Joe increasingly tried to shape the boys' thinking to bring it into line with his Paradox Philosophy. He loved to play the philosopher king, setting up dilemmas for the boys to respond to. One day when nothing more important was going on, he called Tom May into his office. "If you hated somebody, and you could kill them and get millions of dollars for doing it, and you'd never get caught, would you commit murder?"

"No," Tom said warily, knowing that with Joe there was always a right and a wrong answer.

"What if it were you or him?"

"I'd try to find some other way out," Tom said.

Joe pushed further. "What if he'd kill your mother if you didn't kill him?" Finally Tom acknowledged that there were situations in which he could imagine murder. "So," Joe said smugly, "you would kill. You see, it's all a matter of perspective."

Joe frequently found opportunities to lecture his followers on Paradox Philosophy. After taking a group of boys to see one of his favorite movies, *Rambo*, Joe asked them to think about what he saw as the film's crucial moment. In it, Rambo, who is being pursued through the woods by dozens of National Guardsmen and sheriffs, arrives in a clearing where he surprises a young hunter who nearly screams. Rambo grabs the boy and puts a knife to his throat to keep him from speaking. But the former Green Beret cannot bring himself to kill the boy to keep him silent, and so lets him go. The boy immediately cries out, giving away Rambo's position. Ultimately, he is taken into custody.

"What would you have done in that situation?" Joe asked the boys. After some discussion, they agreed that they probably would have done what Rambo did. "Absolutely not," Joe said with the patience of an elementary-school teacher. "He should have killed the kid. You should never, ever act in a way that puts you in jeopardy out of some misplaced sense of wanting to protect others." The discussion ended. "Those of us who didn't agree learned not to ask questions, just to keep silent." a BBC member recalls. "Nothing was worse than to have the light of Joe's contempt turned on you."

For those like Dave May who were less impressed than the others by rhetorical skills, Joe could also show himself to be a man of action. One afternoon he dropped in on the Mays at their Brentwood apartment. The three-story stucco building had been built in typical California Sixties style, with all the units opening onto a courtyard containing a small swimming pool. The May brothers had occasionally jumped from their second-floor balcony into the pool, which was perhaps eight feet out and twelve feet down, and they proposed doing this to Joe. After all three had completed successful dives from the landing, Joe announced his intention to dive into the eight-foot-deep pool from the building's roof, some fifteen feet higher. The twins tried to talk him out of the dangerous stunt. The pool was quite shallow, they reminded him. There was little margin for error. But Joe refused to budge. He pulled himself up onto the roof and, as the stunned brothers watched in amazement, performed a beautiful dive into the pool. "I realized then and there that Joe Hunt was probably crazy but that he was no wimp," Dave May recalls.

As their admiration for Joe grew, many of the boys were becoming increasingly dependent on his approval. Over time, Karny later testified, the BBC boys began relying on Joe. "Everyone came to Joe with their problems . . . because they hoped to gain answers to all the difficulties they have dealing with society," Dean recalled. "The bonds were strong as long as Joe appeared to have the answers, both in terms of philosophies and in terms of coming up with money to keep people happy and activities to keep them busy." As time went on, the boys vied to get close to Joe. "I remember one night when Joe got busted for a traffic ticket," a BBC member recalls. "There were a bunch of us there to bail him out, all waving hundred-dollar bills."

Chapter
15

★

Luan Dosti was very concerned about his son Ben. The boy seemed so involved with this BBC business and with that fellow Joe Hunt. Even after the Chicago debacle, Ben seemed to have complete faith in Hunt.

The Dostis had no trouble seeing why Ben would be attracted to Hunt. The young man had impressed Luan Dosti very much the previous spring when he had watched a demonstration of the attrition mill given by Joe. He was a natural and very slick salesman. But beyond a certain outward charm, Ben's parents could see nothing to recommend the young man. He was not, they felt, the kind of person their son should be associated with. He had "con man" written all over him.

In the fall of 1983 the Dostis invited Danielle and Shalom Karny to dinner. Perhaps if the two sets of parents put their heads together, the Dostis felt, they could figure out a way to convince their sons that Hunt was trouble. After some preliminary small talk, Luan Dosti plunged in. "This Joe Hunt is clearly a loser. Our boys are winners. Why should they be involved with a guy like this? I think we should present a united front in encouraging our kids to break with this BBC."

The Karnys were more than unreceptive to the speech. After listening to what Luan Dosti had to say, Danielle Karny jumped in. "The boys are doing so much," she began. "They are working very hard, but they're just getting going. How can you doubt Joe's sincerity?"

Without help from the other parents, the Dostis felt their efforts to part Ben from the BBC would be futile. They would just keep the channels of communication open and hope he came to his senses.

Chapter
16

Joe was getting very annoyed at Ron Levin. Most days he called or visited the older man at his Beverly Hills apartment, requesting his share of the previous summer's commodities profits. But Levin was used to putting off disgruntled business associates, and he had no problem stalling Joe. Finally, in October, Levin announced that the reason he had been dragging his feet was that he had gotten an excellent deal on a shopping center in Chicago and had used all the commodities money, including Joe's share, to purchase it. Everything was fine, Levin assured Joe, and the BBC now owned fifty percent of a shopping center worth thirteen million dollars.

Joe was in need of some good news for the BBC boys. Lately they had been asking with increasing skepticism when they would be getting the four million dollars and wondering aloud whether Ron Levin was trying to rob them. After hearing about the shopping center, Joe called a meeting at the BBC offices. In their business attire, sitting around the table in the

BBC's lavish conference room, the boys felt very much like up-and-coming businessmen. Nobody knew quite what to expect, but they could tell from Joe's demeanor that he had good news. "We now own a shopping center in Chicago," Joe announced triumphantly. He had been a little disappointed at first, he told the boys, not to be getting the cash, but upon reflection, he was excited about the shopping center. It was the BBC's first holding in real property. After the initial questions had been answered, Joe told the boys that he would be apportioning shares of the center among them. Tom and Dave were promised the largest shares, as they had been of the elusive cash. Others were apportioned percentages, Joe explained, according to their contributions.

There were a few voices of dissension among the boys after the announcement. "What about title? Do we have documents showing we have title?" Dave May asked.

Joe hid any annoyance he felt at Dave for sounding such a negative note on what he hoped would be a morale-building occasion. "Ron's working on that," he assured Dave. "We'll have it soon." The other boys agreed that getting some documentation of ownership would be a good idea.

Joe's meeting about the shopping center was, whether calculated or not, a sophisticated way of keeping the boys believing in him. By including them in the potential gains, Joe had given the boys a reason to want to believe Ron's promises. The group remained cohesive in its excitement about the future.

Shortly after being promised the Chicago shopping center, Joe Hunt made a phone call that would reshape the course of the BBC.

Since concluding his trading for Ron Levin at Clayton Brokerage, Joe had kept in touch with Jack Friedman, the savvy broker he had dealt with there. Sometimes he would call the more experienced trader with questions about the market. At other times he would call just to chat. In late October, Joe called him to get some market prices.

After their business was concluded, Friedman asked Joe a question. "Whatever happened with that story Ron Levin and you were doing on the trading?"

After a brief pause, Joe answered the puzzling question. He was more than willing to cover any lie Levin might have told the trader. "We did it," Joe replied.

"Who explained the trading?" Jack asked. "I thought I was supposed to do that."

"I did," Joe said without hesitation, giving no clue to his confusion.

Then Friedman dropped the bombshell. "So, when did you learn that Levin's account wasn't real?" Friedman asked Joe.

After a moment's silence, Joe mumbled a response. He had known all along, he said. After he hung up the phone, Joe set about finding out just what was going on.

Joe went unannounced to Levin's house and demanded an explanation. "What's this about that commodities account not being real?" Joe asked Levin, keeping his voice and manner calm.

Levin hated being put on the defensive. He would much rather attack, and so he picked up the phone. "How dare you violate my confidentiality!" he screamed at Jack Friedman. "You had no right to discuss my personal business and money with Joe Hunt."

Friedman was good and sick of the eccentric man. "First of all, to violate someone's confidentiality, there had to be some real money, and there wasn't," Friedman yelled back. "And second, we agreed that Hunt would be told after the trading that the account was not real." After Levin, in his usual fashion, threatened legal action, both men hung up.

Levin still had to pacify Joe. "Look, I lied to you about the account," Levin said offhandedly. "It was all a scam. But the reason I did it was to get those phony statements. Using them, I was able to set up an account with another broker without putting up any money." In that account, Levin said, he had made more than a million dollars. He would split that money with Joe.

Joe appeared somewhat mollified as he accepted Levin's offer. But the con man's actions had clearly touched an exposed nerve in the young trader. Like Joe's former fraternity brothers, Levin clearly hadn't taken him seriously. Soon after, when he told Karny about the scam, he vowed to get revenge. "I'm going to kill Ron Levin one day," he said solemnly.

The full story of how Ron Levin tricked Joe Hunt wouldn't become public for more than two years. It was an incredible tale.

The way Friedman tells it, in late June of 1983 he was contacted by Ron Levin, who said he was a producer for Network News. The company, Levin explained, sold stories to television stations across the country. They were now producing a national story on commodities trading, but he needed some help. For the piece, Levin told Friedman, he wanted to do some simulated trading. Several traders would be given dummy accounts to manage. Starting with the same set amount of imaginary cash, the traders would buy and sell commodities, trying to increase the "capital" in their accounts. Many of the large brokerage firms had agreed to participate, Levin assured Friedman. At one, Network News was using a staff trader. At another, Network News would just make random picks, essentially throw darts to determine what to buy and what to sell.

At Clayton Brokerage, Network News wanted to bring in an outside trader, a whiz kid who supposedly had a great system. "And by the way," Levin told Friedman, "we don't want the trader to know that the account isn't real. If he thinks this is just a game, he's not going to be able to get up the kind of emotion he needs to make real decisions."

Friedman realized the positive benefits of allowing such a television documentary to be made at Clayton. It would be free publicity. Levin assured him he would be featured in the program explaining the trading. The brokerage house's management had a few concerns. First, they wanted to make sure that Levin indemnified the brokerage against lawsuits resulting from the program. Second, they were reluctant to send out regular statements of the account's activities and suggested that perhaps the brokerage should send out statements that clearly spelled out that this was merely a test series and not a record of actual transactions.

Later the same day, Friedman dropped in on Ron Levin at his home with papers for him to fill out. When he suggested that the brokerage needed indemnification, Levin immediately sat down at his typewriter. "Attention: Jack Friedman," his memo began. "Network News will indemnify Clayton Brokerage Company of St. Louis, Missouri, from all loss of any kind with respect to their assistance in the Network News, Inc., news documentary entitled 'The Traders.' " The note was signed "Ron Levin, assignment editor."

Later that afternoon, Levin called in the first order Joe had decided on, a thousand September bond calls. Friedman waited a few minutes to fill the order, watching the various prices for September bond calls. Finally he "purchased" them for the Levin account at the highest, most disadvantageous price he had seen during the few minutes. He didn't want to be accused in the future of having fudged in the account's favor. It would be an amusing project, Friedman thought. He suspected nothing more.

Chapter
17

Steve Lopez was a believer in Joe's ability as a commodities trader. In a few months with the group, he had become so impressed with the BBC that he was now ready to go on the road promoting it to friends and family abroad. Based on the promising early returns Joe had announced, Steve believed the commodities trading was going as well as he could have hoped for. He was delighted he had hit on such a good investment for his family. Now, if Joe would permit it, he wanted to share his good fortune.

Joe was more than happy to have Lopez out recruiting other investors. But he did have one concern. Although Steve had been regularly going to observe the trading, he still didn't seem to understand a lot of what was taking place. Before he left, Joe wanted to be certain he could make a good sales pitch.

Joe felt it might help if Steve had something in writing he could study to help him learn sales techniques, so one afternoon the boys sat down in Joe's office with a tape recorder. Joe spent the next hour or two giving his sales pitch to Steve, occasionally stopping to explain a finer point of technique.

During volatile times in the market, Joe told Steve intently, his system could produce yields of one to two hundred percent a month. "Now, things have not been volatile during the past period of time, so we expect to make thirty to thirty-five percent on our money," Joe said.

The BBC founder was shrewd enough to know that such rosy predictions would raise eyebrows among sophisticated investors, so he was careful to also insert some doubt. "In times when there is no volatility, our investors will not make money, but they will not lose money either." His system was based not on any ability to predict, Joe said. Quite the contrary, its most basic principle was that no one can accurately predict what the commodities market will do. Joe's entire system, he told his student, was based on the certainty that no one could predict the future. It was the one statement Joe made that was firmly rooted in fact.

After explaining these basic investment principles to Lopez, Joe stopped to coach his student in sales technique. "Now review that last set of sentences," he said, "because they are a very important set of sentences. This is how you are going to win a lot of sympathy from very wealthy men. They are not going to invest a large amount of money with you on the basis of personality unless you have a long period of time to cultivate it. If you come across with these arguments, they are going to see clarity and insight that is uncommon among people your age. You are going to be sharing attitudes with them that they have come to after twenty or thirty years. You're going to be extremely persuasive on these points." It was a principle Joe had used repeatedly with investors, presenting himself as someone with wisdom far beyond his years.

A transcript made of the tape from that day was stamped CLASSIFIED INFORMATION, as Joe wanted to protect his sales techniques from scrutiny. But as he would later learn, the criminal court system had no respect for his trade secrets.

* * *

Jim Graham was not the type of young man the BBC usually recruited. The security guard at the Wilshire Manning had no money and no social connections. But when Dean Karny got to know him at a party in the Manning's basement recreation room in December of 1983, he realized that Graham might have something the BBC could use.

Graham had the kind of looks that attracted stares. His chocolate brown face had high cheekbones and chiseled features. He possessed the carefully sculpted muscles of a serious bodybuilder, and he dressed conservatively but well. Only his dark, darting eyes suggested anything other than good breeding and polished manners.

It was the promise extended by Graham's eyes that attracted the BBC boys to the twenty-eight-year-old security guard. Graham, Dean decided after talking to him, was streetwise, a quality none of the affluent, protected BBC members possessed. He told Dean he was a black belt in karate, that he had worked as a professional bodyguard and private investigator, and that he had once been a professional football player. Graham also said he had once held the Mr. Universe title, a claim that was not difficult to believe when looking at his perfect body.

Before leaving on a European business trip for Westcars, Dean introduced Graham to Joe. By the time Dean returned a month later, the two had become fast friends. Jim began giving the BBC boys karate lessons in apartment 1505 at the Manning. Soon after, he resigned from his position at the condominium building and went to work full time as director of security for the BBC. As a special incentive to bring him into the group, Joe handed Jim the keys to one of Westcars's BMWs.

None of the BBC boys seemed to question the need for a security director. As one member later put it, "We were engulfed in the notion that we were going to become big businessmen, and big businessmen need security men." The boys also seemed to accept Graham, if not as an equal, at least as an interesting diversion. When Jim was around, the boys got to play at being boys. One afternoon, Tom May was in the mood for horseplay and tried to get Jim into a wrestling match. Finally, Graham agreed to a footrace. "I'll give you a twenty-yard head start and we'll race a hundred yards," he said. Tom, whose quickness had always been an asset on the tennis court, agreed. Jim beat him easily.

The BBC's security director also seemed to know a lot about guns. He carried a Beretta strapped to his ankle. After the BBC rented a warehouse to construct the first attrition mill, he set up a target range there where he liked to fire guns into a barrel he had filled with sand.

Not every black man might have been so readily accepted by the BBC boys, but Jim seemed to know his place. He had little to do with the business operations of the organization, keeping instead to the physical side of things. In addition, he was extremely deferential and well mannered.

Perhaps because of his affable, nonthreatening manner, there were things about Graham that the BBC boys never bothered to question. It was fun to think of Graham as a former pro football player, so none of the boys apparently ever bothered to check whether he had in fact been with the Philadelphia Eagles, as he claimed. He had not. And the rolls of Mr. Universe titleholders don't include a Jim Graham, but again that seemed never to be an issue with Graham's BBC colleagues, who bragged of his accomplishment. Moreover, the boys never questioned Jim's background. Even if they had, they probably wouldn't have learned that Jim Graham was actually Jim Pittman, a small-time hood from Delaware who had fled a felony theft warrant in Virginia and assumed a new identity to escape detection.

The one aspect of Jim's involvement with the BBC that caused some rancor among the troops was his instant high status and access to Joe. The security guard was soon given his own office at the BBC headquarters on Third Street. And although it was only a tiny cubicle, Jim's private space caused some resentment among BBC old-timers who still didn't have established offices of their own. Even more grating to some was the fact that as the winter progressed, Graham spent increasing amounts of time closeted with Joe, discussing plans the others were not apprised of.

The other boys did occasionally get glimpses into the secrets being discussed by Jim and Joe. On one occasion, Jim brought a man named Nick to the offices. Nick was a private investigator, said by Jim to be an expert in firearms, surveillance, and other fringe activities. Nick and Jim went into the office of Joe, who was not there, and shut the door. Soon, Steve Taglianetti, who was in the next room, heard two muffled thuds. After Nick left, Tag went into Joe's office to ask Jim for an explanation. But the security guard offered none. Instead he gathered up a telephone book and left the room. As he passed, Tag could see two bullet holes in the thick volume. Later that afternoon, Graham opened a desk drawer and showed Tag a pistol with a shiny black silencer.

Perhaps it was because the BBC members were boys of the television era raised on video gunfights and staged violence, but none of the boys who were aware of it reacted strongly to the increasing cache of weapons at the BBC. The boys also may have thought of the new instruments of violence as toys, as logical extensions of their male bonding trips to Soledad Canyon to shoot cans with Joe. When Jim Graham turned up one day with a pen gun, an exotic small-caliber, one-shot weapon that looked like a ballpoint pen, none of the boys questioned why he needed it. They thought it very cool. To the BBC members, as one put it, "guns ranked up there with stereos and clothes as good, clean fun." Not one of the rank and file members suspected for a moment that the weapons were part of a strange turn toward violence by Joe Hunt.

Chapter
18

Steve Weiss was quite happy as he looked around the banquet room of the Tail of the Cock restaurant in the San Fernando Valley one evening during the late winter of 1984. Joe Hunt had arranged a banquet for his investors at the old-time restaurant, and many of the sixty or so people who had turned out were somehow connected to Weiss. He was glad to have been able to bring so many of his friends and family into such a good thing.

Joe had selected the restaurant carefully. A far cry from the trendy, West Side cafés favored by the BBC members, the Tail of the Cock, with its prime ribs and thick steaks, was perfect for his middle-aged investors. The large restaurant was appointed with dark wood and leather upholstery. It suggested exactly the kind of wealthy conservative image Joe was trying to portray.

During the presentation he made after dinner that night, the BBC leader was every bit the sophisticated businessman.

His tone was reserved, almost understated. But his news was very good. The commodities accounts were thriving. Investors could expect to see big profits when they got their quarterly statements in a few weeks. That was really all he had to say, he told them. He just wanted the investors to get to know one another and to come together to celebrate their good fortune. Joe's speech received enthusiastic applause, and Weiss and the others went home feeling very optimistic.

When the individual financial statements were sent out several weeks later, none of the investors saw any cause for alarm. On paper, at least, their accounts seemed to be growing at a rapid pace.

The reality was very different. Joe had suffered serious reversals in the commodities market. He was spending at a rapid pace. The BBC was facing severe financial problems. But the company's operations were dependent on a continuing influx of money, and Hunt was not about to give investors the bad news and threaten the flow. He would stall and hope he could make up the money somehow.

Jeff Raymond was exactly the type Joe Hunt liked to recruit for the BBC. A clean-cut, all-American young man with boyish looks and impeccable manners, Jeff had gotten to know Joe Hunt through Dave May, his best friend at the Orange County junior college both boys had attended. Jeff's affluent family had sent him off to finish school in Arizona, but he had remained close to Dave, and through him heard about the BBC. The May twins talked frequently about the group's exclusive makeup and about its lofty goals. After meeting Joe at a party and later talking to him at length at the BBC offices, Jeff was impressed. The organization certainly seemed like a going concern, but he was in no hurry to join up.

Jeff was attractive to the BBC in part because of his father, a successful engineer who ran his own firm. The boys thought the elder Raymond might be useful in connection with the

Cyclotron. As it happened, Jeff's father never got too interested in the Gene Browning technology, but in the end, it was the attrition mill that brought Jeff into the group. Dave was very excited about the prospect of actually constructing one of the massive machines, and his enthusiasm was contagious. The boys could really build a business from scratch. By February, when the BBC rented a large warehouse in Gardena, half an hour south of L.A., to construct the attrition mill, Jeff had decided to join the team. In April he gave Joe twenty thousand dollars to invest in commodities.

As he looked around him during the spring of 1984, Joe was not at all certain that he could expect much help making money from the other boys in the BBC. His band of boys was definitely lacking in ambition. Many didn't even want to apply themselves. After exhorting several of the boys individually to work harder, Hunt still saw no results. Finally he issued an edict. At seven-thirty each morning Joe was going to hold breakfast meetings at a coffee shop down the street from the BBC offices. They would discuss the upcoming day's work, reinforce the group spirit, and then walk the half block to the offices to begin work.

On the first morning, most of the BBC members arrived roughly on time, although some seemed sleepy. Business was discussed enthusiastically. But by afternoon, the new enthusiasm seemed to have dissipated, and, after their usual long lunches, the boys began leaving for home. The second morning just Joe and BBC lawyer Jerry Eisenberg, who was considerably more serious than most of the others, appeared for the meeting. On the third morning, Eisenberg alone made it to the coffee shop. No attempt at BBC breakfast meetings was made again, and the BBC's tailspin continued.

Joe was particularly upset about Westcars. Already the company had spent a couple hundred thousand dollars to import cars and perform mechanical alterations on them. But while the automobiles provided a nice fleet for BBC members, the company showed no sign of turning a profit. The problem was in getting the cars converted. Before a European car can be sold in California, it must be altered to meet the state's rigid emissions standards. Steve Taglianetti, who headed Westcars, had hired a mechanic who worked on the cars at the BBC's Gardena warehouse site. When finished, the cars had to be tested and passed by a certified lab. That was the problem. Again and again, Westcars had sent its cars to an excellent testing laboratory, FCI in Santa Ana. But the mechanic retained by the BBC to make the alterations could not seem to get things right. Very few of the BBC cars had been passed by FCI. And in the meantime, each test cost $750.

In late 1983, when the BBC first decided on FCI, a delegation of BBC members including Joe Hunt and Steve Taglianetti had gone down to meet with lab owners Jerry Coker and Rene France. The boys were particularly interested in how to keep costs down. Might they work out some sort of deal? "If you want to keep costs down," Coker told them, "just make sure the vehicles are well prepared before testing. Otherwise we charge for each and every test. If you have to keep bringing the same cars back, you'll end up paying thousands of dollars per car instead of hundreds."

Despite Coker's admonition, the BBC boys kept taking in cars that hadn't been properly converted. In February, Jim Graham and Steve Taglianetti went down for another meeting with Coker. Wasn't there something they could do? they asked. The meeting was short. Again Coker told the boys to prepare their cars better before bringing them in. Later that month, Westcars received an invoice from FCI for seven thousand dollars.

FCI employees John Paul Redmond and Randy Hatzl were working late at the lab on March 14, 1984. Hatzl was inside a car, Redmond was outside another as the men ran tests. Luckily for them, they were in the back area of the shop. At about seven P.M. they heard what sounded to Redmond "like a strip of firecrackers going off rapidly." But the noise wasn't firecrackers. When Redmond looked up, he saw puffs of plaster dust coming from a wall near his coworker. When Coker arrived after receiving a call from his employees, he said his shop "looked like Vietnam." There were bullet holes in all the windows along the front of the building and glass on the floor. Bullets had even penetrated two Mercedes parked out back.

The next day Coker received a visit from Jim Graham and at least one other of the BBC members. The boys, he said later, acted surprised at the damage, and commented that someone must be angry with the lab. "You know," they then said, "we're also private investigators. Would you like us to find out who did it?"

Coker agreed, and the boys asked for a five-thousand-dollar payment. "First find the evidence," Coker replied, "then I'll pay you."

A week later a couple of BBC boys returned, Coker no longer recalls exactly which ones. "We know who did it," Coker later testified they told him. "It was your former employer." Coker was stunned. "That's difficult to believe," he said. "I've known the man a long time." But the boys sounded sure. "We'll take care of him. We'll kill him. We'll put him in a barrel of acid," Coker recalls Jim Graham saying. But Coker was uninterested. "Just bring me the evidence," he told them. They never did.

A police investigation into the incident was not concluded until more than two years later. At that time, Remington Peters brand bullets recovered from FCI were compared to bullets shot from a .30 caliber Carbine Plainfield rifle belonging to Jim Graham. Markings on the bullets matched exactly.

By April there were strong rumors around the BBC about the FCI incident. Jim Graham had claimed credit for the attack to one of the boys, saying that it had been launched as a way to intimidate the laboratory into passing BBC cars. Another BBC member, hearing through the grapevine of Graham's claim, secretly called the Santa Ana Police Department to confirm that there had been such an incident. But still the boys were skeptical. Joe and Jim were always talking themselves up. They had probably heard about the gunfire and decided to take credit. Besides, if the boys really put any credence in the story, they would have to seriously evaluate their continued involvement in the BBC, and that was something none of them was prepared to do.

Joe was getting fed up with Bruce Swartout, the Orange County businessman whose company, Cogenco, Joe had tried to acquire in a stock swap. Swartout was making noises about suing over the Cyclotronics stock, which he believed to be worthless. He seemed determined to get his hands on the Browning technology, and Joe simply would not allow that.

Friday, April 13, began in the usual fashion for Gerald Lee Rich. At about 7:05 A.M., he arrived at Do-All-Pacific in Irvine, where he worked as a maintenance mechanic. As always, Rich's first task was to clear some space for himself to work. He got out a forklift and began moving equipment out into the parking lot, which Do-All-Pacific shared with Bruce Swartout's company. Between 7:10 and 7:20, Rich noticed something that struck him as a little odd. In front of a parked car, a large black man was crouching down, "like a baseball catcher," Rich would later testify. When the man realized he had been observed, he stood up somewhat nervously. Rich watched the man for a minute or two and then went back to work.

Bruce Swartout also noticed the black man in the parking lot that morning as he drove in and took his usual space at about eight o'clock. The man was leaning up against the building a couple of spaces from where Swartout parked. He appeared to be drinking something from a cup. Swartout assumed the man was waiting for someone. He smiled. The man smiled back.

When Swartout opened the back door of his car to get his briefcase, he was aware of something behind him—a flash he thought might be a knife. But before he could turn around, something hit his back. "I thought I'd been stabbed," Swartout told the police who were summoned to the scene. "Then my back felt very cold. It was very frightening." After a brief scuffle, the assailant ran. Swartout, at sixty-seven, decided he should back off.

Inside his office building, Swartout realized that his shirt was wet. His back was burning slightly where the liquid had made contact. When he took his shirt off, he noticed a slight brown discoloration. He washed it as best he could and waited for the police to arrive.

The bizarre assault on Bruce Swartout remains officially unsolved. (Because Swartout had rinsed out his shirt, the police were unable to analyze the liquid.) But in the weeks preceding the incident, Jim Graham had told at least one BBC member that he was planning an attack on the Orange County businessman.

Chapter

19

One afternoon during the early spring of 1984, Joe called Evan Dicker into his office. "We may have a problem," Joe began confidentially. "We need to find someone to sweep our phones and see if they're tapped. I want you to call around and get somebody, but you've got to do it from a pay phone." Evan readily agreed, always pleased to be included in the inner workings of the organization. Even as he walked several blocks looking for an appropriate telephone, it didn't occur to Evan how strange the request was. In recent weeks, Joe had perhaps begun to get a little paranoid. But he made everything sound so normal, nobody was ready to challenge him.

Those boys who knew about it had only wondered vaguely why there was a need for the sophisticated alarm system Joe had ordered installed in the warehouse. It was logical, they supposed. But Joe's insistence that they take turns sleeping in the Gardena plant to provide additional security seemed a little stranger. For a time, various boys took turns camping out in sleeping bags at the site, but the glamor soon paled and the plan was quietly abandoned.

In some ways, Joe's new paranoia was justifiable. For the first time, his loyal troops were seriously questioning his leadership. Those who had invested their own money were growing increasingly skeptical of Joe's assurances that large profits were just around the corner. Dave May, who had been among the first to publicly challenge Joe, was getting ever more vocal, bad-mouthing Joe to anyone who would listen, primarily to Steve Taglianetti, Gene Browning, and Jeff Raymond, all of whom frequently gathered at the Gardena plant. Joe retained his loyal inner core of Dean Karny, Ben Dosti, Evan Dicker, and a couple of others. There were also a few new members who remained part of the group, like Jon Allen. Dean Karny had met Jon at Whittier School of Law, where he was studying for a law degree, and recruited him for the group. But many of the original BBC members were growing disgruntled.

By April, Jerry Eisenberg was among Joe's most vocal critics. Never a part of the inner circle, Eisenberg had begun voicing questions about the group's direction. With a couple of the other boys, he sat down one afternoon and calculated the amount the BBC was spending each month on its social and business obligations. With rent on two luxury condominiums, a warehouse, a lavish suite of offices, salaries, utilities, equipment rentals, furniture, and entertainment expenses, Eisenberg figured the group was easily spending seventy thousand dollars a month. "It didn't take a math whiz to figure that the money wasn't all coming from profits," the lawyer later said. "It was clear investors' money was going directly into paying expenses."

As Eisenberg became more and more outspoken about what he saw as deficiencies in Hunt's leadership, he became less careful about whom he complained to. One afternoon he made a big mistake. In either late April or early May, Eisenberg went with Jim Graham and Steve Taglianetti to pick up some license plates for Westcars. As they drove down the highway in a Westcars BMW, Jerry complained in his usual fashion about the group. "I'm to the point," he told the others, "where I'll believe Joe when he actually shows me all this money he says he's making. Not before."

Joe could not let the challenge to his authority go unmet. The next day, he called Jerry and Steve into his office. On his desk lay a small tape recorder. "You aren't being loyal BBC members," Joe said, looking at the recorder meaningfully. "The kinds of things you're saying can only undermine the group. If you have things to say, say them to me directly."

Eisenberg was stunned. "You're overreacting, Joe," he said, trying to ease the situation. "It was grumbling. Everybody does it. I'm not here to threaten or jeopardize you." He said nothing about his shock that Joe had apparently ordered Jim to secretly tape their conversation. He was beginning to think Joe was a little nuts. "After that, I figured my office was bugged too," Eisenberg recalls. "We all became more careful. Those of us who complained walked down the hall to do it, and we thought seriously about whom we talked to."

But none of the BBC members except Dean Karny and perhaps Jim Graham had any idea just how crazy Joe had become.

Chapter
20

It was after hours at the BBC headquarters when Dean Karny walked into Joe's office one evening in early May. The two boys were the only ones still working in the large office suite. The phones were silent. Dean and Joe looked forward to times like this, intimate times when they could have uninterrupted discussions. Sometimes the boys talked about weighty matters like Paradox Philosophy or the BBC's future. Sometimes they just chatted. But tonight Joe had business to discuss.

Since the preceding February, when Joe had announced to Dean that he intended to kill Levin one day, Joe had continued to talk somewhat abstractly about his ideas for the murder. Dean hadn't worried. He assumed Joe was just talking. Recently, Joe had spent considerable time with Levin. It was important, he had explained, to maintain a good relationship with Levin so that he "could find a good opportunity to kill him." Recently, Ron and Joe had gone to San Francisco together for a weekend, and the older man had given Joe an expensive watch for his birthday. But as far as Karny knew when he walked into the executive office that evening, Hunt's talk of murdering Ron Levin was still just talk.

Joe told him otherwise. "I am going to kill Ron Levin soon," he said. "I've been doing some planning, and I think I have the right idea." A murder alone would gain nothing, he said. Joe intended to force Levin to make good on some of the money he owed as well. And since a large cash transfer just before Levin's death would be suspicious, Joe planned to take some precautions.

For starters, he told Dean, the boys around the office would have to be prepared. "I want them to get the feeling that Ron is seriously considering going into business with us," Hunt said, "so that ultimately when some money is transferred, it won't come as a surprise." Dean was a willing coconspirator. By now, Joe and the BBC were everything to the weak-willed boy. As a Shading, Dean had fully embraced Paradox Philosophy. If killing Ron Levin was good for the BBC, then killing Levin was inherently good. He readily agreed to help Joe drop hints around the office that Levin was considering investing in Microgenesis.

Joe was also concerned about what anyone investigating Levin's murder would think about a large cash transfer. And so, he told Dean, he had come up with a plan. Joe handed Dean some letters he was drafting. Dean perused them quickly, noting that they were addressed to Ron Levin on the subject of his investing in Microgenesis. To Dean's knowledge, Levin had no intention of investing in the company, and he looked at Joe puzzled.

"It's simple," Joe explained. "When I kill Ron, I'll leave behind at his apartment a correspondence file containing a contract, these letters, and some information about the company. It will seem evident to anyone reading the documents that Ron was planning to invest in Microgenesis. That way, before I kill him, I can force him to sign a large check. When investigators look into why he gave us the money, it will all seem perfectly legitimate."

Written not to be mailed, but rather to be planted in Levin's house on the night of the murder, the letters Hunt showed Karny were a carefully designed mix of business and casual correspondence. In one, Hunt wrote three paragraphs. In the first, Joe struck a conversational tone. He had forgiven Levin, he said, for duping him in the securities scam the previous summer. In the second papragraph, Joe switched to business, alluding to a nonexistent conversation that had supposedly taken place between the two men about possible investors for the milling machine. Was Levin serious, he wondered, about knowing someone willing to pay $10 million for Browning's technological discoveries? In the final paragraph, Joe switched tone again, this time getting friendly and personal. He had been complimented, he said, on the "understated elegance" of the watch Levin had given him for his birthday, and wanted to thank Levin once again "for the very best birthday present I ever received."

As a law student, Dean was particularly impressed with Joe's cleverness. "These letters should create reasonable doubt if it ever comes down to a trial," he said.

"No court in the land could convict me," Joe agreed.

Several years later it seemed clear to Dean Karny that Joe had involved him in planning the Levin murder for a reason. If Dean were an active participant in the planning, he would become, in Paradox fashion, reconciled to it. But at the time, Dean didn't sense any manipulation, and he was happy to help. Joe suggested that Dean try to draft a response, ostensibly from Levin, to one of the letters. In the next few days Dean attempted to do so, but Joe didn't approve of his efforts. The boys discussed it and ultimately decided that Levin would be more likely to make a phone call than write a letter, and so the return correspondence idea was abandoned.

Joe continued to involve Dean in other ways, however. On

May 3, when Joe's secretary typed the first letter and readied it to be sent, Dean removed the letter from the secretary's out-basket. "I'm going to the post office. I'll take this," Dean told her. It was all part of Joe's plan. If the secretary were ever called to testify in a trial, she would have a memory of typing and sending out correspondence that suggested Levin was entering into a business deal with the BBC.

Later in the month, Joe showed Dean a contract he was drafting between Microgenesis and Ron Levin. Levin would be forced to sign the contract before his death, thereby explaining the check he would also be made to write.

At the end of May, Dean went to Mexico for a six-day vacation with his girlfriend. He had become involved with a different woman after Joe put a stop to his earlier liaison. The new girl had been just fine with Joe. A pretty, demure cook for some of the city's wealthiest families, she was not the kind of person to challenge Joe Hunt. Dean would later testify that when he returned from his brief hiatus, he found Joe had continued his planning.

One night shortly after he got back, Dean and Joe were again working late. Dean wandered into Joe's office to see what his friend was up to. Joe had recently learned, he said, that Levin was planning a trip to New York. It was perfect, he had decided. He could murder Levin, and if he hid the body well enough, no one would even notice Levin was missing. People would just assume he had gone to New York. As Joe told Dean about his plans, he referred to seven sheets of paper from a yellow legal pad on which he had made lists. Joe made lists for everything.

Finally, Dean rose and went to stand behind Joe so he could see what Joe was referring to. The first page Dean saw contained numbered items.

1. Jim digs pit.
2. JH cancels his reservations from his phone.

3. Joe arrives 9:00 (see list). Lets Jim in 9:45.
4. Cuffs, tape.
5. Levin his situation.
6. Determination of consideration—Swiss bank checks.
7. Execution of agreements.

Item 10 was perhaps the most chilling: "Kill dog (emphasis)."

Dean was puzzled by the document. It was a basic murder plan, Joe explained. Dean was unruffled by Joe's revelation and pressed for details. "At around nine on the night before Levin leaves town, I'll grab some take-out food and drop by Levin's house," Joe explained. Once there, he would suggest calling a friend to come over, standard operating procedure for an evening at Levin's. At about 9:45 the friend would arrive in the person of Jim Graham, who would pull a gun. They would force Levin to sign over money, then kill him and bury him in a pit they would have prepared up in Soledad Canyon. Before leaving Levin's house, they would plant the carefully prepared correspondence file and contract.

Dean had some questions about the plan. "What does 'Levin his situation' mean?" he asked.

"Well," Joe said, "I'll have to give Ron some explanation of what's occurring. We have to convince him that if he cooperates, he'll live. If he doesn't believe he's going to survive the ordeal, we don't have any hope of getting any money."

Joe had concocted a long and fanciful story. He would tell Levin he had gotten deeply in debt to the Mafia, and that his unsavory creditors were getting impatient. He had stalled them by saying that he was expecting a large chunk of cash from Levin, but he could no longer put the mob off. He had been forced to tell them Levin's name. He would introduce Jim as the enforcer sent by the Mafia to collect the money. If Levin wrote them a check, he and Joe would both live. Otherwise . . .

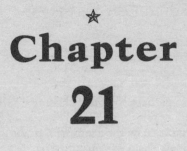

Chapter 21

On May 29, 1984, Joe composed a letter to the more than sixty investors brought in by Steve Weiss and his friends. The letter, written when Joe had already suffered serious market reversals, announced that due to the extreme success of the commodities trading during recent months and to the increasingly unwieldy sums now being traded, the BBC was going to have to stop taking in money. No new investments, the letter said, would be taken for the commodities accounts after June 30, 1984. The letter was sent out with Joe's signature.

The advisory presented a very distorted picture. In fact, Joe had already lost most of his commodities investments. Much of the money put up by Weiss's investors had probably never even made it into the accounts, but was rather used to pay operating expenses or given back to investors as "profits," a classic ploy used to bring in more capital. The BBC's many companies were nearly broke.

In the short run, Joe's letter of May 29 solved the cash

flow problems. Julius Paskan, an older Beverly Hills physician who had already invested $15,000, scrambled to come up with more money before the cutoff date. On June 1 he invested $25,000. On June 3, with money he got from mortgaging his office building, he put in another $140,107.54. On June 16 he kicked in an additional $25,000. And he was not alone. All over the West Side of Los Angeles, Joe's investors were reaching deeper into their pockets to come up with additional money. The BBC's financial problems were temporarily stayed.

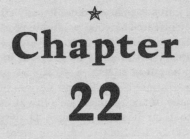

Chapter
22

Joanne Meltzer, one of the BBC's secretaries, was alone in the offices at lunchtime on June 6 when Joe Hunt came in the door with a striking-looking silver-haired man in tow. "Where is everyone?" Joe asked somewhat petulantly. The secretary explained that most of the boys were out to lunch. "Well, then, Joanne, I'd like to introduce you to someone. This is my business associate Ron Levin." Joe said the name with a flourish, as if she should know who the man was. Joanne was puzzled. Never before had Joe made a point of introducing her to any of the people he dealt with in the business world. The two men remained in the offices briefly and then left.

BBC lawyer Jerry Eisenberg was a little puzzled that same day when Joe asked him to draw up a contract between Microgenesis and Ron Levin. The company, Joe said, would be granting Levin certain rights to the Browning attrition mill in exchange for $1.5 million. Jerry hadn't been aware that such a

116

deal was even in the offing. But Joe insisted he needed the contract quickly, and so the attorney drew it up.

Later that night, when Dean got home to the Wilshire Manning, Joe was sitting at the desk in his bedroom looking at the seven-page murder plan he had written earlier. He had decided that this was the night. "You're taking everybody to the movies, right?" Joe asked. It had already been decided that Dean would take Brooke Roberts and Jeff Raymond to dinner and a movie. Later, if it ever came up, Joe could claim to have been with the group. Brooke and Dean would certainly go along with the alibi. With a little luck, by the time anybody got around to asking Jeff if Joe had been at the movie, enough time would have passed that he would be unable to remember with certainty just which BBC members had been along.

"It's all set. We're going to the movie," Dean reassured Joe. He paused. "Good luck," he said finally.

The Westwood movie theater chosen for the alibi was just a few blocks down Wilshire Boulevard from the Manning, past a dozen high-rise condo complexes and a couple of hotels. Dean and his entourage watched the movie *Streets of Fire*. Afterward they went to a Japanese restaurant for sushi. When Dean arrived home that night, he went to bed. As far as he could tell, Joe wasn't home yet.

Sometime before eight the next morning, Joe, who was already dressed in his business suit for the day ahead, went into Dean's bedroom and awakened his sleeping friend. The boys went into the living room and sat on the brown sectional couch Dean had brought with him from Encino. Joe opened his briefcase and removed a check, which he handed to Dean. It was drawn on a Swiss bank account owned by Ron Levin. The check was for $1.5 million. "It's done," Joe said. "Ron Levin is out of our hair. Permanently." Dean pressed for details, but Joe said he would explain it all later. In the meantime, he said, Dean should act very natural around the office and back up Joe's story about the check being part of a business deal. He showed Dean the Microgenesis contract that had been drawn up by Jerry Eisenberg. The document now bore Ron Levin's signature.

Joe was ecstatic at the success of his plan and couldn't wait to show off the huge check to the others. Of course, he couldn't tell them the whole story, but this should increase their respect for his business acumen. After his discussion with Dean, he awakened Jeff Raymond to show him the check. Then he hopped into his Jeep and drove to Dave and Tom May's Brentwood apartment ten minutes away, where he woke up the twins to show them. Later, at the office, the normally restrained Joe was as excited as any of the BBC members had ever seen him. The day's one disappointment was when Joe learned from the BBC's bank that it would take a full month to get the Swiss bank check cashed.

A new attorney who had recently been hired to do additional legal work for the BBC suggested a bank that might expedite the check's cashing, and so later in the day Joe, the attorney, and Dean Karny went to the World Trade Bank in Beverly Hills, where they opened an account with the Levin check. It still might take a couple of weeks, the bank cautioned, but they would expedite the check.

Several days later, Joe and Dean took a walk through the posh residential neighborhood just north of Wilshire Boulevard between Beverly Hills and Westwood. Dean would later testify extensively to the grisly tale Joe told as they strolled along the peaceful tree-lined streets.*

The way Dean says Joe told it, on the night of June 6, after Dean and the others left for the movie, he had picked up takeout chopped salads from La Scala, an old-style Beverly Hills restaurant, and taken them to Ron Levin's house. At a prear-

---

*According to Dean, Joe's version of the events of June 6 connected both Joe and Jim Graham to Ron Levin's murder. Prosecutors believe both men were involved, although both denied that they were. Jim Graham was tried twice for murdering Levin, but each trial resulted in a hung jury. The prosecutor subsequently agreed to drop the murder charge in exchange for Graham pleading guilty to being an accessory after the fact to the murder and to carrying an illegal weapon.

ranged time, Jim Graham had arrived at Levin's house and was let in by Joe. He immediately pulled a gun. Joe told Ron the story he had concocted about being in debt to the Mafia and about how he'd told his creditors that Levin owed him money. Just in case the older man wasn't buying Joe's story, he had thrown in a little extra. "You've never seen me with my shoes off, have you, Ron?" he asked. "Well, in fact, I have no big toe on my left foot. Because of all this, they've cut my toe off. Now they're going to kill me if I don't pay them."

Joe said he had then demanded to know how much money was in Levin's Swiss account. Levin said there was $1.7 million. Joe had told him to write a check for $1.5 million just to be sure it cleared.

At that point, Joe told Dean, Jim had blown his lines. "Is that enough money?" Joe asked Jim. "Yeah, that's fine," Jim responded. But he was supposed to have said, "No, what else have you got?" In that way the boys could have extorted even more.

After signing the check, Joe said, Levin started to whimper, aware for the first time that he might not survive the evening. Jim and Joe took him into his bedroom and ordered him to lie face down on his bed. Finally, Joe told Dean, Ron Levin was shot in the back of the head with a silenced .25 caliber pistol.

At that point in his narrative, Joe turned to Dean. "I remember so clearly the sound of a man's last breath leaving his body," he said. Then he made the sound for Dean, a sort of explosive gasp.

Once Levin was dead, when his blood began seeping out, Joe said, he and Jim had wrapped Levin in the comforter and took him to their waiting Westcars BMW. They hadn't noticed for a time that, along with Levin's body, they had accidentally wrapped up the television remote control that was lying on the bed. Moving Levin had been very difficult. His one hundred and ninety pounds were dead weight, and Joe and Jim were weak with nervousness. Eventually, the two had managed to shove the body into the trunk of the car. But they hadn't counted on rigor mortis, and when they tried to slam the lid, Levin's stiffening knee had put a dent in the gray BMW's trunk.

The final part of Joe's tale was so gruesome that the highly emotional Dean didn't want to listen. Joe said that he and Jim took the body to a pit Jim had already dug in Soledad Canyon. They put the body in, but before they covered it up, they shot it repeatedly with a shotgun so it could not be identified. "At one point," Joe told Dean, "Ron Levin's brain jumped out of his skull and fell on his chest." It seemed to Dean as if Joe thought this detail particularly neat. He chuckled as he spoke.

Dean was impressed with Joe's attention to detail. He had, he said, even remembered to take Levin's watch, because it was a very special brand with a serial number. Joe had thrown it down a storm drain in Westwood Village.

"That's too bad," Dean said. "It was a nice watch."

In the days that followed the murder, Joe and Dean discussed it many times. One afternoon in Joe's office, the boys talked about the need for circumspection. They needed a way, they decided, to be able to bring up Levin and his murder around the other BBC members. "The idea was to have some name, some word so that we could refer to Ron Levin and everything that had happened without people knowing what we were talking about," Dean recalled three years later. By the end of their meeting, the boys had decided on a word. From now on, they would call Ron Levin "Mac."

What Joe didn't tell Dean in the days following the murder, and perhaps had not even yet realized, is that somehow during the night of June 6 he had misplaced his carefully crafted seven-page recipe for murder.

Chapter
23

Dean Factor and Michael Broder knew immediately that something was wrong. Ron Levin had told them to be at his house by seven on the morning of June 7. He was taking the boys, one a Harvard University student, to New York City with him. On the phone the night before, he had repeatedly told them not to be late and had even suggested they spend the night at his house. But when the boys arrived, Ron didn't answer their knock.

At first the two boys were merely puzzled. But when they noticed that their friend's burglar alarm system was not on, they began to worry. Something must have happened. Ever since he had been robbed in his duplex two years earlier, Levin never left the house, even to take the garbage out, without setting the alarm.

Not having a key themselves, the boys called Blanche Sturkey, Levin's housekeeper, and asked her to come. "I don't understand this," she told them when she arrived. "When I left yesterday afternoon he was definitely planning on leaving this morning."

Inside the house the boys and Sturkey discovered other disturbing things. Levin didn't seem to have taken anything with him, including his address book, which he was never without. In his room, Blanche Sturkey noticed that the white comforter that had been on Levin's bed the previous day was missing. In its place was a green one he rarely used. The TV channel changer Levin always kept on his bed wasn't there. Dean and Michael found the remains of two take-out salads in the kitchen. They hadn't been there when Blanche left. Somebody besides Levin had been in the duplex the night before.

Fearing foul play, the boys called Levin's mother. They also went to the Beverly Hills Police Department to alert the officials that Ron was missing. But the police refused to take the report. With adults, at least forty-eight hours had to pass before a missing person's filing could be made. Levin's mother could offer the boys no clue as to her son's whereabouts. More puzzled than ever, the boys sat down at Levin's computer and wrote out a list of all the things they found strange. Then they decided to go on to New York by themselves.

Chapter
24

★

Just after eleven on the night of June 7, 1984, a well-built, nice-looking black man named Ron Levin walked into the Plaza Hotel overlooking Central Park and asked for a room. At $105 a day, the room he was given was one of the hotel's cheapest.

The next day the main desk heard from Mr. Levin again. His room had not been quite what he expected, he told the clerk. He would like something a little larger. That night Levin was transferred to Room 1071, a much grander room that cost $275 a night.

Over the next few days, Levin lived lavishly. He rented limousines in which he visited Delaware, where his family lived, and Pennsylvania. He picked up his kids and took them to church. He visited his mother. The folks in the old neighborhood were impressed with his apparent success.

The Plaza Hotel was less impressed. By June 10, Mr. Levin had run up charges of more than thirteen hundred dollars.

The credit manager had been unable to get sufficient credit approval to cover the charges on the credit card Levin had presented when he checked in. The hotel management left several urgent messages for him to get in touch with them. Finally, with a desperation rarely reached at the genteel Plaza Hotel, assistant manager Richard Lebowitz ordered an additional lock put on Levin's room so that he would have to make contact with management before he could enter.

The lock did its trick. At about six on the evening of the tenth, Levin appeared in the assistant manager's office. Lebowitz was momentarily surprised to see a black man. From the name, he had expected the guest to be Jewish. "There seems to be some problem with my room," Levin began. "My key won't open the door." Lebowitz had been with the elegant hotel for eight years, and he had been well trained in the art of dealing with customers tactfully. "We were very sorry to have to do that, sir," he began. "But you have gone beyond your authorized limit on the credit card you gave us. We need to make arrangements for some alternative method of payment, and we were having trouble reaching you."

Levin immediately took out his wallet and produced an American Express card issued to R. Levin, General Producers. Lebowitz ran a quick check to see if the credit card company would authorize payment. The answer came back quickly: not only would American Express permit no new charges, the company wanted the hotel to seize the card and destroy it.

Levin handled the setback with equanimity. "If I pay the full amount in cash, can I stay on?" he asked.

"I'm very sorry, sir," Lebowitz responded. "But I'm afraid at this point it would be best if you paid your bill and checked out."

Problems like the one with Levin were a rare occurrence at the Plaza, but such things did happen occasionally. Lebowitz had learned over time that the hotel tended to get the cream of the crop of con men, just as it got the cream of the rest of humanity. He was not about to be charmed. Levin seemed to understand. "Okay, Rich, thanks," he said, touching the assistant manager's shoulder. "I'll be back before midnight with the cash and collect my things." The confrontation had been easier than Lebowitz expected.

An hour and a half after Levin and Lebowitz spoke, the Plaza's security supervisor, Joe Vega, cut through a back stairway of the hotel on the way from his second-floor office to the rest room. In the stairwell he encountered a man moving quickly from the third to the second floor. Vega's antennae went up immediately. Not only was it strange to see a guest using the remote egress, Vega also recognized the bags the man was carrying. He had seen them in Room 1071 when he had double-locked the door to that room earlier in the day.

"May I ask why you are using the stairway, sir?" Vega said.

"The elevators on this side of the building are out of order," the man responded.

Vega knew he was lying. As security supervisor he would have been among the first to know about elevator problems. "Are you a guest?" Vega asked.

"Yes," the man responded, still moving rapidly down the stairs.

"May I see your room key?" Vega asked, still being polite, as he had been trained to be with hotel guests. By this time the man was beyond the second-floor landing where Vega was standing. Still hurrying, he held up his key. Vega asked the man to stop so he could continue questioning him. "Look, if you want to speak to me, you are going to have to hurry because I have a limousine waiting," the man responded. At the same time he broke into a run. On impulse, Vega ran after him.

As the two men entered the Plaza's stately lobby from the stairwell, Vega took out his walkie-talkie. "Intercept him before he gets to the Fifth Avenue door," he ordered his men stationed on the hotel's ground floor. By the time the man got to the exit, five security men were blocking the exit. Then, in what was probably the first episode of its kind in the venerable hotel, the man being pursued dropped his bags and assumed a karate stance. "Aaaah-yaah!" he yelled, grabbing the attention of an assortment of genteel ladies and hotel guests sipping tea in the lobby's dignified Palm Court. The security guards paused for a moment. This was a very large, very powerful man. But there were five guards. They encircled the bellowing man, but before they touched him he raised his hands in surrender. "Okay, you got me," he conceded, apparently relaxing.

Vega spoke quietly. "Look, I know what you are trying to do, but if you will just come with me to the front office, I am sure we can settle this matter."

The man offered Vega a hundred dollars if he would "just forget the whole thing." Instead Vega escorted him through the lobby, as curious onlookers strained to see what was happening. In the crowd, Vega and his officers became separated. The man appeared very nervous and was walking quickly—too quickly, Vega thought. He extended his hand to the man's chest in an attempt to slow him down.

"How about five hundred dollars? Will you forget the whole thing for five hundred?"

Vega again declined. Without warning, the man again broke into a run and headed for the revolving door that opens onto Central Park South. This time the five security guards had to take him by force, in the process destroying the glass doors.

Lebowitz was summoned and came quickly. "How did you get into your room, Mr. Levin?" he asked.

"A maid let me in," Levin replied.

The Plaza staff knew he was lying. Only security supervisors could get into rooms that had been double-locked. Vega sent a man up to check Room 1071. He soon reported back. The room's solid and very heavy oak door had been destroyed; it appeared to have been kicked in. The Plaza employees decided to call the police.

NYPD officer Robert Jordan was working burglary detail in midtown Manhattan when he got a call to go to the Plaza Hotel. Vega and Lebowitz explained the situation. Jordan turned to Levin, read him his rights, and placed him under arrest, charging him with burglary. Later the charge was changed to criminal trespass and criminal mischief. Levin didn't resist arrest, but Jordan nevertheless found it difficult to place handcuffs on the man. It was almost impossible to get the large man's hands behind his back because of his muscles. Down at the station, the suspect was booked as Ronald Levin. He was fingerprinted, photographed, and put into a cell. Ordinarily, Jordan removed his prisoners' valuables for safekeeping. But Levin asked to keep his money and his watch. "I let him," Jordan would later testify. "It seemed unlikely to me that anybody in the jail was going to take anything away from this guy."

Early on the morning of June 11, a collect phone call came in on Joe's private line at the BBC offices. Dean Karny answered the phone and handed it to Joe. When he got off the phone, Hunt announced he was leaving for New York. "Jim's gotten himself arrested," he said abruptly.

Central Arraignment Court at 100 Centre Street in Manhattan is one of the busiest courtrooms in the world. The court runs round the clock on three different shifts, as accused criminals of every variety come in and plead to the charges brought against them. The lawyers who work Central Arraignment are a special breed. Intense and scrappy, they often work fifteen-hour days, entering pleas and hustling up clients. In quiet moments, half a dozen of them meet to play poker in the courthouse pressroom until reporters arrive to chase them out. Their more dignified colleagues in the New York legal establishment say that the attorneys who work arraignment court are to the criminal bar what ambulance chasers are to the civil bar. And it is true that many an arraignment attorney has been hired on the courthouse steps.

It was in the courthouse hallway that Joe Hunt met Robert Ferraro at about 6 A.M. on June 12. Hunt was looking for a lawyer to handle an arraignment. Ferraro happened to be one. Joe asked for a card, but Ferraro had none with him. Instead he displayed his Bloomingdale's charge card. Joe was satisfied.

At the clerk's office, Ferraro filed a notice of appearance and in turn was given the complaint against Ron Levin. He then turned to Hunt. His fee, he explained, would be five hundred dollars, payable right then. Joe reached into his pocket and gave Ferraro a wad of cash totaling $4,500. In addition to the lawyer's fee, he explained, Joe wanted Ferraro to use two thousand dollars to pay back the Plaza Hotel. The remaining two thousand was for "Levin" when he was released from jail. The roll of bills remaining when Joe was finished counting out the $4,500 seemed to Ferraro at least as big as the roll he was handing over. Joe never told the lawyer his name.

At around 11 A.M., Hunt returned to the courthouse to see if his friend had been freed yet. Ferraro explained that they were still waiting for his rap sheet to be sent from Albany. An hour later, Hunt came back, but there was still no word. Finally, during the afternoon, the case of Ron Levin was heard. Levin was released on his own recognizance, but was told to come back on August 14 for a hearing. Ferraro urged Levin and his friend to wait around. "We can get this case dismissed if you pay the money." But the two men were in a hurry.

After court recessed, Ferraro called the Plaza and told them he had the money for them. At 3:45, hotel representatives, in the presence of Judge Carruthers, accepted the payment. But the charges still stood, since the defendant was no longer around. On August 14, Ferraro was on hand for the scheduled hearing, but his client never showed up. A bench warrant was issued for Ron Levin. It has never been recalled. The person in the booking photo attached to the police records is clearly Jim Graham.

*   *   *

After Joe Hunt took care of his friend's legal problems in New York, he hopped aboard a plane for London. Steve Lopez had some good prospective customers lined up for Joe to see. In addition, things were getting a little hot in Los Angeles. The investors were asking too many questions. Joe thought a little distance might help until the Levin check went through to solve his problems.

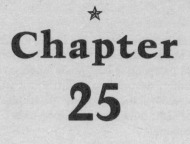

Chapter
25

When Joe arrived back in Los Angeles in mid-June, he found that in his absence his troubles had grown. While he was gone, Ben Dosti had received a phone call from the World Trade Bank. The Levin check had been refused by the Swiss bank on which it was written. Dean broke the bad news to Joe on the way up in the Wilshire Manning's elevator. Joe was obviously upset, but he tried to remain optimistic. "Maybe there's still something we can do," he said after a moment.

A couple of days later, Joe, Dean, and Jim Graham went to breakfast at Shapiro's Delicatessen next door to the Beverly Wilshire Hotel in Beverly Hills. After they finished their meal, they crossed the street to a small strip of grass that lines Santa Monica Boulevard where it skirts the Beverly Hills business district.

"For starters, Dean knows about Levin," Joe said. Jim smiled slightly at the news and nodded. "I've called this meeting to see what ideas anybody has for dealing with the Levin check. We need that money."

Jim spoke quickly. "I know somebody in Washington who can find out anything about Swiss accounts," he said. "I could call him if you want, but it would cost us."

With Jim, one never knew. During his months at the BBC, Joe and Dean had learned that the security man often exaggerated the importance of his contacts and the breadth of his experience. But now they had little choice but to hope Jim was on the level. They needed to know as much as possible about Levin's account in order to plan their next move.

Within a few days, Graham reported that his Washington friend would be able to help. Graham's connection speculated that perhaps Levin might have given the bank some kind of secret instructions. He thought he might be in a position to find out what they were. In addition, Jim said, the man could find out how much money was in the account and get additional checks so that a new draft could be written. There was only one catch. His friend would need thirty thousand dollars up front. On June 19, Jim departed for Washington, D.C. Joe told Dean he had given him the cash.

Within a couple of days, Graham was back. Whether he really met with anyone or not will probably never be known, but he claimed to have picked up valuable information in Washington. "My guy says the check didn't clear because Levin had issued an instruction to the bank not to pay on any check not signed in the upper left-hand corner." The friend had arranged for the bank to send new checks, Graham said, but they would be sent to Levin's mailbox in the Beverly Hills post office.

"No problem," Joe said. "I still have Levin's keys." For the next several weeks, the boys checked Levin's mailbox every day, but the checks never came.

The rank and file members of the BBC were losing faith. All along, Joe had been promising big riches. For many of the boys, the Levin check was the last test. If it came through, then they would continue to believe in Joe. If it failed, as everything else had, that would be it.

Dean was particularly attuned to the feelings of the other boys. For Dean more than for many of the members, the BBC was everything. All the rhetoric Joe had spouted over the last two years, Dean took very seriously. He believed the BBC was founded on noble ideals. His closest social ties were within the group. And now his world seemed to be falling apart.

Finally Dean approached Joe. "I think the cohesiveness of the BBC is failing," Dean began. "We are constantly having to make excuses about why there is no money. We are deceiving the other guys in the BBC, and we shouldn't be doing that." Joe asked Dean what he proposed. "It seems to me that a lot of the members can be trusted," Dean said. "If they understand what we're trying to accomplish, and they understand the goals of Paradox Philosophy, then they will be able to understand the killing of Ron Levin. I think telling them will help bind the group back together so we can get on with what we're trying to accomplish."

It was a strange notion: tell the group about a gruesome murder in order to bring the members closer together. But Dean saw nothing odd about his plan. "At the time, [the Levin murder] was something I was reconciled to, to use the Paradox term. It didn't even occur to me that once we chose the right people who we felt had come along far enough in their Paradox Philosophy, that they wouldn't go along with it," Dean recalled later. He was very nearly right.

According to Karny, during the middle part of June, Joe, Dean, and Ben talked often about who could be trusted with the truth about Levin's murder. Joe decided he would first test the waters with Tom May. He invited Tom along on an errand. On their way to the bank in Joe's black Jeep, Tom gave him the perfect opening. "Something is weird around the office, Joe," Tom said. "You and Dean are always off whispering in corners. It's getting very strange. What is going on?"

Joe hardly paused. "I guess you'll find out sooner or later," he said. "I killed Ron Levin."

Tom was at first incredulous. He had heard Joe's wild stories before. The BBC's founder seemed to love to impress the boys with his wickedness. He often bragged about having tortured and killed neighborhood cats when he was a kid. He used to tell the boys that his mother had taken him to a fortune-teller when he was a boy. According to Joe, the seer had taken one look at the young boy and ordered him out, saying the child was the Antichrist. Once Joe had even bragged about killing two Mexicans he said jumped him one day as he was walking home from school. Tom had learned to discount Joe's stories. Still, this one seemed different.

"You're kidding," he said finally.

"No I'm not," Joe replied.

"Is that how you got the check?" Tom asked.

"Let's just say he signed it under duress," Joe said, grinning slightly. "The murder took place in New York," he added with a sudden fit of caution lest he be revealing too much. "It was the perfect crime."

Back at Third Street, Joe called Tom into his office along with Ben and Dean. "You're close to the other guys. Who do you think we should tell?" Joe asked Tom. "How about your brother?"

After consideration, Tom decided that his brother shouldn't be included. "I don't know if you can trust him," Tom said.

Chapter
26

It was the merest thread of chance that brought Reza
Eslaminia to the BBC in mid-June of 1984. A friend had asked
him to drop some papers off at the group's Third Street offices.
He did, and while there he ran into Ben Dosti. Reza was in
many ways a prime candidate for the BBC. At twenty-three,
the Iranian boy was having some trouble finding his footing
as an adult. He had recently gotten his first job, as a telephone
salesman for an industrial flooring company, but Reza considered the job beneath him. He wanted to start at the top.

There were two other facts about Reza that made Ben
Dosti think the boy was BBC material. One was Reza's girlfriend, Debra Lutkenhouse, a girl from the exclusive San
Francisco suburb of Hillsborough whose very wealthy father
had owned one of the largest moving and storing companies
in the country before retiring to Hawaii. The girl's family
money was very appealing. The other intriguing aspect of
Reza Eslaminia was the young man's own background. His

father, as he was quick to tell anyone who would listen, had been high up in the Shah's government in Iran. When the Ayatollah Khomeini came to power, Reza's father fled to Hillsborough, bringing with him a fortune in excess of thirty million dollars. Or so Reza said.

When Reza asked for information about the BBC, Ben was happy to supply it. "We should really talk business sometime," Reza said. "I have excellent Mideast contacts, and we could probably put together some mutually beneficial deals." In addition, the Iranian boy said, he thought it might be good for the BBC to hook up with his girlfriend's father. Mr. Lutkenhouse had excellent contacts in China, Reza said, and they might be interested in BBC products. At the end of their chance encounter, Ben and Reza agreed to speak soon. Within a week, Ben had made plans to meet Reza in San Francisco, where Debra Lutkenhouse's father was visiting. Reza thought Ben should try to interest him in the BBC's fire retardant chemical. Within a month, the boys were planning business deals of a far different sort.

There was much about himself that Reza Eslaminia omitted in his conversation with Ben Dosti that first day. The Iranian boy spoke only about his father's wealth, but said nothing about his serious troubles with his father. He said nothing about the family's dashed expectations, or about his own erratic history.

As a child, Reza Eslaminia had been groomed with the belief that he would one day be prime minister of Iran. His family's expectations for him had been, if optimistic, not illogical. Reza's grandfather had been one of four generals responsible for the Shah's return to power. His great-uncle had been prime minister. His father, Hedayat, was a rising political star in 1961 when Reza was born, a close ally of the Shah and a powerful member of Parliament. It had appeared back then that the Shah's government would last forever, and if it did, the fortunes of the Eslaminia family seemed assured.

Reza spent his childhood in Tehran's most exclusive section, attended the best schools, and spent his summers in family villas on the Caspian Sea. "My destiny seemed very certain," Reza would later write, "that one day I too would become important to my country."

But events intervened. By the time Reza was ten, the Shah's power was waning. His regime was increasingly linked to corruption and scandal, and Reza's father was right in the middle of it. Over the years, Hedayat had used his position in Parliament to boost his personal fortune, accepting bribes and requisitioning government supplies to build and furnish his lavish homes.

As Hedayat became more corrupt, his family began to deteriorate. In 1972, when Reza was eleven, Hedayat's wife, Mina, learned her husband was seeing another woman. Outraged, she went one day to the home Hedayat had bought for his mistress, expecting to confront the two of them. But when she burst into the dwelling, she instead found her husband smoking opium with some of his parliamentary colleagues and a number of half-clad women. Mina fled, but her husband followed, waving a gun and screaming, furious that he had been embarrassed in front of his colleagues.

Although Hedayat at first demanded a divorce, the couple soon got back together, and the next two years were punctuated by stormy fights and tearful reconciliations. The children, particularly Reza, were caught in the crossfire. "When intoxicated or under the influence of opium, [Hedayat] often beat our two older children severely and to the point they were bruised or bleeding," Mina later swore in court. "On numerous occasions I had to intercede and sustain the abuses rather than allow my husband to continue to beat the children."

In 1974 Hedayat ordered his wife out of the house forever, but battles over the children continued. One day later that year, Reza's father picked him up from his mother's house, saying he was taking the boy for a holiday at the Caspian Sea.

Instead he took Reza halfway around the world to Hillsborough, California, and a whole new life.

Whether Hedayat Eslaminia realized the Shah's days were numbered is unclear, but he certainly saw in 1974 some advantage in establishing a base outside Iran and in funneling a portion of his assets out of that country in case he needed to flee quickly. He chose the San Francisco Peninsula for his new residence. The Peninsula sticks out like a thumb from the middle of California. At its south end, connecting it to the rest of the state, is San Jose; at its other end, sixty miles north, is San Francisco.

Of all the affluent suburban communities that line the Peninsula, Hillsborough, where Hedayat took his son Reza, stands out. Its palatial mansions have served as headquarters for many of the state's wealthiest families. It was here that Patty Hearst grew up. In recent years Hillsborough has also attracted a different type: rich Middle Easterners, particularly exiled Iranians. But the old-line Hillsborough residents have been slow to accept the new element.

Hedayat established his twelve-year-old son in a huge split-level Spanish-style house on a two-acre estate high up in the foothills with a panoramic view of the San Francisco Bay. Then he returned to Iran, leaving Reza—sometimes with a housekeeper, sometimes at boarding school, and sometimes on his own—to keep the household going. The situation was more than the adolescent could handle. Stripped of his identity as an important figure, Reza found himself suddenly considered an inferior person because of his dark skin, accent, and origins. In the strange new culture, Reza soon learned, he had only one real asset with which to attract friends—a house with little or no adult supervision.

By the time Reza was in his teens, his house had become a "party center," according to one family friend. "All the kids in the area knew Reza's was a place they could party without parents looking over their shoulders." As Reza himself later put it, "The wrong crowd started to gather around me, and I started to associate and tried to fit into the wrong crowd in Hillsborough."

Hedayat had little time for his son's problems. In Iran, the Shah's government was beginning to flounder in the face of growing opposition. Hedayat's life was crumbling, and he didn't bear up well under his changing circumstances. "After my mother and father separated, my father gradually began to increase his use of opium," Hedayat's second son, Ali, would later testify in his parent's 1981 divorce case. "What was once a weekly habit became a daily addiction." One room of the Hillsborough house was set aside as an opium room for Hedayat's visits.

In 1977, Hedayat surprised his sons by seemingly taking an interest in their school lives. By now Reza and Ali, as well as Eslaminia's two younger sons, were living in California. Hedayat announced that he was sending three Persian paintings to his children's teachers. He asked a female employee who was traveling to the States to take the paintings with her. She agreed. But at customs the paintings were searched, and officers found sticks of opium wedged behind the frames. After a lengthy investigation, the woman was allowed to leave, and neither she nor Hedayat was prosecuted. It was the beginning of a long pattern of the U.S. government's casting a tolerant eye on Hedayat's activities.

By 1978, when the Shah fell and Hedayat and Mina were forced to flee Iran, Reza had become heavily involved in drugs. His parents' closer supervision did little to stem Reza's decline, and may have furthered it. For one thing, the conflicts between Mina and Hedayat were even more bitter, and now the children were closer to the battleground. Mina settled in a house her father purchased for her in Beverly Hills; Hedayat moved into the Hillsborough house with his children and mistress, and with the children as ammunition, the couple continued their protracted war. Several times Hedayat invited Mina to Hillsborough to visit her children but then sent her away without allowing her to see them.

Yet Hedayat had little interest in being a supportive parent to his sons. After marrying another Iranian exile, named Simin, Hedayat spent his days in an opium daze, allowing the house to get filthy. Dinner was often served after 10 P.M., according to Reza's younger brother, Ali, in order "to accommodate the frequent opium-smoking party guests who are served dinner and entertained in my father's home."

Hedayat also grew increasingly abusive to his sons. Ali later described once coming home from a date at twelve thirty on a Friday night. "I encountered my father at the door. . . . He was obviously high from opium smoking, his eyes were red and he reeked of the odor of the drug. My father refused to let me in except on one of two conditions: either he would shave the hair from my head, or press a burning cigarette against my hand." Afraid to allow either action, Ali "instead, at his command, applied the burning cigarette to the back of my left hand. My left hand still bears the scar from this burn." Next, "because my hair was longer than my father desired, he approached me with scissors, while under opium influence, and knocked me to the floor, knees in my chest, forced on my back, he attempted to cut my hair against my will. With great effort I fought him off."

It was all too much for Reza, who was by then using all sorts of drugs, including marijuana, cocaine, and LSD. After a brush with the law, Reza got on a plane to Los Angeles and checked into a Glendale motel. A family friend, aware of the boy's state of mind, tracked him down there and persuaded the motel keeper to let him into Reza's room. There he found Reza semiconscious, a half empty bottle of Drano the boy had drunk beside the bed.

In 1979, Reza was sent to a drug treatment facility in Texas. There he fell in love with a young woman patient. The staff opposed their relationship, so the two eloped. But after a few months, the girl deserted Reza. During the months that followed, Reza was consumed with grief alternating with rage, much of it directed at his father.

A longtime family friend who had watched with alarm as Reza grew wilder, became concerned about the frequent fights between father and son. On one occasion the friend witnessed a screaming fight in which Reza threatened to kill his father. In another acrimonious exchange, the boy actually attacked Hedayat, breaking one of Hedayat's teeth and bloodying his face.

The family friend was not the only concerned onlooker in the battles between Reza and Hedayat. Reza had begun seeing a Westwood psychologist who soon became so worried that he felt obligated to write a warning letter to Hedayat. "You are in [danger of] potential loss of life and property from your son Reza," the psychologist wrote in 1980. "In the past he made threats when he was very disturbed, which I dealt with while he was in therapy. According to reports I have received, he is once again seriously disturbed. . . . I consider this to be a warning according to the requirements of the California legal system to an endangered person."

Reza had gone to live with his mother in 1980, but the move hadn't helped him find his course. He was arrested three times that year. The first arrest was for possession of a dangerous weapon, the second for drugs. The third was more serious.

On the morning of September 10, 1980, the Palm Springs police received a tip that a local residence would be burglarized that night. The anonymous informant provided police with descriptions of the suspects and license plate numbers of the cars they would be driving.

A Palm Springs detective traced one of the cars to a Beverly Hills address. The family's seventeen-year-old son broke down and gave full details of the planned crime. He had once been to the Palm Springs home of a friend's grandparents, the boy told police, and had discovered that the elderly couple kept fifty thousand dollars in cash as well as valuable jewelry in the house. He had passed along this information, as well as a floor plan of the house, to several friends. The group of Beverly Hills kids was planning to burglarize the house that night.

At around 11 P.M. five Palm Springs police officers under

the direction of Detective Thomas Barton drove to the house and explained the situation to the owner, David Krechman. "My wife and I . . . decided to go to a hotel," Krechman later testified, "because, well, I'm seventy, she's sixty-seven. We were pretty nervous. We decided to get out of there because we thought we'd get hurt or something." Barton and two other officers settled themselves inside the house while the remaining officers took up a position on top of a house across the street.

Several hours later one of the officers across the street radioed Barton: "It looks like it's going down." Two men were scaling the fence. Reports kept coming as the men circled the house; then Barton saw a shadow and heard a scratching noise against the window of the bedroom where he was stationed.

One suspect escaped that night, but police caught the other, Reza Eslaminia. He had a razor blade taped to his ankle, and police found nearby a bottle of ether and a roll of duct tape. Reza claimed later that the officers brutalized him. But Detective Barton told it differently: "When we went to arrest him, he wanted to fight."

After his conviction, Reza wrote to the judge, promising that he had learned his lesson and trying to point out the reasons for his troubles. While growing up in Iran, Reza wrote, he had hopes of becoming an important member of the Iranian government, like his father. Ultimately, though, his dreams were shattered by events in Iran, and, he noted somewhat self-pityingly, "I was left on my own with a house, a school, and no parent or guardian at the age of twelve." He was still uncertain of American ways, he said, and became involved in the burglary attempt as the result of a dare and to impress his girlfriend. Now he realized his mistake. "I am happy to learn the valuable lesson that I did learn," he wrote. "That America is freedom and not jail, and in order to enjoy that freedom that America represents, one must live within the laws and rules of a free society.

"I wish to beg you to give me another chance," he continued, "so that I may restore the love and pride of my loved ones and become a useful member of the society, and, who knows, with a little help from God, maybe even one of the top members of the Parliament in the hopefully upcoming Iranian Government."

Hedayat also responded to his son's plight by writing a letter. His urged that the court release Reza to him, claiming that "any wrong thing he has done [was] caused by his mother, my ex-wife." Hedayat promised that "if he does a single thing wrong, I will be the first one to report it to you or to the local police station."

Mina argued that Hedayat's home was not a fit place for her son. But in the end, Reza moved back to the Peninsula with his father, where he was to receive additional drug treatment mandated by the court.

For a time, Reza appeared, at least outwardly, to bury his animosity toward his father. In March of 1982, when Hedayat asked him to write a letter on his behalf as part of U.S. divorce proceedings, Reza responded with vigor, apparently transferring some of his former feelings for his father to Mina. Reza's story contradicted much of what he had earlier maintained about his life after coming to the United States, but he seemed not to be bothered about that.

"When I was twelve," he wrote to the judge in the proceedings, "my parents got a divorce (valid in Iran) and my father brought us to the United States and enrolled us in the best schools in the country. He also bought us a house in Hillsborough so we would have a home to go to on weekends. Anyway, to make a long story short, the four years that I lived with my father I was an A student and never got in any kind of trouble. As a matter of fact, those years were the happiest years of my life."

At sixteen, he informed the judge, he had been lured away to his mother with lies about his father. It was, he said, "one of the biggest mistakes of my life." Reza spun a wild tale in his letter, claiming that the moral climate in his mother's house was even worse than that in his father's. "While I was working, she was in a different nightclub every night," Reza claimed. "About six months ago, I caught her in bed with three black men," he wrote, clearly hoping the judge would think his mother more immoral because of the men's race. "I truly wish I never had a mother. She thinks she is still twelve years old and is constantly trying to pick up on men and have a good time to a point where she was even paying some of these men money."

In a further contradiction of both the truth and his earlier statements, Reza also praised his father to the judge. "I have never seen my father use any sort of narcotic drug. He even hates cigarettes and does not allow us to smoke cigarettes in his house. He is a good man, a very religious man. He is a good father and a very good example for us, and we love him very much."

Despite his statements to the judge, Reza had not completely buried his hostility toward his father. Later in 1982 he discovered a perfect means for venting it. Reza, always seeking approval from those in power even as he flaunted their authority, had gone to the police with an offer to inform for them about Peninsula drug activities. During 1982 and 1983 he received more than fifty payments of between twenty and three hundred dollars for information he passed along to law enforcement. The biggest fish he knew about in the drug sea, he kept insisting, was his father. But Reza couldn't seem to interest any agency in taking action against his dad. If he wanted revenge, he would have to seek it elsewhere.

On June 24, 1984, Ben accompanied Reza to San Francisco as planned to meet with Debra Lutkenhouse's father. The older man was impressed with the BBC member's style and intelligence, but in the end he was not interested in Fire Safety. Ben was in a hurry to catch a plane back to Los Angeles. He had a very important meeting to attend.

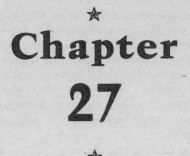

Chapter 27

The afternoon of June 24 was a perfect day for polo. Since May, a contingent of BBC boys including the Mays, Jeff Raymond, Ben Dosti, and Evan Dicker had been learning the game at the Los Angeles Equestrian Center. They had hoped to play on that warm Sunday in late June, but Joe Hunt had insisted most of the boys attend a meeting at his apartment in the Wilshire Manning. The organization had not met as a group for some time, and Joe said he had urgent business to discuss.

The boys arrived in casual clothes and flopped down on the brown sectional sofa Dean Karny had brought with him when he moved into the apartment. By two o'clock, most of the BBC's inner circle had arrived. There were the Shadings, Joe, Ben, and Dean; there was Jim Graham, who had by then become a de facto Shading even though he didn't officially hold the title or have much understanding of Paradox Philosophy; and there was a good proportion of the other boys—Evan Dicker, Jon Allen, Steve Taglianetti, Jeff Raymond, Tom

May. Brooke Roberts played hostess, providing sandwiches for the boys as they waited for the meeting to begin.

Dave May was conspicuous by his absence. Joe had told them all in advance that the important business he had to discuss didn't involve Dave. He would appreciate it, he said, if Dave was not told about the meeting. Inviting Jeff Raymond had been a bit of a gamble for Joe. The boy was very close to Dave, but since he was now living in apartment 1505 with Joe, Dean, and Brooke, Joe hadn't felt he could exclude him. And besides, Jeff didn't seem like someone who would rock the boat.

After everyone arrived, Joe stood tall above the seated group. "I want to discuss some very sensitive things," Joe said to his curious audience. "We have discussed before how sometimes in the world, if you want to acquire greatness, you must take risks. Occasionally, you must even transgress the law. What you are about to hear is going to require you to stretch to new heights. You are going to need to accept much more responsibility than you ever have had to before. Anybody who doesn't want to take on this higher knowledge can leave the room now. If you do stay, you will have to be responsible and disciplined about what you hear." Joe looked around the room, making eye contact with each of the boys in turn. Not one left.

At that point, Joe called a break to the meeting. "Before I can continue, I need to have a final conversation with certain other people," he said. He then gathered Dean, Ben, and Jim and went with them into his bedroom. Dean later testified to what happened there.

"Are we all agreed to tell this group here about Mac?" Dean says Joe asked the other boys in his bedroom. Dean and Ben affirmed that they were in favor of telling.

Jim had reservations. "I still don't know," he said. "It seems to me that when you tell a bunch of people something like this, somebody always talks."

Dean, Joe, and Ben broke in with their assurances. "We've

handpicked these people," Dean said. "They can definitely be trusted."

"Well, if you think so, then it's okay with me," Graham said finally. "You know these guys better than I do, and if you think they can be trusted, then go ahead and tell them."

Wanting another few moments privately with Graham, Joe sent Dean and Ben back to the living room. Several minutes later, he and Jim rejoined them.

The long break had heightened the sense of drama in apartment 1505 considerably. When Joe began speaking again, it was to a silent and serious group of young men. "Jim and I knocked off Ron Levin," Joe said almost casually. As the boys sat stunned by his revelation, Joe continued. "We're also broke. There was a major setback in the commodities markets, and our funds there were wiped out. We still have a little money and certain assets, including the attrition mill. We may still be able to get the Levin check cashed. We can definitely get back on our feet if we stay together and work hard, but I thought you all needed to know exactly where things stand."

When Joe quit speaking, the BBC members began asking questions, carefully avoiding mention of Levin and instead focusing on their concerns about money. "Does that mean the twenty thousand I invested is gone?" Jeff Raymond asked. Yes, Joe told him, but he hoped to pay the money back eventually.

As the meeting was winding down, Joe Hunt made a final point. "You had an opportunity to leave the room and not hear what I said. None of you took it. Therefore, you are bound by your own decision never to reveal the secret you learned here," Joe reminded them. "You may at some point decide to leave the BBC, and that's fine. You can do anything you want. You can go fishing in the outer Adirondacks. You just can't ever tell anyone what you heard here today. Anyone who does so will be dealt with severely."

Dean was both impressed by Joe and encouraged by what he saw in the faces of the boys at the meeting. Joe had really mastered Paradox Philosophy, Dean thought. It was amazing how he had taken something black—a murder—and turned it into something white. He had started out with bad news and then had blended in hope and optimism until by the time the meeting ended, none of the attendees had appeared upset to Dean. He was optimistic that the announcement would bring the boys back together, as he had hoped. He would soon learn how wrong he was.

Chapter
28

The morning of June 25 was unusually warm for early summer in Southern California. Dave May had arrived at the Gardena warehouse early and was attending to paperwork in the plant. He liked working in the big, empty warehouse. He had learned a lot from helping Gene Browning assemble the massive metal attrition mill, and he was proud of his work.

Dave was feeling quite contented when a clearly worried Jeff Raymond came in. "What's up, bud?" Dave asked casually.

Jeff responded in a whisper. "This place may be bugged." Then, gesturing, he directed Dave to the front office that Joe's father had used for Fire Safety. Still in a whisper, Jeff continued. "Joe's killed Ron Levin," he said.

Dave didn't respond as he tried to assimilate the bizarre information. It was unbelievable. "You're fucking kidding," he finally said.

In low tones, Jeff told his friend about the preceding day's meeting. Dave was uncertain quite what to think. Joe Hunt was a liar. Was this just one more lie? But as they reviewed all the strange things they had heard during the last several months—the purchasing of weapons, Joe's paranoia about the warehouse—the boys became convinced that it was likely Hunt actually had killed Levin. The next step was to decide what to do.

By the end of their discussion, the boys had decided to approach Dave's father. It was true David May II hadn't always been the most involved parent, but he was the one person Dave felt certain would know what to do about the bizarre situation. Dave didn't relish the thought of going to his father. Ever since the elder May had written his sons the caustic letter dismissing Hunt as a fraud, the twins had looked forward to the day when they could announce to their father they had made large profits through the BBC. Now Dave would have to admit his father had been right.

He also worried about his brother. Why in the world hadn't Tom told him about the meeting? Dave and Jeff discussed whether they should talk to Tom, but in the end decided he was too close to Hunt. For now they would proceed alone.

Over the next couple of days, they prepared for their meeting with Dave's father, making notes on a steno pad of everything they had to relate. The night before Dave rehearsed what he would say. On the morning of June 27, the day Dave later recalled as being "the worst in my life," Jeff and Dave drove to David May II's imposing house near Sunset Boulevard in the most expensive part of Beverly Hills. Dave had insisted his friend come along. "If I'm going to put my tail between my legs and eat crow, you're going to share the dinner with me," he told Jeff.

When the boys arrived, Dave's father was in bed, where the seventy-three-year-old often conducted his morning business. After being shown to his room, the boys pulled up chairs. "Dad, I don't know where to start," Dave began hesitantly, his carefully worded speech now forgotten. "It has just come to my attention that everything I've believed about the BBC up to now has been a lie. Tom and I lost all our money. And to top it off, I think this guy has killed somebody, and we don't know what to do."

The elder May was stoic. If he was surprised at his son's story, his face didn't reveal it. "Where's Tom in all of this?" he asked.

"I don't know," Dave replied. "I think he's mesmerized by the guy."

Dave plunged ahead, wanting now to tell his father everything, but David May stopped him. "It's best if I don't hear all the details," he said. "If you're involved, let's see what we can do to get you out." It would be best, Dave's father said, if the boys saw his attorney. The lawyer would have a far better notion of what to do. "You can count on my support," the elder May concluded.

Dave left his father's house feeling as if an enormous burden had been removed from him. Without being condescending, as Dave had feared he might be, his father had come through. He was confident now that everything would work out.

During the next week, the boys met with David May's attorneys. They were clearly uncertain, Dave felt, about what had actually happened. "This guy is a compulsive liar, right?" they asked Dave after hearing his story. "How do you know the murder story isn't just another of his lies?" They would make the contacts with law enforcement agencies for the boys, but in the meantime, Jeff and Dave should keep their eyes and ears open. Anything they could gather would increase their credibility with the police. It all might take some time.

Chapter 29

Reza Eslaminia made a note. "Get tuxito" (sic), he wrote on a list of things to do on July 6. Reza wasn't accustomed to dressing formally, but the printed invitation to Evan Dicker's twenty-third birthday party was specific. In small print at the bottom were the words "Formal Attire." Reza Eslaminia didn't own a tuxedo, unlike most of the BBC boys, but he was determined to rent one. The party was the first major BBC social function to which he had been invited, and Reza wanted very badly to be accepted by this group of young men. Finally, after ten years in America, he felt he had fallen into exactly the right sort of company.

By the time Reza arrived at Evan's one-bedroom Beverly Hills apartment on the evening of July 7, the party was in full swing. Champagne flowed freely. Limousines, arranged for by Jim Graham, stopped frequently at the curb to deposit various BBC members.

Even by BBC standards, the party was a gala affair. Evan

had wanted to do things right. Even more than the others, the stylish young man loved lavish entertainment. He liked the way people looked in evening clothes. He loved drinking good champagne.

Joe Hunt had his own reasons for wanting the party to be special. The group had faced some serious stresses lately. Joe felt it was important for the members to have something to celebrate together. In honor of the occasion, Joe had taken twenty thousand dollars of the group's dwindling cash reserves and purchased ten identical motorcycles, one for each of the core BBC members. He had parked Evan's in the middle of his living room, a sort of centerpiece for the party.

Reza was very impressed by all the splendor. As the evening progressed, he hoped he was making a hit at the party. His girlfriend Debra, or Debi as he called her, had for years urged him to downplay his background, not to brag, and he was being careful to do as she advised. But the boys all seemed interested in his unusual history. Ben was being especially attentive, making sure the Iranian boy met the right people.

By the end of the evening, Reza Eslaminia was very pleased with the way things had gone. He felt the group was going to accept him.

Ben Dosti's girlfriend, Kate Johnston, wasn't so happy when she left Evan's house. In the middle of the evening, Jeff Raymond had pulled her aside. "I can't be very specific, Kate, but you've got to be very careful. There are some very strange things going on in the BBC. Ben may be involved. If I were you, I wouldn't count on ever seeing the money you invested again. And there are other things, too." Kate was alarmed and pressed him for more details, but Jeff, while he wanted to warn the young woman, didn't want to jeopardize his plans for going to the police. "Just don't discuss this with Ben," he warned, "or I could get in big trouble."

Jeff's puzzling words confirmed what Kate had suspected for some time: Ben was involved in something he didn't want her to know about. Lately he had seemed very distant. When she asked him about business, he was circumspect. She was beginning to feel that Ben was pushing her away. Now she realized it must have something to do with what Jeff was talking about. Kate was very worried.

Chapter

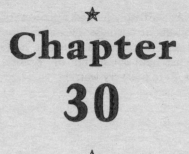

30

Prosecutors believe Dean Karny's version of what transpired next with Reza Eslaminia. This is what he has told them happened.

On a hot summer afternoon shortly after Evan's party, Joe called an impromptu meeting of the Shadings. "Come outside," he told Ben and Dean. "We need to talk." Out on a busy street corner in front of the BBC offices, Joe began. "Reza wants to enlist our help. He's interested in forcing his father to turn over some assets, and perhaps we can help." During the next five minutes, the boys discussed the facts as presented by Reza. His father, Hedayat, was a monster, a violent drug dealer who had cut Reza, his mother, and his siblings off without a penny. There might be a fair amount of money for the BBC if the boys agreed to help. The three Shadings agreed they should meet with Reza and discuss the possibilities further.

A few days later, Joe, Ben, Reza, Dean, and Jim Graham

got together at the Wilshire Manning. Reza explained more about his father's background, about his career in Iran. "Because of his position in the government, he was able to get a lot of money, about thirty million dollars, out of the country before the Shah fell," Reza told the eager boys. The money was stashed in various banks around the world. Most important, he told them, his father had lots of enemies. In addition to his drug dealing, Hedayat Eslaminia was very involved in an international movement aimed at overthrowing Khomeini, according to his son. He was on a hit list maintained by the current Iranian regime. "No one would ever suspect us. Everyone will assume that either the Ayatollah's people got him or that some drug dealer finally caught up with him."

The BBC boys were extremely interested. For one thing, Reza would split any money he got evenly with the BBC, and the group's situation had become desperate. For another, as crazy as Reza's plan might sound to many of their peers outside the BBC, Joe, Dean, and Ben had already crossed the line into madness. Joe had engineered and carried out the execution of a business enemy; the others had given him their tacit approval. Nothing bad had happened as a result of the crime. What was one more felony?

Over the two weeks that followed, the boys met frequently, and by late July they had formed a concrete plan. They would abduct Eslaminia from his house and transport him back to Southern California. They would keep him hidden there until he could be forced to reveal where his assets were and to sign papers granting everything to Reza. Then, at least the Shadings understood, he would be killed. By the way, Joe told the boys, he'd been thinking. They needed a code name for the operation. From now on, they would refer to the planned abduction as Project Sam.

Reza urged the abduction be carried out quickly. "My father is planning a trip to Europe soon," he told them. "If we do it soon, people may just assume he left for his trip. If we don't, we may lose the opportunity." That was something no one wanted. Project Sam was scheduled for July 30.

At a meeting in his apartment in mid-July, Joe assigned tasks to each of the Project Sam participants. Dean was to purchase two trunks large enough to hold a human being. One would be used for Eslaminia; the second would be used only if they ended up having to abduct Eslaminia's girlfriend, Olga Vasquez, as well. Dean was also to get gags, handcuffs, and disguises. The boys discussed just what they would need and finally decided on either police uniforms or delivery uniforms as a way to gain access to Hedayat's security-gated condominium complex.

Reza was to get kitty litter and a bucket for his father to use as a toilet, and also chloroform in case they needed to subdue Hedayat. Ben was to get air freshener, to mask the smell of the chloroform, and spray-on plastic bandage material so the boys wouldn't leave fingerprints. Jim would be in charge of surveillance. He was to figure out how to get into the condominium and to make sure no one else was watching Eslaminia.

Together, Ben, Dean, and Joe would look for a house suitable for keeping Hedayat hidden in. After Joe had assigned everyone but himself tasks, he looked up at the group. "I'll take it upon myself to go to the library and get books on torture. I think I'm the only one among us with a stomach for that sort of thing, and one of us is going to have to *encourage* Mr. Eslaminia to sign some papers."

At the end of the meeting, Reza raised an additional item of business. He had been thinking, and it seemed to him that they might need to purchase some opium. "My father's an addict," he told the others. "He may really need the stuff. Besides, it could be a great way of getting him to do what we want." The boys agreed immediately, and Joe assigned Reza the task of procuring the drug.

By the time the boys met again a few days later, many of the Project Sam assignments had been completed. Dean hauled out one of the trunks he had purchased to the center of his living-room floor, and the others set their things on top. The trunk seemed as if it might be too small for Hedayat, who was five foot ten and weighed one hundred seventy pounds. But Dean had already tried it out. A human would definitely fit, he assured the others. If there had been prizes awarded that evening, Dean would probably have gotten the one for the most innovative purchasing. He'd found a gag in the shape of a penis at a store called the International Love Boutique in Hollywood, and it proved to be the hit of the evening.

Before Dean could get the uniforms, the boys needed to decide who would be participating in the actual abduction. "I don't think you should be seen," Joe told Reza. "Your father will be a lot more afraid if he doesn't know you're part of the team. It's better if he has no idea who sent us." Reza readily agreed. By the end of the evening it had been decided. Joe, Ben, and Jim would be the ones to actually go into the apartment. Dean and Reza would act as lookouts on the street. In the meantime, Reza needed to get his father's exact address. Due to economic circumstances, Hedayat had been forced to sell his Hillsborough home the previous year. The two had been on the outs for so long that Reza wasn't sure just where he lived.

Chapter
31

By mid-July, the BBC was clinging to one last business hope—Microgenesis. Gene Browning believed the attrition mill he had built with Dave May and Jeff Raymond was finally ready. Tests performed at the warehouse had demonstrated the machine's ability to crush rocks. In anticipation of the machine's entrance into the marketplace, the boys had prepared a projected profit statement for Microgenesis of North America that reflected their unbridled optimism about the device's possibilities. For 1984, the report projected profits of $14,143,719. Each year, revenues were expected to grow, until in 1988, the report estimated, the company would be making an annual profit of $68,200,000.

Of far more practical interest to the BBC members, the group had actually received an order for one of the Cyclotrons from a Mesa, Arizona, miner, Bill Morton. He agreed to pay a large sum for the machine, and had expressed an interest in acquiring more if the device lived up to its promise.

Dave May and Gene Browning worked hard for more than a week setting up the machine for Morton in the 120-degree heat of the Arizona desert summer. But in many ways they enjoyed their work. In the months they had been assembling the machine, Gene and Dave had developed a close friendship, almost a father-son relationship. Dave had been looking for an opportunity to clue Browning in on the developments in the BBC, and one afternoon he did. "I think Joe killed Ron Levin," he said.

After hearing Dave's tale, Browning believed the young man absolutely. "Have you gone to the police?" Browning asked. Dave told him they were planning on going. He and Jeff Raymond had already picked up Steve Taglianetti as an ally. They were recruiting others and gathering information. Then they would go.

Dave's revelation came as a major blow to the older man. Time and again he had come close to finding funding for his invention, only to have the deal fall through. With Joe he had been sure his troubles were over. Just recently Joe had assured Browning that the BBC would soon purchase a house for him. Now the BBC would certainly collapse, and Browning's future would be as uncertain as ever before. Even as he reassured Dave about the importance of going to the police, he cursed Joe Hunt. Another dream dashed.

On July 20, when the machine was tested, it was clear Browning had other problems as well. The machine didn't work. Dave and Gene tinkered with the huge milling device's parts for hours in the hot sun, but the rocks they fed in were not being properly pulverized. Bill Morton was extremely upset. Browning apologized and said he would go back to Los Angeles and solve the problems. But the machine's flaws were not easily remedied.

Shortly after the two men returned, Morton made clear that he would not pay the BBC any further money. But by this time, both the BBC leaders and Gene and Dave had other preoccupations.

*   *   *

Dave had been looking for weeks for a way to approach his brother about the Levin murder. The twins had grown so far apart that they were barely speaking. As Dave later put it, "If we could have stopped being brothers, we would have." Everything about Tom's BBC persona grated on Dave. Sometimes in the evening when Tom came home in his three-piece suits, Dave, in his stained, sweaty work clothes, couldn't resist baiting his brother. "Work hard today, Tom?" he'd ask. "Make any big deals?" It was one of the few times in their lives that they had kept secrets from one another, and Dave didn't like it. He realized that the distance between them would soon be unbridgeable. He had to find out just where Tom stood.

Dave wanted Jeff to be around for moral support when he confronted Tom about the Levin murder, so one afternoon the two boys went together to the Mays' Brentwood apartment. Eventually Tom came in and sat on the pastel sectional couch that dominated the living room. Jeff and Dave sat down on either side of him.

"Tom," Dave began dramatically. "Don't you have something to tell me?"

Tom looked nervously at Jeff, uncertain how to respond. "Should we tell him?" he finally asked hesitantly.

Jeff shrugged. "It's up to you," he said.

After several moments of silence, Tom turned to his brother. "Hunt killed Ron Levin."

"I know," Dave said imperiously. "I just needed to hear you say it. We've already gone to Dad and spoken to his lawyers. We're going to go to the police. We're really moving on this thing."

Before Dave could continue, Tom had stood up on the couch and begun jumping up and down hooting with high-spirited joy. He hugged Dave enthusiastically, and then Jeff and then Dave again. "I've felt so all alone," he said finally.

It was a moment of triumph for Dave. In the relationship between the two brothers, Tom was more often in the lead. Outsiders would have had trouble discerning the subtle differences between the twins; in fact, many people simply could not tell them apart. But within their world, they both on some level believed that Tom was perhaps a little smarter, perhaps a little handsomer, and certainly the leader. In recent months Joe Hunt had heightened the brothers' shared perceptions, reinforcing Tom's notion that he was superior and Dave's that he was somehow lacking. Dave's secret campaign against Joe Hunt had changed the balance of power. It was Dave who had seen through Joe Hunt, Dave who was now in control. He, when it came down to it, was the one who had rescued Tom.

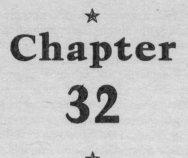

Chapter 32

During the last weeks of July, Karny later told prosecutors, the five boys involved in Project Sam operated with a strong sense of mission.

From Western Costume Rental, a huge Los Angeles company that works frequently with the movie studios, Dean Karny rented three identical police uniforms complete with badges, utility belts, and imitation service revolvers. At a surplus store he purchased three sets of brown pants and shirts to serve as delivery uniforms.

Joe, Dean, and Ben were also trying in the days before July 30 to resolve the last remaining glitch in their plans: they desperately needed a place to hide Eslaminia after the abduction. The hideout had to be near enough to Los Angeles that the boys could easily come and go, yet it must be remote enough, as Joe reminded them, "that the screams won't be heard."

On the morning of the twenty-sixth Joe and Dean drove

to Lake Arrowhead, a mountain resort community approximately two hours away from L.A. Stopping in at a Century 21 realty office, Joe spoke to a part-time high-school teacher, part-time realtor who happened to be working in the office that day. "I'm wondering if you could help us," he said politely. "We have a rather special need." Joe went on to explain that he was an economist writing a paper for the government on a very tight deadline. He would be needing a place to write for the next six weeks or so. "I don't want any distractions," he said. "I'm looking for someplace remote."

The realtor showed the boys several properties, but they seemed uninterested in all of them. After a few hours, they promised to keep in touch and left.

From a phone booth, Dean and Joe called the office. Ben was looking at houses in Palm Springs. He had left a message that he had located a few places he thought they should see. So the boys headed down the mountain and east on Highway 10 to meet Ben in the desert community. But none of the possibilities there seemed right either. No closer than they had been to finding a hideout, the boys returned home.

Back at the BBC, the boys had an idea. Los Angeles just might be the ideal place to find the perfect house. There were many remote homes in the various canyons, and it would be a good thing to have Eslaminia close enough that they could get to him quickly. The other BBC members wouldn't be as suspicious as they would if the Shadings had to keep leaving town. Besides, the Olympics were about to begin. There might be fully equipped houses available for short-term rental as a result.

A Beverly Hills realtor whom the boys contacted thought she had the perfect house for the young "government writer" looking for seclusion. One day during the last week of July, she showed it to him and Dean Karny. They were impressive young men, she thought, bright, articulate, and personable. There was just one thing that was strange. When she showed them the two-story house tucked away behind dense shrubbery off Sunset Boulevard near UCLA, they didn't seem very interested in the house's appointments. They didn't even want to see the upstairs. Instead, the boys focused their attention on the concrete basement, which was entered through a trap door at the back of the hall closet. After spending some time down there, they ascended the stairs. "It's perfect," Joe Hunt said. "We'll take it." The realtor had been selling high-priced real estate in Beverly Hills for years; she knew better than to ask questions.

During the final two weeks before Project Sam, Ben Dosti and Jim Graham flew to San Francisco for a weekend surveillance run. Ben's job was to try and make sure Eslaminia was as rich as his son said. Jim was to begin scoping out the condominium complex. At the airport, Ben rented a car with his American Express card, the only general credit card any of the boys had, and then checked himself and Jim into a hotel in Palo Alto.

Ben Dosti had little training in techniques with which to determine a person's assets. The only thing he had was the address of Hedayat's former home in Hillsborough, so he decided to see what he could find out there. He got lucky. On the grounds of the large, empty estate, he found an old brochure from an open house. The flyer described the house as a "split-level Spanish-style house with a panoramic Bay view." The asking price was $715,000, reduced from $799,350. It was enough for Dosti. Clearly the man had some money if he had lived in such a lavish house. Satisfied, he returned to Los Angeles.

Jim Graham's work was not so easily accomplished. Reza had managed to get his father's address by employing a private investigator, and so, over the next several days, Jim spent a lot of time outside the condominium complex in Belmont where the elder Eslaminia lived. Several times he called Los Angeles asking his BBC colleagues to get license plate information for him from cars he noticed outside the buildings.

Finally, on July 29, the day before Project Sam was to be

implemented, Graham made his move. Gaining access to the security complex was an easy step for a man with his talents. But once inside, Graham was confronted by the building's maintenance man, Kenneth Hickson. After the men exchanged polite greetings, the worker asked Graham for his name. "I'm Jim Graham," he responded without hesitation.

Later in the day when Hickson saw the affable, well-built young man again, Graham asked Hickson to help him open the automatic gate to the parking garage. Hickson was happy to oblige. "Are you in the Olympics or something?" Hickson asked. "You look like an athlete." Graham affirmed that he was an Olympic boxer and offered to get Hickson tickets to see him fight down the Peninsula at Stanford University.

Hickson thought nothing of it the next day when he saw the same man enter the security building from the lobby.

On the morning of Sunday, July 29, Project Sam was officially put into action. The way Dean Karny later testified, it came off as follows. In one of the BBC's gray BMWs and in a yellow pickup truck borrowed from Joe's father, Ben, Joe, and Reza took off from the Wilshire Manning. In caravan, the boys headed north on Highway 101. Seven hours later they were in Belmont, where Ben used his credit card to get two rooms at the Villa Motel.

Dean remained behind in Los Angeles temporarily to attend to an important detail. Early on the morning of the thirtieth, he went to the realtor's office with nine thousand dollars in cash, some of the last of the group's ready money, which would cover six weeks' rent on the house she had shown them. He picked up a key and departed for Los Angeles International Airport.

Chapter
33

★

By the time Dean arrived at the Villa Motel at three o'clock on the afternoon of the thirtieth, most of the preparations for Project Sam had been completed. That morning the other boys had rented a U-Haul truck, which was now parked on the dirt shoulder of a nearby road. Later in the day Ben purchased brown wrapping paper.

After Dean helped wrap and address the trunks, he surveyed Ben and Joe in their delivery uniforms. The boys had decided they would attract less attention in those outfits than in police uniforms. Jim decided not to wear his. If he was seen by anyone he had met at Hedayat Eslaminia's condominium complex, he felt it would be better if he was wearing sweats. At approximately three-thirty they left the motel and piled into the BMW and the pickup.

★ ★ ★

Hours later, after the long drive down Interstate 5, after Dean discovered their captive was dead, Joe began to evaluate the group's options in light of the unexpected development. "This really isn't going to make much difference," he said soothingly to Dean, who was much more visibly upset. "We still have Reza in our ranks, and he's the oldest son. We'll be able to get his assets in the end anyway." Almost as an afterthought, Joe broached another subject. "I don't think we should mention what happened to Jim just yet," he said. "He would think we had blown it, and I don't want him to lose confidence in the operation as a whole because of one unfortunate occurrence." Dean readily agreed. They could tell Jim about Hedayat's death later, after they had concocted a good explanation. He wasn't eager to tell anybody about the events of the last several hours.

When the BBC caravan from northern California pulled up outside the Wilshire Manning late that night, Dean hopped out of the pickup. Ben and Joe drove on to the house they had rented. Dean stayed behind to intercept Jim. On the way up to Ben's apartment, where Dean needed to gather a few things, the two boys spoke. "Everything's under control, Jim," Dean said. "Joe says you can just go on home." With Jim safely out of the way, Dean sped off to the house on Beverly Glen, his mind in turmoil.

In the vestibule of the rented house, Dean stepped around the trunk that was now Eslaminia's coffin and went into the living room to talk with Joe and Ben. At first the boys talked about money, about how perhaps they could get Reza appointed conservator of his father's assets and still get their hands on large sums. Then they spoke of their more immediate problem. What should they do with the body?

There wasn't, the boys felt, any reason to destroy the corpse. Even if it were found, no one would suspect the BBC. People would be far more likely to assume Eslaminia's death had been the work of the Ayatollah. They would dump the body in Soledad Canyon. Joe felt it was unlikely anyone would find it there. After all, he had certainly had good luck using the site for Levin's body. If someone did come across the Iranian man's corpse, so be it.

While Dean stood lookout upstairs, Ben and Joe dragged the body into the basement to remove any identification Eslaminia might be carrying. At Joe's insistence, the search was done on a blue plastic tarp so that no traces of hair or other evidence would be left behind. When they were finished, they carefully folded the tarp. Then they put the corpse back into the trunk and loaded it into the pickup. Since Ben had already helped with one unpleasant task, searching the body, he was excused to go back to the Wilshire Manning. Joe and Dean headed out on the Antelope Valley Freeway toward Soledad Canyon.

Despite the late hour—it was by now long after midnight—the boys noticed a truck parked high up on the canyon road where they had hoped to dispose of their load. Instead, they pulled off the dirt road at a turnaround beside a steep hillside. In seconds they had the trunk out of the back and had opened it. With a huge heave, they rolled Hedayat Eslaminia's body over the cliff.

On the way back to Los Angeles, Dean and Joe stopped frequently to dispose of evidence. They tossed the trunk in a Dumpster in the San Fernando Valley town of Sylmar. The tarp went into another Dumpster. Smaller items were thrown along the road. After all the incriminating items had been pitched, the boys opened the windows in the back of the camper to get rid of the smell.

Chapter
34

When Olga Vasquez left for work at 7 A.M. on July 30, 1984, Hedayat Eslaminia was sleeping off a hangover. The twenty-five-year-old secretary hated to leave the apartment. She and Hedayat had fought the evening before over his having gotten drunk, and she wished she could set things right before work. But she knew it was best at times like this to let things settle.

Olga Vasquez and Hedayat Eslaminia were an unlikely couple. Not only was he more than twice her age; they were also from very different cultures. Olga was of Puerto Rican descent, raised in the Catholic religion. Hedayat was a practicing Muslim and spoke little English, the only language in which they even tried to communicate. But nevertheless, when Olga met Hedayat through friends who arranged for the two to have drinks, she fell for him immediately.

It didn't seem to matter to Olga that in recent years Hedayat had been in something of a tailspin. Since coming to the United States, the Iranian had lost significant amounts of money in bad real-estate investments. His opium problem had worsened, and he was given to petty thievery. After his second wife, Simin, left him, Hedayat seemed to thrive only when meeting with other exiled Iranians to discuss the state of affairs in Khomeini's Iran.

But if Olga Vasquez recognized Eslaminia's troubles, they seemed unimportant to her. She had never before met a man with such a range of experiences, and she was enthralled with the expanded world view he gave her a glimpse of. Soon they were living together. And although communication was difficult, for the most part the relationship worked. The way Olga saw things, it was really more on the surface that their backgrounds were so different. In many ways, she told friends, their cultures were similar. Even the spices they liked in their food were compatible.

Olga had learned during the months they had been together to give Hedayat space when he needed it, and after a fight was such a time. She waited until eleven on the morning of July 30, figuring Hedayat would need time to get up and compose himself. Then she called. He was lying down in the spare bedroom, he said, and he was feeling better. He would look forward to seeing her later. Olga called later, just to chat. Hedayat seemed just as he always did.

When Olga got home that evening, her lover wasn't in the apartment. Later she wrote down her recollections of just what she noticed after arriving home. "I came home about five-thirty. I opened the door very nervously, because I could see in my mind Hedayat in the kitchen preparing dinner. I opened the door and looked in the kitchen and it was dark, but the hallway light was on. I called out Hedayat's name, and no answer. I went into the living room and the curtains were completely drawn. I went into the bedroom without using the key to open the door because the door was open. I noticed the curtains were drawn also. I went to open them and noticed the window about twenty inches open. Hedayat's wallet and checkbook were in their usual places, and no clothing or luggage was missing."

They were seemingly small details, but taken together Olga was worried. Hedayat rarely went out at that hour, and he never left the apartment without locking the windows and the door to his bedroom. She knew he worried about agents of the Ayatollah. He had told her about how his name had been scrawled in blood on a wall in Tehran by the new regime. It was a message that he was to be assassinated. He met frequently with other exiled Iranians planning ways to overthrow the Ayatollah. He always slept with a gun by his bed. Olga was panicked by the possibilities.

By dinnertime, Olga was sure something was amiss, and she began calling Eslaminia's friends. None had heard from him, and they agreed that things did not seem right. At five the next morning, Olga and Hedayat's friend Ali Bani called the Belmont police to report the disappearance.

Police on the San Francisco Peninsula were familiar with Hedayat Eslaminia. In Hillsborough, they had been called in to settle the sometimes violent domestic disputes between the Iranian man and his second wife. The police had dealt with Hedayat during the time of Reza's various legal problems and at the time of his suicide attempt. Hedayat's most serious brush with the law had come when he was caught shoplifting sheets from Macy's. On that occasion, Eslaminia at first claimed he had paid for the merchandise. Then he tried to blame his son Ali, who was with him. In the end, however, Eslaminia was convicted of the misdemeanor.

Police had also received reports of suspicious traffic in and out of Eslaminia's Davey Glen apartment that had caused neighbors to believe he was dealing drugs out of his home. All in all, he was the sort of man who was responsible for the increasingly negative attitude some residents felt the Peninsula police had developed toward Iranian exiles.

The Belmont police were quick to put aside any preconceived notions, however, when they heard about Hedayat's disappearance. They took Olga Vasquez's concerns very seriously and went to take a report from her immediately.

The afternoon after the disappearance, Olga was interviewed by local newspapers and television stations. The media loved the story and ran pictures of Eslaminia along with the story of how he had been kidnapped. It was probably the work of the Ayatollah Khomeini's forces, the media tended to agree.

Joe Hunt's Harvard School
yearbook photo. (*Daily News*
Photo Dept.)

From the May twins' high-school yearbook photo. (*Daily News*
Photo Dept.)

One page from Joe Hunt's "recipe for murder"—the seven-page list he drew up outlining his plan for Ron Levin's murder. It was this list that incriminated him. (*Daily News* Photo Dept.)

Prosecutor Fred Wapner preparing for his final arguments with a blow-up of the incriminating list. (*Daily News* Photo Dept.)

Ron Levin (*Daily News* Photo Dept.)

Ron Levin's brother Robert waiting to hear the verdict in Joe Hunt's Santa Monica Trial. (*Daily News* Photo Dept.)

Ron Levin with his mother. (*Daily News* Photo Dept.)

Evan Dicker testifying in Joe Hunt's trial for the murder of Ron Levin. (*Daily News* Photo Dept.)

Joe Hunt's attorneys for the Levin murder trial: Richard Chier (left) and Arthur Barens. (*Daily News* Photo Dept.)

Jim Pittman during a court appearance in Santa Monica. (*Daily News* Photo Dept.)

Tom May testifying for the prosecution in Joe Hunt's Santa Monica trial. (*Daily News* Photo Dept.)

Joe Hunt during his Santa Monica trial for Ron Levin's murder. (*Daily News* Photo Dept.)

Brooke Roberts on the witness stand during the Santa Monica trial for Ron Levin's murder. (*Daily News* Photo Dept.)

Joe Hunt turns to speak to the bailiff after his conviction for Ron Levin's murder. His attorney Richard Chier looks on. (*Daily News* Photo Dept.)

Hedayat Eslaminia (*Daily News* Photo Dept.)

Indian Canyon Road in Soledad Canyon where Hedayat Eslaminia's body was dumped. (*Daily News* Photo Dept.)

San Mateo Superior Court, Redwood City, California: Arben (Ben) Dosti after he was sentenced to life imprisonment without possibility of parole. (AP/Wide World Photos)

Reza Eslaminia in San Mateo Superior Court. Reza received a sentence of life imprisonment for the 1984 scheme to kidnap his father resulting in his death. (AP/Wide World Photos)

Joseph Gamsky, a.k.a. Joe Hunt, the mastermind of two murders for profit, in his prison garb. (*Los Angeles Times* Photo)

Chapter
35

⋆

As Olga Vasquez fretted about her missing lover, and as the rest of the Project Sam participants headed for Los Angeles, Reza Eslaminia relaxed over an elegant dinner.

Reza and his girlfriend, Debi Lutkenhouse, were sentimental about their relationship. They had gone out for the first time on July 30, 1982. Each year on the thirtieth they celebrated the event. In 1984 the couple celebrated their anniversary with a trip to Ciao, their favorite Italian restaurant in San Francisco.

When Reza first met Debi, he expected her to be his salvation. Deeply troubled and still dangerously attracted to drugs despite repeated treatment, Reza was attending a broadcasting trade school in San Francisco, hoping to become a sound engineer. Debi attended the same school. They met and quickly fell in love.

In many ways, the couple was an odd mix. Short, slightly chubby, with an upturned nose and long blond hair, Debi could at best be considered cute. Reza liked glamour. But the Iranian boy also liked money, and Debi's family had lots of that. In addition, she possessed self-confidence and poise. She was competent and articulate. The horribly disorganized side of Reza was very attracted to her stability.

Reza's family thought Debi was very good for the troubled young man. The Hillsborough girl strongly disapproved of drugs, and she communicated this to Reza in no uncertain terms. When he proudly told her about his family's wealth and position, she came down on him hard, telling him not to be boastful. Moreover, she wanted him to look around himself and face reality. Whatever his family's position had been in Iran, things didn't appear to be going well in the United States. Eslaminia's Hillsborough mansion was falling into a state of disrepair. Purchases of such household necessities as toilet paper and soap were often not made. It seemed clear to Debi that Hedayat Eslaminia no longer had much money. Reza should just face up to that, she urged, and realize that status and money were unimportant in the overall scheme of things.

Debi quickly became an integral part of Reza's life, organizing outings for his younger siblings, spending time with Reza at his father's house, and trying to interest him in business. In late 1982 she brought her brother together with Reza and his father to try to organize Mideastern business deals. Hedayat Eslaminia had bragged of his excellent contacts in Saudi Arabia and promised that the business would prosper. But after six months, Debi's brother had absorbed ten thousand dollars in expenses for travel and telexes. The business had brought in no revenues. In February 1983 he pulled the plug on the operation. Under the terms of their initial agreement, Debi's brother and the Eslaminias were to split expenses evenly, but despite repeated requests, the Eslaminias never repaid any of the money.

As Debi became closer to Reza, her contempt for his father grew. He had no respect for anyone, she felt, and was always just trying to see how he could use people. Her feelings toward him were crystallized by an incident involving her own father. In mid-1983, when her father was visiting Hillsborough from Hawaii, Debi took him to the Eslaminias' house. Upon learning that Debi's father owned a sixteen-acre botanical garden, Hedayat Eslaminia offered him seeds that he said would grow "pretty little flowers." What he neglected to mention was that the pretty flowers were actually opium poppies. Debi and her father were not amused.

But if Debi could clearly see Reza's father's failings, she was blind toward those of her boyfriend. She ignored the fact that Reza had quite an eye for the ladies, she overlooked his lack of fiscal responsibility and unwillingness to get a job, she didn't object to his frequently borrowing her Porsche, and she bailed him out when he got in trouble. In late 1983, Reza obtained a Social Security check in the amount of $486 made out to a Hillsborough woman. After endorsing the check over to himself, Reza cashed it at a Bank of America where Debi maintained an account. When authorities threatened to prosecute Reza, Debi immediately made up the funds.

When Reza finally hooked up with the BBC, Debi was very pleased. She met Ben Dosti during the trip north that he and Reza took to meet with Debi's father. Later she traveled to Los Angeles, where she had dinner with many of the BBC members at a trendy Beverly Hills restaurant. Years later, testifying in court, she would still remember the evening as special. The cast of "Hill Street Blues" was seated at a nearby table, but as Debi remembers it, "we seemed to be getting more attention than they did." The Hillsborough girl was particularly impressed with Ben Dosti. "I was happy to see that Reza had met a person of Ben's caliber," she later recalled.

At their anniversary dinner on July 30, 1984, Debi says there was no mention of abducting Hedayat Eslaminia. They talked about Reza's alienation from his father and his dashed hopes for a reconciliation, but beyond that, according to Debi's later statements, nothing more was said about Hedayat Eslaminia.

Chapter
36

Reza was triumphant when he returned from the Bay Area on August first. "It worked," he told Dean and Joe. "Everyone believes my father was kidnapped for political reasons. All the papers are saying so."

Dean and Joe looked inexplicably serious. Finally Joe spoke. "Reza," he said soberly, "your father is dead. He died during an interrogation. Things didn't go exactly as we'd hoped."

Reza was silent as the words sunk in. "I want to see his body," he said finally. "I want to make sure he's dead."

Joe thought about Reza's request and then denied it. It wouldn't do to give Reza so much leverage.

During the next several days, the boys brainstormed about how to salvage Project Sam. Their situation was helped when a friend of the Eslaminia family called Reza and told him that as eldest son, he should take charge. Now Reza had a quasi-official imprimatur for taking control of his father's assets.

Assisted by the BBC, he would go to Belmont, go thro
father's papers with an eye to locating assets, and g
pointed conservator by the courts, so he could contro the
family fortunes.

Things did not go quite so smoothly.

Olga Vasquez was immediately suspicious when Reza
called shortly after Hedayat's disappearance. Her lover, she
knew, had not gotten along with his eldest son in recent
years. She just didn't believe he would want Reza pawing
through his things. Olga agreed to talk to the young man and
the friend he had come up with. But she wouldn't do it alone.

After receiving Reza's phone call on August 5, she called
the Belmont police and asked for an officer to accompany her
to pick up Reza at the nearby convenience store from which
he had called. The young man was waiting there along with
Joe Hunt in Debi Lutkenhouse's gold Porsche. After taking
the boys up the hill to the Belmont condominium complex,
the policeman and Reza spoke privately. "My mother asked
me to come up and try to figure out what happened to my
father," Reza said sincerely. "We're very worried about this
whole affair." The policeman cautioned Reza about not bothering Olga. He wasn't to try to stay at the apartment, as it
belonged to her. Reza politely agreed. Olga then took the
policeman aside and told him she now felt comfortable talking to the young man. The officer could leave. A friend of the
young woman's had agreed to remain with her during the
visit. She would call if there were any problems.

Upon conversing with Reza, Olga's suspicions of the boy
sharpened. There was something she just didn't like about
him. At one point in their conversation, Reza got serious.
"You know, my father loved you very much," he said. Olga
was made suspicious by the statement. "Why do you refer to
him in the past tense?" she demanded. But the boy was
evasive.

Because it seemed to her somehow important to document Reza's visit, Olga got out her camera. "Do you mind if I take your picture?" she asked him. "I want a souvenir to remember you by." The young man agreed, although Olga thought he was somewhat reluctant. Reza then asked if he could take a picture of her, and she agreed. But as soon as he had the camera, he tore it open and ripped out the film. "He's crazy," Olga thought immediately. She ordered him out of her home.

Shortly after Reza's meeting with Olga Vasquez, Jerry Eisenberg got a phone call from Ben Dosti, who said that the boys needed some immediate legal help. Reza's father had been kidnapped, Dosti explained to Eisenberg, who up to then had heard nothing about the disappearance. Reza and several others were up in the Bay Area attending to details. They wanted to gain access to Hedayat's apartment to go through his papers, but his girlfriend refused to let them in. They needed Jerry's help.

Later that day, Jerry flew up to San Francisco with Dean and rented a car. He first met with Joe and Reza at their Palo Alto hotel, to be filled in on details. "My father has a lot of important papers that may shed a light on his disappearance," Reza explained. "His girlfriend is a horrible person and may even have had something to do with his disappearance. She is refusing to let us go through his things. Can you see what you can do?"

Next, Jerry went to the Belmont Police Department, where he explained Reza's dilemma. It was really out of their hands, the officers explained. The FBI was now handling the case. But they could set up a meeting for Eisenberg with the investigating agents. That afternoon, Eisenberg met with the FBI and explained his request. By the end of the meeting they had reached an agreement. The Belmont police would go in and take all of Hedayat's papers. They would hold them, and Reza could look at them if the court wanted him to.

Eisenberg felt he had achieved a victory. The papers would be in safekeeping, out of the hands of the scheming woman. He was surprised that Joe did not seem pleased with his accomplishment. But he didn't spend much time worrying. He had tickets for the Olympic volleyball finals that evening, and he intended to be back in Los Angeles for them.

After the hour-long flight back from San Francisco, Eisenberg stopped in at the BBC offices. Jim Graham was the only other member there. Graham wandered into Eisenberg's office and chatted idly for a couple of minutes. After hearing what Jerry had done that day, Graham looked at him. "Did you know Eslaminia is dead?" Graham asked. "We kidnapped him to get his money, and he died of a heart attack while we were working on him."

"You're kidding," Eisenberg said, disbelieving. He studied Graham intently. Graham smiled meaningfully, and Eisenberg's doubts were erased.

Jerry Eisenberg had no hesitation about his course of action. He was a lawyer, and he intended to continue being one long after the BBC was out of business. Before leaving for the volleyball match, he picked up the phone in his office. He had the card of the FBI agents he had met with earlier. He dialed the number. "This is Jerry Eisenberg, the person who spoke to you on Reza Eslaminia's behalf earlier this afternoon," he said. "It has just come to my attention that Reza and some of his colleagues may have had some responsibility for Mr. Eslaminia's disappearance." The FBI agent was very interested. After a long conversation, he advised Eisenberg to remain a part of the group so as not to raise suspicion. He should keep his eyes and ears open. He should also be careful, the agent said.

After their setbacks in Belmont, Joe realized the boys needed more help. Shortly thereafter he approached Evan Dicker, who was now attending law school and had become a notary public. "Look, Evan, Reza's father once granted him power of attorney, but the form got lost. Now his girlfriend is giving Reza all sorts of trouble. We have a new power of attorney form here, and we've signed his name to it. Will you notarize it?" Evan didn't hesitate. He got out his stamp and affixed his signature to the document, swearing by so doing that Hedayat Eslaminia had signed the document in front of him. It now looked to all the world as if Hedayat Eslaminia had granted a power of attorney to his son on April 14, 1984. The paper would make getting Reza named conservator of his father's assets vastly easier.

Next Joe approached Eisenberg for help in filing conservatorship papers. Eisenberg readily agreed so as not to raise Joe's suspicions, but his lawyer's mind was wary. He would fill out the papers, he decided, to appear to be going along with Joe. But he would insert some errors. Perhaps a judge would notice the problems and not grant the conservatorship. That would give the FBI time to put its case together and arrest Reza before he got hold of his father's money. Before going into court, Eisenberg again called the FBI and informed them what he was going to do. If they wanted to step in and stop things, he figured, they could.

On August 16, Eisenberg appeared before a judge in Redwood City. He stated his case and presented the papers. He had filled in the wrong date, as well as other minor errors. But the judge never noticed. Without even coming out of his chambers, he granted the conservatorship to Reza. Ben, Reza, and Jerry went to lunch to celebrate their success.

On the day after the conservatorship was granted, a group of BBC boys gathered in northern California. Over breakfast at a coffee shop, Joe made assignments. The boys were divided into teams of two. Each team was given a set of the conservatorship papers and made responsible for inquiring at specific Bay Area banks whether Hedayat Eslaminia maintained accounts there. When they regrouped later that day, the news was disappointing. After inquiring at virtually all of the likely financial institutions, the boys had discovered just one bank account, with a tiny balance. "I think most of my father's money is in Switzerland," Reza explained. "That's where he liked to do his banking." Joe would have to think of something else.

Chapter
37

★

The Morton attrition mill demanded much of Joe's attention during early August, when he would have liked to concentrate solely on finding Eslaminia's assets. The Arizona miner was quite angry that the machine didn't work. He wanted something done. With decisiveness, in the middle of trying to secure Eslaminia's assets, Joe took action. "Go to Arizona and bring the machine back," he ordered Dave May, Steve Taglianetti, and Jerry Eisenberg. "Rent a truck and get it back here however you can." The boys agreed.

At the Phoenix airport they rented a car for the twenty-mile drive to Mesa. Out at the mining site, they encountered a guard; they told him they had come to fix the machine. Once inside, Eisenberg turned to the others. "Look, we clearly can't get this thing out of here with this guy here," he said. "Let's just take whatever makes it work and leave the shell." The others agreed, perhaps in part influenced by wanting to get out of the scorching desert.

After loading the components, the boys headed back to town, where they had lunch and called Joe. He was furious. "Can't you do anything right?" he demanded. "Stay where you are. I'm coming out. We are going to get this machine."

The boys had some five hours to kill before Joe arrived, and during that time they began talking about the BBC. Dave grumbled. Jerry grumbled. Dave made a tentative step. "Things are getting really weird around there," he said.

"You don't know the half of it," Jerry replied. Each was dancing around the real issues, trying to see if he could trust the other. Finally Dave took the plunge.

"Did you know that Joe says he killed Ron Levin?" Dave asked Jerry. The attorney was silent. "He announced it to a meeting of a bunch of the guys," Dave continued.

"I think you'd better tell me everything," Eisenberg said. "Then I'll tell you about a whole other murder."

By the time Joe Hunt and Jim Graham arrived, Dave May, Steve Taglianetti (who had already been recruited by the Mays), and Jerry Eisenberg had agreed to join forces in their previously separate campaigns against the leader they no longer believed in. Bolstered by their new comradeship, the boys stood up to Joe immediately. "Help load this truck," Joe ordered the boys, "and then you can drive it back to Los Angeles." They would help load, the boys said, but Joe and Jim could drive it back to Los Angeles themselves. Steve, Jerry, and Dave were flying back. Never one to fight a losing battle, Hunt backed down. But it was clear to him that the loyalties of the BBC boys were shifting.

On an August afternoon in the law offices of Arthur Crowley, high above the Sunset Strip in Hollywood, representatives from the FBI and the Beverly Hills Police Department sat down with the renegade BBC boys and Gene Browning. In the end, Dave had been able to recruit only his brother Tom, Steve Taglianetti, and Jerry Eisenberg in addition to Browning and Raymond. He had been too nervous to approach any of the others. Dave had already met with officers from the Beverly Hills Police Department. Now he was providing the corroboration of others.

After a brief meeting in a conference room, the BBC members were taken individually to be interviewed by the various assembled agents. After several hours, the law enforcers excused the boys. It looked like they had themselves a case.

Chapter
38

Beverly Hills detective Les Zoeller wasn't exactly proud of the way his department had handled Ron Levin's disappearance, but he wasn't ashamed either. The affable, sandy-haired officer and his partner, Rick King, had been assigned the Levin matter back when the missing persons report had first come in. Zoeller was an excellent detective with a solid reputation, but in this case there had simply been no leads, nothing to pursue. Privately, the two men had assumed that Levin was probably dead, that somebody finally got him. The officers, like most Beverly Hills policemen, had known Levin for years, and they realized that a man with his particular style of bad habits probably had enemies. But it was hard to base an investigation on a hunch. Zoeller was glad to finally have a concrete lead.

After talking to the Mays on August 9, Zoeller decided to search Levin's apartment. If they were right about what had happened, he should find a contract between Ron Levin and

Microgenesis. Joe would have planted it there when he forced Levin to write the check for $1.5 million. But getting permission to search the Peck Drive duplex proved thorny. After consulting with his son's attorney, Martin Levin told Zoeller he was reluctant to have Beverly Hills police officers on the premises. Ronnie was facing grand theft charges, after all, and the Beverly Hills Police Department had been the investigating agency on the crime.

Zoeller was reassuring. "We're not interested in anything relating to that," he told the worried father. "We're only interested in things that will help us find out what happened to your son." Martin Levin finally agreed.

At 9 A.M. on August 16, as Jerry Eisenberg attempted to get a conservatorship for Reza in northern California, Zoeller became the first police officer to search Ron Levin's house for evidence of foul play. It was strange entering his house again, Zoeller thought. The last time he had been there was to investigate a robbery. Levin had been the victim that time. He had opened his door to a young woman who said her car had broken down. She asked to use the phone. Once inside, she was joined by a man who roughed Levin up and robbed him. Zoeller had gone to interview Levin about that robbery a couple of years earlier, and had gotten to know the eccentric man in the months that followed. Far too often, Levin would call to ask how the investigation was proceeding. He was a terrible pest, and Zoeller knew all about his repeated scams, but he had come to be somewhat amused by Levin in spite of all that. Now it looked as if he might be dead.

Martin Levin apologized for the stuffiness inside the apartment. It had been shut up for the last two and a half months, he explained. As Levin opened windows, Zoeller walked quickly through the apartment. The May twins, relying on the lie Joe had told Tom, said the murder hadn't taken place here, so Zoeller was not particularly interested in more than a cursory examination of the con man's living quarters. He was interested in Levin's papers.

In a lot of cases, it would be difficult to work with the

victim's father standing watching, but Martin Levin seemed genuinely interested. Zoeller explained as he went through the papers on Levin's desk that he was looking for specific documents he thought might have been left behind during an abduction or murder. After a few minutes, Martin Levin approached Zoeller tentatively. "I found these papers next to Ronnie's desk when I was going through his things after he disappeared," he said, offering Zoeller seven sheets of yellow legal paper. "I just don't know what to make of them. I wonder if they have any significance." The papers had puzzled Martin since he discovered them. They had seemed disturbing, but he simply hadn't known what to do. With a denial common in such circumstances, Martin Levin had decided to ignore his find. Now seemed the time to turn them over to someone who might be able to glean their meaning.

Zoeller glanced at the top sheet. "At Levin's: To Do," it was headed. He quickly scanned the page, his eyes catching on phrases like "Close blinds," "Tape mouth," "Handcuff," "Kill dog (emphasis)." In a quick flash of realization, Zoeller dropped the pages. They appeared to contain a murder plan, and he didn't want to get fingerprints on them. He looked up at Martin Levin. "I think, Mr. Levin, that these do indeed have some significance," he said.

After four hours of searching, Zoeller was ready to call it a day. He hadn't found the contract he was seeking, but he had a far better piece of evidence. Before leaving, he decided to alert Martin Levin to be on the lookout for the other documents. "There's something else I'm looking for," the detective explained. "If you come across anything bearing the names of Joe Hunt, Jim Graham, Dean Karny, or Microgenesis, please let me know." He wrote the names down on a piece of paper.

The older man studied it. "Hold on," he said, and left the room. He came back with a folder he had stashed away when he first went through his son's apartment. "Is this what you're

THE BILLIONAIRE BOYS CLUB **187**

looking for?" It was the Microgenesis contract exactly as the Mays had described it.

In San Francisco, four hundred miles away, Oscar Breiling was having a slow day. As a special agent for the California attorney general's crack Special Prosecutions Unit, the fifty-year-old officer had just finished a massive auto theft case. For the past several months he had been working like a maniac. Today, he thought, he would take things easy. But after several hours of paperwork at his desk, Breiling was getting antsy.

The dapper, six-foot-tall investigator still craved action, even after twenty-two years as a lawman. So what if his hair and carefully trimmed beard were now entirely silver? Breiling had no intention of letting age get in his way. He was always happy to brag to younger officers about how he consistently got among the highest marks on the target range. During an evasive driving course, he had outscored even the instructor on the simulated road tests. Breiling enjoyed the prestige of his position as a special agent for the bureau's San Francisco office, but he sometimes missed his days as a street cop and was always quick to volunteer for action.

Breiling had been in his office for some time when a colleague poked his head in. "Hey, Oscar, want to drive down to Belmont with me?" the other investigator asked. "I've got to follow up on a request for state assistance on a case. I don't think we can do anything, but I've got to go talk to them." Breiling looked at the papers on his desk. The invitation hardly qualified as exciting, but it was the best one he'd had all day. "Sure," he replied.

On the way down the Peninsula, the officer filled Breiling in on the details. The Belmont Police Department had approached the State Bureau of Investigation to ask for help. "Some rich Iranian guy's been kidnapped down there. They think it might be a political thing," Breiling's colleague said. Unfortunately, the state just didn't have the manpower at the moment to tackle what looked like a complicated case.

In Belmont, Oscar and his colleague listened as a group of Belmont officers again pled for help. Two FBI agents explained that their agency couldn't take the case, in part because they were too busy with the Olympics. But the FBI had an informant. They no longer thought the case was politically motivated. If the state agreed to take the case, the FBI would provide its informant, but only once the state had committed to tackling the case.

As Breiling listened, he began to get angry. The various officers were treating this whole affair as if it were a hot potato. He was sick of the reluctance of a lot of law enforcement agencies to take on big cases. The prevailing attitude, he felt, was big case, big problems; little case, little problems; no case, no problems. This Iranian guy had once been somebody, and now he was missing and probably dead. The Belmont police were making a sincere request for assistance. They deserved help.

Breiling carefully considered the facts he was hearing. He would love to take the case himself, but the Special Prosecutions Unit for which he worked had certain case criteria, and Oscar needed to think about whether what he was hearing fit them. In 1979 a publicity-conscious attorney general had established the unit as a prestigious section of the state prosecutor's office. Some of the best criminal attorneys and investigators working for the state had been brought together with a mandate to take on the tough cases. The group could take cases, its guidelines said, that involved organized crime, that were multijurisdictional, or that involved large amounts of money. But Oscar knew that there was another criterion far more important than the others: cases had to be capable of garnering a lot of publicity.

After some quick calculations, Breiling decided to take a chance that he could convince his bosses the case would fit all the criteria. It looked like the crime had been committed by an organized group, perhaps by an Iranian hit squad, or if the FBI was right, by a group of kids. The case clearly involved money, it looked like it would be multijurisdictional, and most important, it would be a headline grabber. "I think I can take this case," Oscar told the assembled officers. "Now tell me everything you know."

Back at the office that afternoon, Oscar called the main SPU office in Sacramento. "I just heard about a case I think it's very important for the unit to tackle," he told his superiors. By evening he had obtained permission to look into the case a little further to determine whether or not it deserved a full investigation by the unit. But in getting the go-ahead, Breiling had promised a lot. He hoped he could deliver.

That night on the six-acre ranch he shared with his wife, Breiling took a few minutes before he went to sleep. "Lord," he said, praying earnestly, "I'm going to need your help with this one. I promise that when it's solved, you'll get the credit, but I'm going to have to rely on you." It was something Breiling had never done before. A deeply religious man who served as minister to a small Pentecostal congregation, Breiling had always kept his work and his religion to some extent separate. God had enough to do, he felt, without having to help Oscar Breiling out with his cases. But this time was different. After his prayers, the investigator went to bed confident. The next morning he approached Ron Bass, the competent, ambitious lawyer who had been assigned the case. "Ron," Oscar said, "we're going to get a body, and we're going to get the suspects on this case. The Lord's on our side now."

But if Breiling was confident, the rest of the office had doubts and ribbed him good-naturedly. "Oscar's got a murder case," the office joke went, "but there's no body. It involves millions of dollars, but there's no money. It was done by the Ayatollah or a gang of kids, but there are no suspects." In the words of a current television commercial, they wondered, "Where's the beef?"

Breiling had only a week or two to work the case before he was scheduled to leave on vacation, and he chose a cautious approach. He was going to treat the case like a cookie, he told Bass. He would nibble all around the edges before he ever took a bite out of the middle. He didn't want to frighten anybody into running before he solved it. Breiling's first step was to read all the police reports that had been prepared. If what Eisenberg told the FBI was correct, it looked like this BBC group was at the heart of the matter. With that in mind, Breiling approached Olga Vasquez, who told him of her visit from Joe Hunt and Reza Eslaminia.

As a last note before taking his vacation, Breiling decided to look at the documents that had been seized from Eslaminia's house in Belmont after his disappearance. But on checking with the Belmont Police Department, he learned that many of the pages in the four-foot-high stack were written in Farsi. Before leaving town, Breiling asked Ron Bass to see about getting a translator to look at the documents.

Two weeks later, when Breiling returned, he asked Bass about the documents. "All hell broke loose while you were away," Bass said. An interpreter had been called in to begin translating the documents, but he had taken just a quick look. "I can't translate these," the linguist had told the police. "They involve matters of national security. I don't even want to read them." Before consulting Bass, the Belmont police had called in the FBI, which swooped in with "an allied agency," presumably the CIA, and confiscated all the papers. Breiling hoped the FBI's informant was right about Eslaminia having been kidnapped by a bunch of kids, because if it was the Ayatollah's gang, Breiling had just lost what might have been his best evidence.

Chapter 39

⋆

Joe Hunt remained unaware of the full extent of the trouble that was brewing for him. But he did know one thing: Tom May was stealing BBC documents. Joe viewed Tom as an inconvenience more than a threat. It was inconceivable, he felt, that that little twerp could cause him harm. Even his clumsy attempts at espionage were pathetic. Tom had long been the butt of office jokes for his clock-watching ways. Usually the last to arrive at the office and the first to leave, Tom was suddenly staying late. "I have a little work I want to finish," he would say by way of explanation. Something would have to be done.

One Friday night in August, Tom and Dave were summoned to Evan Dicker's apartment. When they arrived, Evan escorted them to the study, where Joe was waiting. "It has come to my attention that someone is stealing documents from the BBC," Joe said formally. "If we find out who it is, we'll take action." After Joe left the room, Evan looked at the twins, who at times had been his closest friends in the BBC. Every weekend the three boys made pilgrimages to the local late-night clubs to drink and chase girls. But all that was secondary to the BBC in Evan's mind. "I wouldn't fuck with the BBC," he said meaningfully.

Within a few days, Joe and others in the BBC's current inner circle were at Evan's apartment. "I've got something to discuss. Let's go for a walk," Joe proposed. On the way to a nearby delicatessen, Joe told the boys what was on his mind. Now that there was a risk of the Mays talking, the group had to pin suspicion for the Levin murder on someone else. Joe had a plan. They could kill Renee Martin, Jeff Raymond's girlfriend, in such a manner that it would appear to authorities that Jeff had done the murder in a fit of sexual passion. The BBC inner circle would then tell police that they believed Jeff had been a little kinky and that he had been sexually involved with Levin. They had long suspected he was guilty of murdering Levin as well, they would say.

One evening when Evan and some of the others were at Joe's apartment, Joe took several boys into the basement recreation room. He had a very simple plan for disposing of the Mays, he told them. "We'll rent a big truck and simply run them off the freeway," he said, as if he was proposing a social event. None of the boys responded enthusiastically to Joe's proposals. Evan Dicker went home hoping the plans would simply die. Joe was beginning to sound like an absolute nut.

After meeting Joe Hunt at Evan's, the May twins were very frightened. Joe was beginning to seem capable of anything, and he was clearly suspicious of their activities. Now that they had been to the police, they felt they should keep a very low profile, perhaps even take a trip, until Joe was arrested. At the end of August the perfect opportunity presented itself.

A miner with some acreage outside of Las Vegas had

purchased an option on the Cyclotron. Somebody had to deliver the massive machine. Arrangements were made for the Mays and Jeff Raymond to do the moving. Afterward, they decided, they would go on a long fishing trip. But on the morning the three boys showed up with a rented truck to pick up the milling device, the warehouse's large doors had been chained shut to keep them out. Joe must have decided he didn't want the Mays to leave. Panicked and unwilling to stay behind for any reason, the boys got a blowtorch from the building's office and went to work on the lock. Within minutes they had the doors opened. They quickly loaded the machine and left for the high desert.

To allay suspicions they called Joe that afternoon. "It was weird, Joe," Tom told him. "The doors had been chained shut, so we had to torch them open. Oh, and by the way, as long as we're going up there, we thought we'd take a while and go on a little vacation," he added. Joe was silent.

After hanging up the phone, Joe went into action. He departed immediately for the mine site, but by the time he arrived several hours later, the Mays were gone. He did, however, find their briefcase, and in it was the pink slip to a classic Corvette the boys had spent months restoring. He pocketed the paper and returned to Los Angeles.

For the next two weeks, Dave, Tom, and Jeff had the kind of fun they hadn't thought about for months. They stayed in a small cabin and spent their days like little boys, lazing in the sun, fishing, and eating.

Joe was furious. He was not about to be beaten by the likes of the May twins. He really needed to know exactly what they were up to. One afternoon Evan was driving Joe home. "I wonder what's happened to those records Tom took," Joe said.

"Why don't we just go investigate?" Evan suggested. "It's a piece of cake to break into their apartment from the balcony."

"We don't even need to do that," Joe said. "I have a key."

The two boys drove straight to Brentwood and within

minutes were inside the twins' apartment. After going through papers without much success, Evan suggested they listen to the answering machine. Among the usual sorts of messages was one from a person the boys didn't know. "Dave or Tom," the caller said. "This is Les Zoeller. Would you please give me a call at 550-4955?" When the message had played out, Joe picked up the phone and dialed the number. "Beverly Hills Police Department, detective division," a voice at the other end said. Joe hung up the phone.

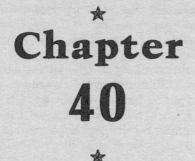

Chapter
40

During the final days of August, the Mays and Jeff Raymond were beginning to feel a little trapped in the mountains. Every few days they called Les Zoeller to ask whether Joe had been arrested, but he always said no. They were getting antsy to see just what was going on back home. Low on money and clean clothes, the boys decided to return, at least briefly, to pick up more supplies. They were a bit nervous, but it was an almost pleasant nervousness. It had become increasingly hard to believe, up in the forests of the Sierra Nevada, that Joe Hunt's threats were real.

By the time the boys arrived back in Los Angeles, they were once again feeling wary. Out of what they hoped was an abundance of caution, they parked the Oldsmobile they were driving around the corner, out of sight of their apartment. But within minutes Joe was at their door. Joe grabbed the keys to the car, which he said belonged to his father. Did they have a few minutes to talk? Joe wondered. Jeff explained he had to leave. The Mays said they were expected at their mother's house.

"How about if I drive you," Joe said. "We really need to talk."

Panicked but unwilling to raise Joe's suspicions further, the twins agreed. Tom explained he would have to call his parents. "We're on our way there," he told his mother. "Joe Hunt is giving us a ride. We should be there in twenty minutes." He hoped the call would help insure their safety, but he was still very nervous as he climbed into Joe's jeep.

Once he had started the car, Joe turned to the boys. "You're out," he said. "You're no longer BBC members." The twins were silent, hopeful that this was all Joe had in mind. "We're really going to have to talk," Joe added. "Not today, but soon. How about if you meet me at the warehouse tomorrow?"

The boys had no intention of seeing Joe at the remote site. They saw too clearly in their minds the barrels leaking sand that Jim Graham had used for target practice there. "How about the Chart House for dinner," Dave said, picking one of the twins' favorite Westwood restaurants.

"That's fine," Joe agreed. "Tomorrow." He let the Mays off and waved good-bye.

Dave and Tom were scared to meet Joe at the Chart House, but they were more scared not to. He had issued an order, and to defy it would be to escalate things considerably. At the appointed hour the next day, they appeared at the restaurant.

After the boys were seated, Joe began. "As we discussed previously, you two are no longer BBC members," he said. "That leaves us with a few matters of parting to be resolved. For starters, I believe you have some documents that belong to the BBC," he said calmly. "I would like them back." Dave and Tom were silent, uncertain how much Joe knew. Perhaps he was just bluffing.

"Now I know you've gone to the police," Joe continued matter-of-factly, "and that's a problem. You must call Detective Zoeller back and explain that you were lying." Joe paused and waited, but Dave and Tom still did not speak. "And by the way," Joe said, "you might want to tell him that he should be more circumspect when he leaves you telephone messages." The twins realized with a sinking feeling exactly how much Joe knew. There would be no bluffing their way out.

"Look, Joe, I'm not sure just what you want from us, but there's not much we can do," Dave said.

"What I want is quite simple," Joe answered. "I want you to call the police back and tell them the truth, that Ron Levin and I are dear friends and that you know I didn't kill him. Explain that this was all a misunderstanding, and ask him to return the documents you supplied." Joe paused for effect, looking from one twin to the other. "You know I would never have killed Ron Levin. You know it."

"There's no way we can get the stuff back," Tom said.

"Look," Joe said, "I hoped it wouldn't have to come to this, but it looks as if it has. I have the pink slip to your car. I'll return it to you if you return the documents. It's that simple."

Dave thought longingly of the classic Corvette he and Tom had worked so hard to restore. "There's just no way, Joe," he said finally.

Joe looked fiercely at each boy in turn. "Then I declare war on you guys," he said calmly. He rose and left the restaurant.

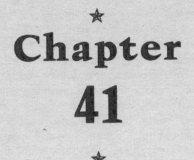

Chapter
41

Ben Dosti had never before been to Europe, and he was excited. His family had come from there, and he had always wanted to go. When Joe decided that someone must go abroad with Reza to try and locate Hedayat Eslaminia's assets, Ben had hoped he would be the one chosen for the trip. Now, at the end of August, Ben and Reza were about to leave for the Continent.

Kate Johnston was not sorry to see Ben go. By mid-August, the bright young woman had realized that her relationship with Ben was in serious trouble. He never had any time to spend with her. He had become completely absorbed in his increasingly secret affairs with the BBC.

It wasn't simply that Ben was very busy. Kate could accept that. It was that he had shut her out of his life completely. He was always running off to San Francisco, but when Kate asked him why, all she got were vague answers. The BBC was helping Reza deal with his father's disappearance, he would tell her. Nothing more. On the occasions Kate really tried to get him to talk to her, he was downright evasive. There was one night that stood out. After avoiding her questions, Ben had gotten quite serious. "Listen, Kate," he had said. "Whatever happens, just remember that I love you." He would say no more. The words were somehow very disturbing.

Kate held on for a while. There were so many things she loved about the ambitious young man. But things had finally come to a head. If Ben wouldn't share what was going on in his life, then they no longer had any basis for a relationship. Over dinner in a restaurant, the couple agreed to stop seeing each other. Intellectually, Kate knew it was the right thing to do, but emotionally she must have had doubts. Right there in a restaurant full of people she burst into tears. Ben's leaving for the Continent was a good thing. It would put the final seal on their breakup.

Ben and Reza's European trip began inauspiciously. They first flew to London, intending to spend a few days there checking into Hedayat Eslaminia's financial matters. But Reza was detained by customs. His visa was not in order, the customs officials said. He would have to return to the United States and get the proper approvals. After arguing briefly, the boys decided to go to New York, where the matter could be attended to. They returned to London a few days later without trouble.

Within a few days of arriving, the boys began their search in earnest, contacting Eslaminia's friends in Britain and talking to banking sources. But in London they found nothing. They would have to move on to Switzerland.

Chapter

42

The summer of 1984 should have been idyllic for Steve Weiss. In his travels through Germany, France, and England he had seen beautiful scenery. He had visited old friends. He had lived the sort of European existence he felt really suited him. The whole summer had been special.

Forty years earlier, Weiss, then only eighteen years old, had arrived in Europe for the first time under very different circumstances. A first scout in a rifle division of the general infantry, he was sent into France as part of the planned Allied liberation of that country. Ten days later, after a night attack, he had found himself cut off behind enemy lines. After being smuggled through France in a policeman's uniform by members of the French underground, the young soldier had fought with the Resistance for forty-five days until the country was liberated by the Allies.

It had been a life-altering experience for the young man. After the war, he was one of only eight Americans to be awarded the French Resistance Medal. Now, at fifty-eight, he was returning to France for anniversary celebrations. But despite the awards, the celebrations, and the general good feeling of being back, Weiss could not entirely forget his worries about what was going on at home.

During the nearly four months he was gone, Weiss heard from his cousin and fellow investor Chester Brown repeatedly. Brown was worried about the commodities trading. Joe Hunt seemed increasingly reluctant to face his investors. He was being evasive about when profit disbursements would take place. Brown was nervous.

At first Weiss and Brown tried to reassure one another during their phone conversations, but by the end of the summer it was clear to both men that something was wrong. Weiss was staying at Plombières, a spa town in eastern France once frequented by Napoleon III, when he got the most disturbing news of all. Joe was behaving really strangely. He had become positively reclusive. Brown was becoming convinced that something was very wrong with the investments.

After the conversation, a feeling of dread settled over him. Weiss had encouraged so many people to invest with Hunt—the people he cared about most in the world. He had thought he was doing them all a big favor. If they lost their money, how could he face them? And that wasn't all. In the weeks before he left, after Joe had announced his intention to stop taking new money, Weiss had mortgaged his house to raise an additional fifty thousand dollars to put into his account. His earlier investments had all been with money he could afford to gamble; this time he was playing with money he might someday need to live. Weiss was becoming anxious to get back and size things up for himself.

By the time he returned to Los Angeles in late August, Weiss had made a decision. He was going to remove ninety percent of his money from the trading accounts. Even if everything was going well, he was determined to never again risk money he couldn't afford to lose. Unable to reach Joe by phone, Weiss wrote him a letter informing him of his decision to divest. Then, on a Thursday in early September, just before a scheduled disbursement of funds, Joe agreed to meet with Weiss, his cousin Chester Brown, and a couple of other investors.

Joe greeted the men warmly, inviting them to sit down in his office. "What can I do for you gentlemen?"

Weiss was determined to keep things cordial and not to appear unduly concerned. "We just want to make sure that there are no problems with the distribution scheduled for Monday," Weiss said.

Joe was reassuring. "Everything is fine. Profits are holding steady, and checks will be mailed out on Monday."

The leery investors weren't completely convinced. On Monday they returned to the Third Street offices. Joe was unavailable to see them, the secretary said. But the men insisted. Finally Joe came out of his office, dressed immaculately as always in a well-cut suit. He looked at his investors for a few moments, then said quietly and without emotion, "There is no money. I lied to you last week."

For a few moments, the men were too stunned to speak. Finally Weiss found his voice. "You cheated us," he said furiously. "You told us everything was fine, and now it turns out you've stolen all our money." Joe tried to offer explanations and reassurances, but the men were too upset to listen. "The only thing for you to do now is to call a meeting of all the investors and explain to them where their money has gone," Weiss said.

More than seventy grim-faced investors turned out the following Saturday to hear from Joe Hunt what had happened to their money. Joe had rented a conference room in a Beverly Hills lawyer's office to accommodate the crowd, and he arrived flanked by his secretary and a new BBC attorney, Lauren Raab. There was little conversation in the room before Joe rose to speak. When he finally did, a woman in the front row asked if she could tape his speech. After a moment's thought, Joe agreed. When his audience became absolutely still, Hunt began.

"In late April or early May, a position was undertaken with the Financial Futures Trading Corporation. . . . That position proved to be a disastrous one," Joe began. "As a result of an administrative mistake—and mistake is a very soft word for a very difficult problem," Joe continued, everyone who had invested before June 15 had lost everything, or as Joe put it, "was involved into the vortex of loss that occurred at that time."

Joe then reminded investors that he had no legal obligation to pay restitution. "Under the contracts that exist between us, a loss of up to the higher amount of the limited partnership is a loss that the individual has to bear personally. That is the written contract." Joe paused and the investors remained absolutely silent.

When Joe continued, his tone was comforting. "There is a difference," he said earnestly, "between a written contract and the basic obligation and responsibility that I feel in this situation." While legally he had no mandate to make restitution, Joe reminded them again, ethically he felt "a different responsibility." But before telling them more, Joe said, he wanted his secretary to take a roll call.

Joe resumed his speech with the explanation of why he felt responsible to his investors. "First of all, I had a situation which is my reputation. Setting aside any moral issues or ethical responsibilities, quite pragmatically, seventy individuals is a large number of people to have had bad experiences with me personally. I'm not interested in poisoning myself in the community to that extent.

"Secondly, and more importantly, there are the ethical considerations. I feel a higher obligation."

Joe's final consideration in accepting responsibility was a last-ditch effort to restore some confidence in his abilities. "I also have an interest in protecting my trading approach," he told the investors, "and that is significant because I intend to continue to exploit the opportunities in my butterfly system in the futures market." If Joe had to make public his trading records, he said, people would be able to figure out "exactly what my approach is. I do not wish to make that sort of disclosure."

Before divulging his plan for compensating his investors, Joe again reminded them that they were also responsible for what had happened. "I think it should be recognized before I proceed that the responsibility is not entirely mine. Now I choose to accept it, but it must be recalled that many of the individuals in this room never chose to come to my office to hear from me a discussion of my history. . . . Very few people, or perhaps only half of the people, chose to hear what the trading approach was, and made the investments blind. It must also be recognized that in the relative sense a large potential profit like this is usually only coupled with a large potential risk. I endeavored in many ways to minimize that risk, and had the approach been executed faithfully, there would have been no loss. There would have been a mirror image, or the exact opposite gain, for that period of time."

Steve Weiss was astounded. Here was a young man who had just lost the investments of more than seventy people, and he was blaming them. He was also blaming some unnamed person who didn't follow Joe's instructions in trading. Blaming everybody, it seemed, except the person who had caused the disaster—Joe Hunt. But Weiss decided to hold his tongue until he heard what Joe was proposing.

Finally Joe Hunt got to the real point of the meeting. "I have drawn up and I have present with me today some promissory notes with two elements in them." The first part, Joe explained, contained a payment schedule, which obligated Joe to repay investors in six payments during the next year. At the end of the year, the investors would have received their initial investments back plus hefty profits. To avoid disappointment to the investors, Joe said, he had drawn up a schedule he knew he could meet. "I took numbers and dates that I was sure I could live with," he assured them.

The second element of the promissory notes didn't please Joe's audience. "I do not wish to try to put myself in a situation of double indemnity, and I do not wish to try to put myself in a situation where I compromise my investment approach," Joe said. "For these two reasons, I am requesting at the same time and on the same document as the promissory note, a release for Financial Futures Trading Corporation of North America." It took a few moments for Joe's words to sink in. If the investors signed the notes obligating Joe to repay them, they were giving up all claims against the company to which they'd paid their money.

With Joe's position firmly laid out, the investors began hurling questions at him. "How could you accept any investments after the disaster date?" "Wasn't that kind of dishonest to suck people in?" "When do we have to decide about this?"

Joe fielded the questions calmly, relying on his vocabulary and rhetorical abilities to reassure his listeners. Nothing was his fault, he told them over and over. The disastrous trade occurred only because someone didn't follow his directions. He had planned to repay the investors for that out of his pocket, but outside circumstances prevented him from doing so. As Joe put it, "There has been recently a maddening concatenation of problems on other fronts occasioned by some disloyalty of my partners."

Even with all the problems, Joe said, things should have been fine, because in late June he had received a check drawn on a Swiss bank for $1.5 million. He had intended to use that money to repay investors and so had sent out statements indicating the profits that would have been obtained had the money been properly invested. But then, before Joe could cash the check, the man who wrote it vanished.

Joe's full explanation of the Levin matter to the investors was strange. "When [Levin] disappeared, since the check was actually sort of a draft arrangement on a Swiss bank, he was unable to approve the disbursement of the funds. I had checked before concluding that the amount was good on the Swiss bank, and there was way in excess of the necessary funds to cover the check. I had no reason to believe that the check would become problematic. It took about a month and a half for me to have exhausted every other possibility for getting this check through and to realize that the fellow wasn't coming back, that he wasn't just on a junket. It took me about a month and a half to realize that it wasn't going to go through. Now I was in a situation of a moral quagmire. I tried to do every good and honorable thing, and I found myself in a situation where I had compromised myself."

The investors, growing more hostile, weren't entirely buying Joe's self-portrait as the noble benefactor. "On August thirtieth you sent out SEC letters saying the disbursements would be coming shortly thereafter, didn't you?" one investor shouted.

But Joe still shirked any responsibility. "Unfortunately, this situation is interwoven with a lot of personal circumstances. . . . Some of the people who were employees in my organization have apparently made off with substantial assets of mine in the last month or so, and debilitated my ability to take care of these disbursements. What I still intended to do, even after the disappearance of [Levin], was to take personal funds and resources, money that was coming in on substantial contracts, and divert it. I had these resources that were necessary to do so in my estimation." Circumstances, including dishonest employees, had put Joe in a position where he didn't get anticipated revenues, he said, "so once again, I was not able to handle this in the manner that I had planned."

A concerned woman in the audience interrupted Joe. "Did you report this man who gave you this check and the people in your office who had been stealing from you to the police and the SEC?"

"I have reported the individuals to the police, and I am working with a couple of people in the police department on recovering."

"And the man who gave you the check, too? I mean, it's over a million dollars."

"The man who gave me the check is on the FBI's missing persons list, not as a criminal but as, I guess, a natural situation when somebody disappears without a trace. He comes from a very substantial family. It's an FBI matter. Kidnapping's an FBI matter."

"So you reported it to your local FBI?" the woman persisted.

"I didn't have to report it. The family ended up reporting it about two weeks after he disappeared."

"But I mean did you report that he had given you a check for one point something million?"

"It is well known to the authorities and to the family," Joe said.

As Joe's announcements about the loss really began to sink in, the investors got even more aggressive in their questioning. One man summed up what many were thinking. "There is obviously evidence of failed expertise here," he said accusingly. "The reason we are sitting here is because your expertise didn't work, and now you're telling us that you feel it's perfectly proper for us to turn you loose to continue your securities operation. You know, we're just a bunch of normal people here, and it's kind of like the fox got into the chicken house, didn't kill the chickens but wounded the chickens, got caught, and now feels it's appropriate to be turned loose to go out into other chicken houses."

Joe was quick to respond. "Number one," he said, "no one has caught the fox."

When some of the investors said they wanted to talk to lawyers or the SEC, Joe was quick to point out why they should not. "What might a lawyer be able to do for you?" Joe asked. "Let's assume the worst. Let's assume that I was a pathological liar, a criminal of immense ability, and that I misdirected these funds. The lawyer might be able to prove what occurred, and I would be jailed. That certainly doesn't help you." A lawyer might be able to get a judgment against Financial Futures, Hunt said, but since there was no money left, that would have little effect. And since he had already agreed to pay them back and was ready to sign a promissory note to that effect, Hunt said, what more could a lawyer get?

As to the SEC, Hunt questioned how that agency could

help the investors. "The SEC is an enforcement agency, and its penalties are money or time out of my life," Hunt said. "The money penalties certainly don't help you because money is being directed away from you. I would think that the SEC's objects and goals are competitive with those of the people in this room."

The notes were the investor's best hope, Joe told them. When a woman asked how long they had to think about things, Joe answered quickly. "I'll address that. I would like them to be signed today."

Steve Weiss was the first to voice his outrage at Joe's suggestion. "It seems as if you're holding a gun to our heads, and you're saying on a weekend, when no trading takes place until Monday, that we're supposed to sign this document as laymen before we leave this room. I say no."

Another investor spoke up quickly. In August, he said, he had received a letter that the investments were all fine. "You said I could get my money out. And now you're asking me to trust you?" the man asked incredulously. "How am I going to trust you?"

Another man spoke up almost apologetically. "We're a little shaky about what's going on here," he said. "We would like to be able to find out whether in fact the offers are really the way you laid them out. Maybe there's a way of recovering money other than signing these promissory notes. If you say no, you may be right, but it's a little hard to figure out so fast. If you are really interested in doing this without some kind of litigation, you might be doing yourself as well as ourselves a favor if you gave us a few days to look this stuff over and not create a mood where we feel like it's panic time—you've got to sign it or you're going to lose everything.

Sensing the hostile mood of his audience, Joe caved in. "If you want to have time to reflect, you can have until Wednesday." Then, trying to end the meeting, Joe encouraged the investors to get copies of the tape that had been made and listen to his remarks again. He offered to make himself available to investors with questions until Wednesday, when anyone wishing to sign the promissory notes must do so. Then he closed the meeting. By Wednesday, a majority of the investors had signed the promissory notes Joe wanted.

Chapter
43

During his vacation in mid September, Detective Les Zoeller had a hard time putting the Ron Levin murder case out of his mind. He was hopeful that he would soon have enough evidence to arrest Joe Hunt and Jim Graham. Zoeller was aware that the Mays couldn't understand why he hadn't arrested Joe yet. But the detective knew the judicial system and its occasional failings. He wanted to arrest the two men together, and he was determined not to do it until he could make the cases stick.

When Zoeller returned to work a few weeks later, he learned that events had outpaced him during his absence. Zoeller's partner had run a routine computer check on Jim Graham and had hit paydirt. Under the bodyguard's real name, Jim Pittman, Graham had nine outstanding warrants in Virginia on charges of grand theft and other, lesser crimes. From officers familiar with the case, Zoeller's partner, Rick King, had discovered that Pittman had owned a cleaning company in Virginia. After a rash of thefts from places cleaned by his service, police searched Pittman's house. They found much of the property there.

King decided he shouldn't wait. He had excellent grounds now for arresting Jim Pittman—or Jim Graham, as he was known in Los Angeles. Why not get him off the streets?

By the time Zoeller got back from vacation, Hunt had already arranged for the thirty thousand dollars' bail to get his friend out of jail. Now both men were out on the streets and wary. It was not, Zoeller felt, an ideal situation.

All the remaining BBC members were stunned at the news of Pittman's arrest, but Dean Karny took it the hardest. For weeks, ever since the Eslaminia abduction, Dean had felt as if he was living in a very disagreeable dream. Try as he might, he couldn't forget the evening he'd spent with the trunk in the back of the truck. Graham's arrest terrified him. It seemed as if it would only be a matter of time before the police came for him.

A week after Jim was taken in, Dean went to Joe. "I'm going to move out, Joe," he said seriously. "You don't need to worry. I'm not going to go to the police or anything. I just feel like I need to walk away from all this and start my life again." Joe accepted Dean's explanation. A few days later, Dean left the Wilshire Manning and went to stay with his parents in the Hollywood Hills.

At 10:45 on September 28, Joe climbed into his Jeep and pulled out of the Wilshire Manning garage, turning east onto Wilshire Boulevard toward the BBC offices. He accelerated quickly, weaving in and out of traffic. Within a block he noticed flashing red lights in his rearview mirror and pulled over. It was an event he had been expecting. Detective Les Zoeller introduced himself politely and placed Joe under arrest.

Back at the Beverly Hills police station, Zoeller went through Joe's possessions to decide what to book into evidence. He quickly decided to hold on to a maroon leather combination briefcase, various identification cards including a California driver's license in the name of Tom Frank May, and a Malibu Grand Prix card in the name of Joseph Gamsky. When Zoeller asked Joe for his Rolex watch, Joe removed it. "Ron Levin gave this to me," he said.

At 2:05 that afternoon, Zoeller took Joe from his cell to a jail interview room. Earlier in the day he had reviewed fingerprints lifted from the seven-page list. They were clearly Joe Hunt's. He had done a lot of thinking about Joe Hunt in recent weeks; now he wanted to have a little talk with him.

After reading Joe his rights, Zoeller asked him when he had last seen Ron Levin. "I last saw him in early June, but without a calendar I can't be more specific," Joe answered. "You know, we are extremely good friends," he volunteered. "A couple of months before he disappeared, we spent a weekend in San Francisco together. We were negotiating a business deal just before he disappeared."

Zoeller asked Joe about the check for $1.5 million. Had he received such a check from Levin? Joe said yes without hesitation, but when Zoeller asked him whether the check had been cashed, he was unwilling to speak further. "I don't want to answer that without an attorney present," he said. Ten minutes later, he apparently changed his mind. Microgenesis was now in serious financial trouble, he said. The check would have solved all the company's problems, but the bank had refused to honor it.

"What about that watch?" Zoeller asked, changing subjects. It had been a birthday present about a year ago, Joe said. He had been with Levin at Tiffany's when the watch was purchased. It had cost six hundred dollars. "Have you ever been to Levin's house?" Zoeller asked. "Yes, at least a hundred times," Joe answered.

Zoeller kept the conversation cordial, asking Joe about his businesses and the attendant problems. Then, hoping to catch the BBC leader off guard, he pulled out the seven pages he had gotten from Levin's father.

"What do you know about these?" he asked. For the first time, Zoeller thought, Joe looked really shaken. He said nothing, and began nervously going through the papers. After several minutes of silence, Zoeller asked again, "What do you know about these?"

"I don't know anything about them," Joe answered.

"Did you write them?" Zoeller pushed.

"On an issue like this, I want to confer with my attorney," Joe said. He continued to look at the pages for several more minutes until Zoeller took them from him.

"Do you have a key to Levin's house?" Zoeller asked after putting away the lists.

"I don't want to answer that without my attorney," Joe said. Zoeller took him back to his cell. He had gotten what he wanted.

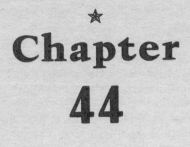

Chapter 44

Brooke Roberts had left the Wilshire Manning at approximately the same time as Joe on September 28, and so she witnessed his arrest. Within minutes she had conveyed the news to key BBC members, and they moved into action. Lauren Raab, a new BBC attorney who had been kept in the dark about both murders, was immediately sent down to the police station to gather what information she could.

When Lauren Raab returned from the jail, she gave Brooke a letter from Joe. Joe was unsure what would happen, he told Brooke, but he was proud of her for remaining strong. At the bottom of his note, he had written a postscript. "Don't make yourself available to my investors too much," it said.

The next day, Brooke accompanied Lauren to the police department. Joe's cell had a window, and he had requested that Brooke stand outside so he could see her. She had composed a brief note in the car for the attorney to take in. After assuring Joe of her love, Brooke got to the point. "We have been doing terrific work. Everyone is staying together," she wrote.

Within a few days of Joe's arrest, Dean received a phone call while he was visiting his girlfriend. It was Joe Hunt. "I don't have much time to talk," he said, "but there are a few things I need to say. Your recollections about several things are going to become critical. First, everything you can remember about the check and the contract is very important. Also, your recollections of the night Levin allegedly disappeared. Now, I think we may have been at the movies together that night."

Dean answered quickly. "I think that's right."

"I think you'd better work on really polishing what you remember about that whole period in early June," Joe said. "I've got to go." With that, the BBC leader hung up.

At Joe's request, Evan agreed to sleep at the Wilshire Manning temporarily so that Brooke would have someone there. On the third morning after the arrest, Evan was awakened by a banging on the door. Detective Zoeller handed him a search warrant. "We have a warrant to search this apartment," Zoeller said. "If you'd just have a seat in the living room, we'll try to be quick." The officers then awakened Brooke and had her sit in the living room as well.

The search turned up several things that would become important in later criminal cases, including a notebook of Reza Eslaminia's in which he had made numerous notes about his activities during the month of July. But it had another major effect as well. For the first time, Evan Dicker realized just how serious the situation had become.

During the search Zoeller asked Evan if he had been at the June 24 meeting where Joe announced he had murdered Levin. The frightened boy answered no, but the question filled him with terror. If the officers had fixed him with one more mean look, he later reflected, he would have signed anything they put in front of him. How had he gotten involved in all this? he wondered.

A few days after Joe's arrest, Zoeller met with Assistant District Attorney Anna Lopez about the case. After reviewing the charges Zoeller wished to file, she looked up. "You have plenty to make a case against Joe, but you don't have enough against this Jim Pittman yet. I really think you should charge them together so the preliminary hearings can be held at the same time. I'm going to reject this for now." It was a tough blow to Zoeller, but after reflecting, he agreed. The young attorney was right.

Joe was very pleased and more than a little smug when he was released without being charged. "They just don't have a case," he told the other BBC members. But he was also very worried. Karny's estrangement from the group had left a potentially lethal situation. Dean had been talking about Joe to certain BBC members. If he talked to the police, Joe knew, he would be in serious trouble. He would have to speak to his former lieutenant.

Dean agreed to meet his ex–best friend shortly after Joe's release, at the Old World Cafe, a health-food restaurant in the heart of Westwood. At first they exchanged small talk. Joe told Dean about jail. It wasn't too bad, he said. He had washed his socks out in the sink. Joe also told Dean about his questioning by Detective Zoeller, but he put it in the best possible light. Joe had been very surprised, he told Dean, to see the seven-page list, but he had been able to mask his reaction.

"Clearly the lists don't constitute sufficient evidence against me, or they wouldn't have let me go. I'd have to say Zoeller wasn't very bright," Joe added. "After I made him look ridiculous in his questioning, I pointed out to him that he hadn't done very good police work. There was simply no evidence to hold me."

Finally Joe got to the heart of what had brought him to the meeting. "I hear you've been criticizing me behind my back," he said sorrowfully. "I guess the time has come for us to really part company." There were, Joe said, just a few details to work out. After a long conversation, the boys reached an agreement. Dean would go his own way for the time being. They wouldn't see each other for a while. Maybe someday they would get together again and pursue some of the things they had always wanted to accomplish. In the meantime, they would stick together on their secrets.

Dean left the meeting with a heavy heart. Joe had been more than a best friend these last two years. He had been a teacher, an employer, and a mentor. Dean would miss their relationship.

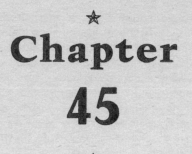

Chapter
45

In Switzerland, Ben was very relieved to hear Joe had been released. He had been dismayed shortly after the arrest when he called the BBC offices and spoke to Joe's secretary, Loree Leiss. "Joe's in jail and everything's in chaos," she had wailed. Ben hadn't been able to get the straight story until he spoke to Dean. He had been deeply disturbed by the developments back home.

Now things seemed much better, both in Los Angeles and in Europe. After many false starts, Ben and Reza were still hopeful. They believed they had located a bank in Zurich where Hedayat maintained an account. They had gone in and presented their papers. The officials would get back to them soon. But as the boys had already learned, Swiss banking operated on its own rules. They would be attended to when it was convenient for the bankers to see them.

In the meantime, Ben was enjoying Europe. In the bars of Zurich he had met others like himself, bright, ambitious young men from around the world who wanted to make a lot of money without a lot of work. They were dabbling in arbitrage, putting investors with money together with businesses that needed to borrow it. The sums they were dealing with practically made Ben salivate. Figures in the billions rolled off their tongues easily. None of the young men Ben met had actually made a killing yet, but each was on the verge. It was a feeling Ben had known many times.

As he waited for the slow wheels of banking to turn, Ben tried to learn all he could about arbitrage.

In San Francisco, Oscar Breiling had been making methodical progress. He had been deeply bothered by the release of Joe Hunt in Los Angeles. Les Zoeller was an excellent officer, he knew, yet apparently Zoeller hadn't been able to get enough to make Joe on the Levin case. On that one, Joe had admitted his guilt to ten people. Still, Breiling was confident he would eventually make his case, even though he had no body and no witnesses.

In mid-October, Breiling received a phone call that suggested a break in the case. One of Hedayat's best friends, a man who lived in Los Angeles, wanted to let the investigator know about a call he had received from Switzerland. A Swiss banker who had been a friend of Eslaminia's as well as of the Los Angeles man had been visited by someone representing Hedayat's son Reza. The man had produced documents, including a power of attorney, which seemed to grant Reza legal rights over his father's assets. He wanted to withdraw more than a hundred thousand dollars from the account. The papers seemed to be in order, but the banker was suspicious and had called Los Angeles in an attempt to get more information before releasing the funds.

The Los Angeles man told the banker to stall as long as he could. Then he called Breiling. "Hedayat never would have granted his son control of his affairs," the friend insisted.

"Not under any circumstances." Oscar took down information about the power of attorney. Then he got busy.

First Breiling approached Olga Vasquez. "Do you have any way of knowing where Hedayat was on April fourteenth?" he asked. "He supposedly signed a power of attorney in Los Angeles that day, and I wonder if he was really there," the investigator explained.

Breiling had gotten lucky. "I remember exactly where we were," Vasquez told him. "We were in Mexico." A calendar confirmed that the couple had been in Mexico that day visiting with friends. On their way back across the border the next day, they had been detained. There should be a record of that.

It had been a simple step for Breiling to confirm Vasquez's information. Border officials had kept records of Eslaminia's car license, what time he crossed the border, and in which lane of traffic he had been traveling. The friend in Mexico remembered Hedayat's visit distinctly. Breiling hoped desperately he would be able to use his new information to prevent Reza Eslaminia from getting his father's cash.

Much later that night, Oscar reached the Swiss banker at his home. "Please just hold everything," Breiling begged the man. "I have reason to believe those papers Reza has were fraudulently obtained." Suspicions were fine, the banker said, but unless he had some legal reason to withhold the funds, he could not do so much longer. Reza was being represented by a lawyer who was putting considerable pressure on the bank.

After hanging up, Breiling called Ron Bass, the deputy attorney general assigned to the case. It was now well after midnight, but the lawyer didn't seem upset at being disturbed. First thing the next morning he began drafting papers to revoke the conservatorship. As soon as they were completed, Oscar had the documents before a judge in Redwood City, who agreed to cancel Reza's authority over his father's estate.

By the end of the day, Breiling had sent a cablegram off to Switzerland:

BY COURT ORDER OCTOBER 18, 1984, REZA ESLAMINIA NO LONGER CONSERVATOR OF HEDAYAT ESLAMINIA'S ES-

TATE. DO NOT RELEASE FUNDS TO HIM. LETTER AND
COURT DOCUMENTS TO FOLLOW. SPECIAL AGENT OSCAR
BREILING.

When Reza and Ben went in that afternoon to pick up
their funds, the bank official politely informed them that they
had received information that Reza's authorization to withdraw funds was no longer valid. They were sorry to say they
could not release any money.

Chapter
46

Les Zoeller was ready. He now felt he had enough of a case to arrest both Joe Hunt and Jim Pittman. The district attorney's office agreed, and on the morning of October 22, Zoeller took his warrants to be signed by the judge in Division Six of the Beverly Hills Municipal Court. Zoeller had a special reason for selecting that particular courtroom.

At 9:45 that same morning, Joe Hunt, too, was in Division Six. He had still not been charged with any crime and was feeling increasingly certain that he was home free on the Levin murder. His cockiness about his circumstances had grown to the point that he had decided to do battle to get back his briefcase, which the Beverly Hills police had seized at the time of his arrest but had not yet released.

By the time Joe arrived in the courtroom, Zoeller had already gotten his warrant signed. But he waited patiently while the young man argued for the release of his property.

After the hearing, Zoeller approached his adversary. "I'm placing you under arrest," he said.

Across town that night in West Los Angeles, Zoeller didn't anticipate that Jim Pittman's arrest would be so simple. He arranged for six officers to stake out the powerful man's apartment. At 9:18, after waiting for some time, the men saw Pittman drive up in his black BMW. The officers approached swiftly. "On the ground, spread-eagle!" one of the men shouted. Pittman responded immediately. As some of the men handcuffed him, others confiscated his possessions.

Back at the station, after Graham was booked, the officers went through a blue nylon gym bag he had been carrying. There were twelve books in the bag, including such titles as *Improved Munitions From Ammonium Nitrate, Getaway Driving Techniques for Escape, Hit Man: A Technical Manual for Independent Contractors, 100 Ways to Disappear and Live Free,* and *How to Rip Off a Drug Dealer.* But the book the officers hoped Graham would have the most use for was one entitled *Survival in the Slammer.*

On the morning of October 23, Zoeller and another officer took Graham from his jail cell to an interview room. After reading him his rights, the men asked Graham if he would like to talk to them. "Sure, I want to talk," Graham answered. During the interrogation, Pittman attempted to downplay his relationship with Hunt, insisting that he was a private investigator who did most of his work for a former governor of Wisconsin who lived in the Wilshire Manning. When pressed, he said he had done some work for Joe, mostly "following people around for him."

Zoeller decided it was time to get down to business. "I have evidence implicating you in the murder of Ron Levin," he said calmly. Graham considered his plight. "When am I supposed to have done that?" he asked. Zoeller told him that the murder took place on June sixth or seventh. "I wasn't even in town at all in June," Pittman insisted. "I was in Washington at the beginning of the month and in Hawaii at the end. I didn't even get back to town until June twenty-ninth."

Zoeller pressed Graham for details. Where had he stayed? What dates exactly had he been gone? Who was he working for? After the interview was over, he tried to verify Graham's story. Yes, the former governor said, he had on occasion employed Graham. Had Graham ever gone to Hawaii for him? Zoeller asked. Yes, the man said, but it had been a strange thing. He had asked Graham if he knew an investigator in Hawaii because he needed some work done there. The next thing he knew, Graham was in Hawaii. But that was at the end of June or the beginning of July, and he had only spent a few days there.

Zoeller hoped that this time Hunt and Graham were in jail to stay.

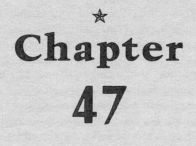

Chapter
47

Dean was a mess. During the time between Joe's arrests, he had almost convinced himself that life would be normal again, that he could walk away from the BBC, become a lawyer, and forget that he had helped plan two murders and actually participated in one of them. Joe's second arrest destroyed that illusion.

Shortly after the arrest, Dean received a phone call at 2 A.M. "We've got to talk, Dean," Joe said.

Dean's heart began beating rapidly. "I really don't want to discuss anything on the phone," Dean replied.

"Whether you like it or not, you are going to be involved in this case," Joe insisted. "And even though you don't want to talk, we have got to discuss a few of the issues on which your testimony is going to be required."

Dean must go to the jail soon to see Joe in person. In the meantime, he had better be aware that one of the key issues was going to be whether or not a meeting took place on June 24. "We'll discuss it when you come to see me," Joe said.

During the next couple of weeks, Dean had difficulty sleeping or eating. He took to his bed for long periods, and his old nervous reaction of vomiting returned. The lanky boy was even thinner than usual.

Finally he told his parents part of the horrible story that was haunting him. Danielle and Shalom Karny rallied immediately behind their son. They knew him to be a good, moral boy. They had raised him that way. It was Joe Hunt who must be the monster. They would do whatever they could to extract their son from Hunt's clutches.

A lawyer retained by the Karny family advised Dean that his first move should be to get any existing police reports so the attorney could assess Dean's exposure. Dean made contact with Ryan Hunt. He would like to pick up some of his personal belongings from Joe's father, Dean said, and also he wondered whether it would be possible to get copies of the police reports. Ryan Hunt agreed.

On November 14, accompanied by his mother, Dean went out to Ryan Hunt's San Fernando Valley office. Brooke Roberts was there waiting for him. "You've got to help Joe, Dean," she began urgently as soon as she saw him. "A lot of people are coming forward against him now. They're saying there was a meeting at which he said he killed Ron Levin. You've got to come forward and contradict that." Dean listened as the impassioned Brooke spoke. If Dean didn't want to go directly to the police himself, she said, he could sign an affidavit Joe's lawyer would draw up. But there were three specific points Dean had to address: he must say there was no meeting, he must say Joe didn't kill Ron Levin, and he must say Joe never threatened him.

"I can't do anything right now," Dean insisted. "My attorney says I can't do anything, at least until he has a chance to see the police reports and evaluate my position."

"Come on, Dean," Brooke cajoled. "Signing an affidavit is

not going to hurt you at all, and it could help Joe so much. He may not even get bail without this."

"An affidavit is a statement," Dean replied. "It has consequences. Unless I can see the police reports, I can't say anything."

Brooke wouldn't give up. "They want to send Joe to the gas chamber," she said emotionally. "And if he gets convicted, you can bet they're going to come after you."

After Dean got the reports from Ryan Hunt, Brooke continued to try and encourage Dean to come forward, explaining to him that the evidence against Joe was insufficient and that if Karny would just support him, Joe would get out on bail. Aware that she had lost the battle, at least for the present, Brooke left Dean with one last request. "If you talk to Ben, tell him it's safe for him to come home and that he should come back and help Joe."

When Dean next talked to Ben, he told him something else entirely. "Things are a mess here," he said. "Just stay put. I'll tell you when it's safe for you to come back."

Chapter
48

At three o'clock on the afternoon of October 24, Jon Allen walked into the headquarters of the Beverly Hills Police Department to be interviewed. He hadn't come forward earlier, he told Les Zoeller, because he was scared. Joe Hunt had threatened him. He was now ready to tell everything.

Allen was a breakthrough witness in certain ways, although he was able to add very little to what the Mays and others had said. But up until now, the BBC members who had come forward were ones who had broken with the group in the aftermath of the Levin killing. They were boys who hadn't been trusted for some time. Allen had remained a part of the BBC during the crucial months following Eslaminia's abduction. His defection was a sign that the united front presented by the BBC might be crumbling.

Zoeller treated Allen carefully, encouraging him to speak and reassuring him as he told his tale. His story about the June 24 meeting matched the Mays' account closely. Joe had threatened the boys after the meeting, and Allen had taken this very seriously. At the end of their conversation, Zoeller asked Jon if he would be willing to talk about the Eslaminia matter to an agent for the state of California. Allen agreed, although he knew little about Eslaminia. He had decided to cooperate fully.

Soon after talking to Zoeller, Jon called Dean Karny. By now Dean was making notes of every conversation he had about the BBC and the murders. "Jon Allen called me, I believe as a friend," Dean wrote in his notebook after the phone call, "and told me that he had decided to make a statement to the authorities rather than to potentially 'get in trouble' for things he was not responsible for. He advised me that I should also seriously consider making a statement, as he felt it would alleviate both my emotional stress and the potential risk of becoming a target for prosecution. He said that he preferred not to come over and visit me when I asked him to, but said that he did want to acquaint me with what he had said and with whatever other information he had concerning the overall situation."

Later in his record of his conversation with Jon, Dean noted the most terrifying thing he had learned. "Jon also feels from his conversation with Zoeller that if Dean doesn't do something soon (such as come forward and make a statement), that he might soon be arrested," Dean wrote, referring to himself in the third person. "Zoeller really wants to talk to Dean."

On November 27, Dean learned just how badly Zoeller wanted to speak to him. First thing that morning the Karnys' doorbell rang. It was Les Zoeller with a subpoena for Dean. He was being called to testify at Joe's preliminary hearing.

Danielle Karny opened the door to the polite, handsome detective. "Dean's sleeping," she told him after he had stated his business. "If you'll wait in the living room, I'll get him." After fifteen minutes, Mrs. Karny reappeared. "He's brushing his teeth now. He should be here shortly," she explained. After another fifteen minutes, Danielle Karny returned with a telephone. "I'm sorry to have taken so long, but Dean's lawyer is on the phone and he really wants to talk to you."

"We're not trying to give you the runaround," the attorney, Ron Morrow, told Zoeller, "but you're in the wrong place. I'm up in San Francisco talking to the Special Prosecutions people now. I promise you we're going to have something big for you. Just be patient." Zoeller decided he would ride things out.

Dean's attorney, Ron Morrow, was comfortable dealing with prosecutors. He had been an assistant U.S. attorney himself before leaving for private practice. The bright, aggressive young lawyer now maintained a small practice in which he could pick and choose his clients.

When Dean came in seeking help with his problems, Morrow hired a private investigator to verify the young man's story. It all checked out. They were in an excellent position to cut a deal.

Breiling was glad to be called in to the meeting Ron Bass had scheduled with Ron Morrow. "I'm representing a client who can provide you with very specific information about the murder of Hedayat Eslaminia," the lawyer said. Breiling thought about the options. Reza and Ben, he believed, were still abroad. Joe and Jim were facing other charges as well. It was unlikely any of them was trying to negotiate a deal. "How is Dean?" he asked Morrow.

Bass then handed his investigator the report Morrow had prepared. When Breiling was finished reading, Bass turned to him. "Well? Is it worth granting immunity?"

"Yep," the investigator answered without hesitation.

Neither Bass nor Breiling liked the idea of granting full immunity to an admitted murderer, but there was little alternative. Dean was clearly not going to say a word unless he was promised a very good deal. And the prosecution needed a witness who could tell what actually happened on July 30, 1984. With Dean Karny, the men realized, they could probably recover Eslaminia's body. They could also learn for the first time exactly what led up to the abduction of the Iranian man. Breiling at last had his big break.

By afternoon, the details had been worked out. The next morning, Dean flew to San Francisco. With a tape recorder running, Oscar Breiling read the boy the deal that had been worked out. He was to have blanket immunity from prosecution for the murders and related acts. The state would try to intervene on his behalf should he be sued or prosecuted by the Securities and Exchange Commission. And finally, because Dean had insisted on the condition, the state would put in a good word for him with the California State Bar Association when Dean applied for admission. It was Dean's great panic that his participation in the BBC would keep him from the one goal he had in life—to be a lawyer.

During the hours that followed, with the tape recorder still running, Dean gave Breiling and Bass the full story of the BBC.

Chapter
49

On November 29, Les Zoeller had his first chance to talk with Dean Karny, and the conversation was all he could hope for. In addition to supplying full details of what Dean knew about the Levin murder, the young man said he knew exactly where Hedayat Eslaminia's body had been dumped. Zoeller made plans to go with him to look for the remains the following morning.

Detective Les Zoeller had no trouble finding his way to Soledad Canyon on the morning of November 30. He had been out there several times with various BBC members searching for a possible dumping spot for Levin's body.

After a twenty-minute drive through the arid, high desert canyon, Karny indicated a dirt road. "I think this is the road," he said. "Turn off here." About half a mile up the winding fire road, Karny told Zoeller to pull off into a turnaround. "This is the spot we threw him over," he said grimly, pointing down a steep hillside covered with chaparral.

Coyotes had long since scattered the former Iranian leader's bones by the time Zoeller and his team of officers arrived at the site. But it nevertheless took them only a few minutes to confirm that Karny had brought them to the right place. Just ten feet down the hillside, Zoeller and two other policemen spotted a bone fragment. Moving downhill some sixty-five feet further on, they found a piece of a rib cage and some hair fragments. It was enough to warrant a full-scale search. Zoeller made his way back up the steep hillside to the car, where he radioed the coroner's office to send out a team to really scour the hillside.

By the end of the day, the searchers had assembled, photographed, and labeled a femur, an ulna, a lower jaw, a scapula, some vertebrae, a skull, and a pair of black Jockey Classic Briefs, size 36. It was the jawbone that proved that the remains were those of Hedayat Eslaminia.

★

Chapter

50

★

One evening in November, Rose and Luan Dosti received a disturbing phone call at their Hancock Park home. A Detective Zoeller from the Beverly Hills Police Department wanted to speak to Ben about the disappearance of a Beverly Hills con man named Ron Levin. It was urgent that he speak to him. Could the Dostis tell him how to contact their son?

Ben's parents were deeply disturbed. They had seen their son in London during September, when Luan had had to go there on business. He had seemed fine then. Wouldn't they have known if something had been seriously wrong? The Dostis immediately contacted a lawyer. They definitely needed some good advice. They also spoke to their son.

"Is there anything to what this Detective Zoeller says?" Luan Dosti asked his son during a phone conversation.

"Absolutely not," Ben replied.

His father pushed further. "There is talk about immunity. Do you need immunity from anything?"

"Look, Dad, I have nothing to hide," Ben said insistently. "I'll come back to Los Angeles and clear this thing up."

For weeks prior to going to the police, Dean had been telling Ben not to risk returning to the United States. "I think you should wait until things calm down," Dean had urged his friend during their occasional phone calls. Ben was safe and untouchable in Europe, Dean reasoned; who knew what would happen if he returned? But there was another element of Dean's interest in Ben's remaining abroad. The authorities were unlikely to grant immunity to two people with the same information. Dean had desperately wanted to be the first man in.

Dean had asked Evan Dicker directly to wait to talk to authorities until Dean had his chance. After all, he had pointed out to Dicker, Dean had much greater exposure in the murders. Evan had known nothing in advance. He hadn't even known anything about the Eslaminia homicide until Dean told him about it in November. As a friend, Dean pleaded, would Evan please wait to come forward? Evan had agreed. In early December, after Dean had spoken to police, Evan went in as well.

Now was the time, Dean felt, for him to urge Ben to come back and try to negotiate a deal with the authorities. Dean could honestly say he had been more than fair to Ben in his talks with Breiling and Zoeller. He had of course had to tell them truthfully about Ben's involvement. But he had bent over backward to let them know it was Joe who controlled things, that he and Ben had been puppets. On November 29, Dean spoke to Ben in Europe. "I went to the authorities and told them everything," he said. "Come back and you can probably make a bargain. I'll do what I can to help, but you may have to spend some time in jail."

A few days after he talked to Dean, Ben Dosti headed home with Reza Eslaminia. They had just boarded a People's Express plane at Newark Airport outside New York and were waiting for the plane to take off for Los Angeles when an airline representative entered the plane with a message. Would Ben Dosti please come forward? There was an urgent phone message for him.

Ben got off the plane and contacted his parents. "Don't come back," Ben's mother told him on the phone. They had gotten a call that morning from the attorney they had hired to represent Ben. He had been in San Francisco that morning and seen in a paper there that a warrant had been issued for Ben's arrest. Until he had time to sort things out, Ben decided he would remain in New York.

Ben quickly grabbed Reza, who had been with him on the flight to Los Angeles, and the two boys checked into a New Jersey motel to wait for further developments. During the next several days, Ben met with his attorney, who flew to New York. It was best, Ben felt, not to return to California, at least for the moment.

Chapter
51

Soon after Ben made his decision to remain in New York, his parents got a phone call from Danielle Karny. "We simply must meet to talk about this disaster the kids are involved in," she said insistently. "Can you come tonight?" The Dostis agreed.

That night the Dostis arrived at the Karnys' house and were ushered into the living room. Dean was brought in and somberly began telling the Dostis the story of the BBC, which their own son had never told them. He spared no details, explaining how Ben had participated with the others in planning and carrying out the kidnapping of Eslaminia.

"Ben has got to come in and make a deal," Karny insisted. "I was able to tell them a lot, but Ben was actually inside the apartment. He was in a position to see much more than I saw. They need his testimony."

Dean continued his narrative through Eslaminia's abduction. As he began to tell them about what happened inside the back of the truck on the way home, Danielle Karny interrupted. "Stop," she commanded her son in a near hysterical tone. "I don't want to hear it. Stop talking."

The Dostis had heard enough, too. They were certain their son couldn't have been involved in such hideous events. He had told them he was innocent; that was enough for them.

After leaving the Karnys, the distraught couple saw their lawyer, who was appalled that they had met with Dean. "He's the last person you should be talking to," he told them. In addition, he said, they weren't to discuss anything further with their son.

Chapter
52

Ben Dosti was not at all sure what the future would hold. All he knew was that for now, he would remain in New York with Reza. It wasn't that he particularly enjoyed Reza's company; it was simply that Ben couldn't think of anything else to do with his associate. Reza had no money and no place to go. He couldn't rely on his family for support the way Ben could. And it would be dangerous to leave Reza entirely on his own. So for now, Ben was stuck with the Iranian boy.

For the first few weeks, the two boys remained in New York City, moving frequently around Manhattan from cheap hotel to cheap hotel. Ben realized that they should not use their actual names and always registered them under pseudonyms, but living under a false name without identification was difficult. Ben decided to see what he could do about getting some ID.

Ben had read once about how to get false identification, and he put the information he had gleaned to work. At the

New York Public Library, he went through newspapers from the Sixties, looking for the name of someone roughly his age who had died during that period. Soon he found a story about two young boys, Christopher Lee Potter and Lansing Lee Potter, born about the same time as Ben, who were killed with their parents when the private airplane they were flying in crashed. He then wrote away to Kentucky for the brothers' birth certificates, ordering both "just in case" as he later put it.

Armed with the birth certificate of Lansing Potter, Ben began applying for identification around the city. He first got a false New York State identification card, and then, using that, got a valid New York Public Library card. He registered to vote. Lansing Lee Potter was off and running.

After the first of the year, Reza and Ben left New York for Fort Lauderdale. The weather in New York was getting to them, and they wanted to be someplace where they could sleep outside if they ran out of money. After more than a month in Florida, Ben was getting good and tired of Reza. He wanted him to contribute something for lodging and meals, but Reza insisted he had no money and couldn't get any. Finally, although it made him very nervous, Ben suggested that they split up. Reza agreed to leave for Las Vegas. Ben gave him five hundred dollars to live on until he could find a job. Before Reza left, Ben gave him a piece of paper with a code on it. It was a list of numbers, zero through nine. Each had a different number next to it. If Ben needed to reach Reza, he would call Debi Lutkenhouse and leave the number of a pay phone and a time to call it. Reza should take the numbers and translate them with the code sheet. He should return the calls only from a pay phone.

From Florida, Ben went to Boston, where his father was living temporarily on a job. At first Ben stayed with his father in suburban Lexington, but soon it was decided that he should live elsewhere. They couldn't be sure Luan Dosti's house wouldn't be watched by the authorities. Soon, Lansing Lee Potter, or Lee as he liked to be called, had established himself in Cambridge. He got a post office box at a mail drop on Massachusetts Avenue, he grew a beard, and he began looking around for something to occupy himself.

There were things Ben missed about the BBC. He had loved the feeling of being a businessman, of being just on the verge of a big killing. If only he could have seen things through, Ben still thought, some of the BBC projects would have paid off big. Bored and alone in Boston, Ben began planning new business ventures.

Large-scale arbitrage projects, like those he had heard about in Zurich, still seemed wildly alluring to Ben. He spent many of his days in Massachusetts trying to arrange business deals. In a letter to a potential money source, he wrote that he was seeking amounts "up to five billion U.S. dollars" for a European arbitrage deal.

In another burst of entrepreneurial zeal, Ben wrote a letter to the Xerox corporation. He realized, he said, that people overused superlatives. But the idea he had for a Xerox television advertisement could only be called "sensational." The company should advise him, he concluded, about whom he should send his idea to so that the commercial could be quickly produced.

During the spring of 1985, Ben decided he should be prepared to go to Europe if it became necessary for one of his arbitrage projects. Besides, he could always use another piece of identification. By summer, he had applied for and received a passport under the name of Lansing Lee Potter.

After some time in Las Vegas, Reza made his way to Lake Tahoe. Prior to leaving Florida, Ben had given Reza the extra birth certificate he had procured. "You shouldn't use this unless it's an emergency," Ben had cautioned him. "You don't look like a Christopher Potter. You should try and get a birth certificate with a Spanish surname. It will be much more believable." Ben had carefully instructed Reza on how to go about procuring false identification.

Back in California, Reza decided Ben's way of getting identification sounded like a lot of work. He had a perfectly good birth certificate, after all; why shouldn't he use it? Ben, he felt, was being ridiculously overcautious. Soon Reza had used his birth certificate to get himself a California driver's license, and using his new name, he soon had himself a job working at a Tahoe ski resort.

After some time in the mountains, Reza moved to Santa Cruz, south of San Jose, where he landed a job with an old family friend. Upon hearing from Ben that the other boy had successfully gotten a passport, Reza decided he would do so also. In a final burst of caution, Reza made himself a list of things he must do before going in to file his application if he wanted the officials to believe he was Chris Potter. It read: "Memorize bairthdate [sic], birthplace, father's birthplace, father's name, mother's birthplace, mother's name."

Chapter
53

In late February of 1985, Oscar Breiling was driving in to San Francisco from his ranch across the Bay. The congested commute was just like always, until the investigator had to brake for slowing traffic ahead. When he eased his foot down on the pedal, the left front brake grabbed, spinning the state-assigned car so that Breiling slammed head on into the center divider. It was not the way he had hoped to begin his morning.

Breiling tried to open his door, but the car had crumpled in such a way that a traditional exit was impossible, so the six-footer instead crawled out the window. Standing beside his auto on the busy freeway, Breiling noticed that his knee and back were quite sore. But that, he figured, would heal. Mostly, he was angry.

After getting a ride into work, the investigator filled out paperwork about his accident. Then, disgruntled and sore, he decided to take the rest of the day off. It was now Friday afternoon. Surely, he thought, he'd feel fine on Monday.

Through the weekend, Breiling felt worse and worse. Early the next week, he went in for X rays. The lawman could see the problem himself on the hazy picture: his back was broken between the shoulder blades. Two vertebrae were crushed. He would be off work for many months.

Breiling tried hard to be a good patient, but he was not cut out for convalescence. Through the daily physical therapy and traction, he worried about what he should be doing around the ranch. He also worried about his case. He was itching to get back on the job.

While Breiling was at home nursing his injuries, Joe Hunt and Jim Pittman had gone through their preliminary hearing in the Levin matter, and the judge there, as expected, had ruled there was enough evidence to bind the young men over for trial. In May of 1985, while the investigator was still out on disability, Pittman had gone to trial for that killing. Breiling had found the results disturbing and disappointing. The proceedings ended in a hung jury: ten of the jurors had felt beyond reasonable doubt that the bodyguard killed Levin, but two had not. Pittman would have to be retried.

The Pittman verdict made Breiling all the more determined to get back on his feet. When his case was brought to trial, he wanted the evidence to be incontrovertible. There were still so many leads he wanted to follow up on. Soon it would be time for Joe and Jim's prelim in the Eslaminia case. He definitely wanted to be back for that.

Chapter
54

Reza Eslaminia was getting very tired of life on the lam. With his girlfriend Debi's help, he was now in contact with a San Francisco attorney who was trying to arrange some way Reza could turn himself in.

Debi, too, was growing frustrated with the state of affairs. She had never wavered in her devotion to the troubled young man, but she wished she could safely see more of him. As she waited for some sort of action, Debi wrote Reza a letter expressing her frustration. Addressing him as her "dearest Christopher," Debi chastised Reza for not calling when he had promised to. She worried, she told him, when he didn't call. Moreover, she said, she was very lonely without him and couldn't wait to be reunited permanently. "I imagine this house with . . . you out in the living room making business calls and me in the kitchen making breakfast," she said.

Despite the negotiations for Reza to turn himself in, he continued to pursue getting a passport. On August 1, he drove to the Federal Building in San Francisco in a red 1985 Ford Mustang. He had rented the car several weeks earlier, and it was now seriously overdue. But today Reza couldn't worry about that. He had received word that his passport was ready.

After a brief wait in the building, Reza heard the name of Christopher Lee Potter read over a loudspeaker. It was his turn to pick up his passport. As he rose to walk to the counter, a man in a suit approached him. "Are you Christopher Potter?" the man asked.

"Yes," Reza responded.

"Then I'm afraid you are under arrest for passport fraud," the man said.

Passport investigators are trained to look for fraud, and Christopher Potter's application contained several red flags. His Social Security number indicated a recently issued card, which is unusual for someone in his twenties. His California driver's license indicated he had no previous license experience, also an oddity in California, where most youngsters get their licenses upon turning sixteen. Finally, the swarthy young man pictured on the passport hardly looked like a Christopher Potter. Analyzed together, the factors had been enough to raise questions.

Taking information from the passport application, San Francisco passport officials wrote to the recorder in the county where Potter had been born and inquired whether there had been any recent requests for Potter's birth certificate. Also, the fraud investigators wanted to know, was there perhaps a death certificate for him?

The response was quick. Christopher Potter had been dead for more than ten years. His birth certificate, as well as that of his brother Lansing Lee Potter, had been requested in late 1984 by a man who had identified himself as a New York genealogist.

On a hunch, the officials ran the name Lansing Potter through the agency's computers. A passport in that name had been issued recently to a person living in Cambridge, Massachusetts.

Picking up fugitives is often a difficult task, but the FBI hoped the case of Lansing Potter would be a simple one. It was. Taking the address listed on Potter's passport, a federal agent went on August 2, 1985, to the mail drop where Potter had, at least at one time, maintained a post office box. After presenting his identification, the FBI man began his inquiry. "Do you still maintain a mailbox for a Lansing Potter?" he asked. Yes, the clerk said, although they knew him as Lee. Did he come in regularly? Yes, usually each morning, the clerk said. The agent decided to wait.

After a time, the dark-haired, bearded young man walked in. The clerk nodded to the waiting agent. "Are you Lansing Lee Potter?" the FBI man asked. After giving an affirmative response, Ben Dosti was placed under arrest.

In California, Oscar Breiling's bedside phone rang shrilly. The investigator answered. "You're going to have to come back, Oscar," a jubilant Ron Bass said. "They've caught your boys."

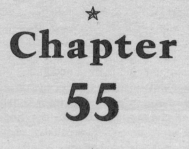

Chapter 55

The Roberts family had a cause. They wanted Joe Hunt freed. In the months since Joe's arrest, they had changed their feelings toward their daughter's boyfriend; the family had come to see Joe as a martyr. For the two years prior, Brooke's father, Bobby, had viewed Joe Hunt as an evil corrupter of his young daughter. He had despised the arrogant young man. Now he had made a complete turnaround.

On the night of Joe's second arrest, Brooke had gone to her parents late at night and poured out an emotional story of his innocence and wrongful arrest. Her parents seemed to hear only one thing: their adored only daughter was in pain. She needed them. The whole family rallied at once.

Brooke's parents and brothers began visiting Joe regularly in jail. Her father retained a lawyer to handle the young man's legal problems. They closed in tightly and protectively around Brooke. It was the oddest thing, friends of the family said to one another. Bobby Roberts couldn't stand Joe Hunt until he got arrested for murder. Then he embraced him like a son.

By the fall of 1985, jail was really getting to Joe. He had always dreamed of one day being a world leader, but it was hard to even imagine such a thing from a six-foot-by-ten-foot cell. Joe spent some time each day trying to learn Japanese, which he told himself would one day serve him well in business. If he could just be in isolation, things might be better, but the other prisoners were often frightening. Some of them were willing to respect Joe, even asking for his help with their legal troubles. But others were less respectful.

During the year Joe had been in jail, Bobby Roberts seemed to have become ever more convinced that Joe was being wrongfully held. It was outrageous, the movie producer felt, that such a boy was sitting in a cell surrounded by criminals. In the fall of 1985, Roberts called Arthur Barens, the lawyer he had hired to represent Joe, and told him to do whatever it took to get Joe out on bail.

Arthur Barens had heard nothing about the Billionaire Boys Club when he was approached by a friend of Bobby Roberts about representing Joe Hunt after his arrest in 1984. Barens was a strange choice for an attorney in a complicated murder trial. The wealthy Century City lawyer was primarily known as a personal injury lawyer; he handled car accidents. He was very good at what he did, as his busy office suggested. But he had not practiced much criminal law. The one high-publicity criminal trial he had handled was that of Marvin Pancoast, the mentally disturbed young man who killed Vicky Morgan, Alfred Bloomingdale's mistress, with a baseball bat. With Barens as his lawyer, Pancoast was convicted of first-degree murder. Many people in the legal community felt Barens should have been able to do better by his client, who had been in and out of mental institutions. Barens was very happy to be asked to take Hunt's case. It would be, he believed, a chance to redeem himself, and he planned to pour himself into the case, body and soul.

If anybody could make up for lack of experience with sheer determination, it was Arthur Barens. Abandoned by his mother when he was very young, Barens, a bookish, timid boy, had been raised in a foster home in the sprawling black ghetto of South Central Los Angeles. One of the few white children in the neighborhood, the boy felt isolated and mis-understood. He decided at an early age that education would be his ticket out of the world he hated. At UCLA he had done extremely well, graduating Phi Beta Kappa. After completing his undergraduate work, the short, stylish young man married his college sweetheart, the pretty, accomplished daughter of a wealthy Beverly Hills man. But Barens vowed he would not live on his father-in-law's money. He wanted the best for his wife, but he would earn it for her himself.

After law school at the University of Southern California Barens began practicing law, first with the flamboyant pali-mony attorney Marvin Mitchelson, and then with another firm. Ultimately he started his own practice, which quickly began to thrive. By 1979, through working frequent fifteen-hour days and seven-day weeks, Barens had amassed a small fortune, enough to purchase a huge Tudor-style mansion in the best part of Beverly Hills. He served on important chari-table boards, had standing in the Jewish community, coached his adored daughters' soccer teams. And although he still sometimes felt like a visitor in his luxurious home, he had become, at last, an insider in the world he had always coveted.

Barens had been immediately intrigued by the Hunt case. After meeting the young BBC founder, Barens realized Joe was someone he could identify with strongly. Like Barens, Hunt had been very attracted to the highly seductive culture of Beverly Hills. Joe, too, had wanted desperately to be a part of it, but he had made some mistakes. Barens could even identify with that; Barens himself had made serious mistakes before getting on the right track, but he had been able to recove.

from his. Joe needed a chance, and Barens was determined to give it to him.

Barens was in the middle of vigorously preparing for Hunt's northern California preliminary hearing when he got a call from Roberts. "See what you can do to get Joe out on bail," Hunt's patron had said.

Getting bail set for a defendant accused of a capital crime is no easy matter, and Barens was a bit daunted at the prospect. Zoeller, he knew, had several people who would swear Joe had threatened them. Barens didn't believe the threats were real, but no judge was likely to take a chance. Barens had recently brought in Richard Chier, a very bright, iconoclastic criminal specialist, to assist on the case. They had met by chance in a courthouse one day when Barens admired a suit the other man was wearing. Both men were devoted followers of fashion, and they soon discovered they had a lot of other things in common too. After Chier was brought on board, the two men worked for days drafting a bail motion they hoped would get Joe released.

Fred Wapner, the capable young deputy district attorney who had recently been assigned the Levin murder case, was surprised when he received Barens's motion for a bail hearing, but he was not particularly alarmed. Joe Hunt was accused of two murders. Wapner's case against him was a death penalty case. The witnesses who had been threatened by Joe would give strong statements. Surely no judge would take the risk of letting Hunt out.

Wapner was the kind of hardworking, straightforward deputy who made up the backbone of the district attorney's office. Diligent and well schooled rather than brilliant and flashy, low key in his presentations, Wapner had gone to the district attorney's office straight out of law school. From the beginning he had enjoyed being a prosecutor.

In law school, Wapner had decided he wanted to be a trial lawyer. Wanting the stability of a steady paycheck, he opted, despite being from a liberal family, for becoming a prosecutor. He had never regretted his decision. Wapner had a lot of respect for law and order. He felt people should do what was right and good for society, and that, he believed, usually translated into what was legal. He had worked hard at his job, first prosecuting misdemeanants and drunk drivers, and then moving on to bigger cases. But the complicated no-body case of Joe Hunt was clearly the most challenging Wapner had ever worked.

Wapner and most of the other people in the Santa Monica branch of the DA's office knew he had been given the case because he was ready for it and because he deserved it. But there were a few people downtown who felt that he had been assigned the Levin murder because of his famous father.

Wapner's name had always meant something in Los Angeles legal circles. His father, Joseph Wapner, had been among the most respected judges in the county. In recent years, Fred's father's fame had spread beyond the courthouse walls and into the living rooms of America as the stern but fair Judge Wapner of the television show "People's Court."

Famous father or not, Wapner realized that the only way he could win this case was with hard work, and with that in mind, he prepared diligently for the first real test, the bail hearing.

Barens and Chier planned their strategy carefully. They knew they had one trump card. Judge Laurence Rittenband, the feisty octogenarian assigned to hear the case, badly wanted to have the trial in his courtroom. Over the years, the highly qualified but often imperious justice had heard many of the biggest cases in the Los Angeles courts' Western Division. He had presided over court proceedings in the sex crime case of director Roman Polanski, and over numerous high-publicity murder trials. He enjoyed the press attention on his Department C.

Hoping that Rittenband's enjoyment of the limelight and

interest in complicated cases would have an impact on his ruling, the defense team made it clear to the judge that they were worried about his ability to be impartial. Earlier in the year he had presided over Jim Pittman's trial on the Levin matter. The jury had split ten to two for conviction on that case, and so it would eventually have to be retried. It would be difficult for Rittenband not to have formed some opinions about Joe Hunt during those proceedings. By letting the judge know their concerns, Barens and Chier hoped the judge would be eager to show his lack of bias by granting bail to their client. After the hearing, much to Fred Wapner's amazement, the judge set bail at $500,000.

What all the parties had failed to take into account was what probably motivated Rittenband to take the action he did. Even after all his years on the bench, the judge took the premises of the American legal system very seriously. The Constitution guaranteed that people were innocent until proven guilty. In his courtroom, although he had a reputation for toughness on convicted criminals, Rittenband frequently asserted the rights of the untried.

Soon after his success in Santa Monica, Barens appeared before a judge in northern California to request bail in that case too. Appearing for the state was John Vance, a deputy attorney general who had recently been assigned the Hunt case because Ron Bass was overburdened with other cases. Over Vance's vigorous objections, the judge granted Hunt bail of $500,000 in that case, too.

If Joe, accused of two murders, could somehow raise one million dollars, he would be released on bail.

Chapter
56

If anyone had doubted Bobby Roberts's belief in Joe Hunt, Roberts demonstrated it categorically in late October 1985 by putting up his two-million-dollar Bel Air estate to secure Joe's bail. If Joe skipped out, Roberts would lose his home, which was his biggest asset by far. And the Hollywood producer didn't stop by posting Joe's bail: after the young man was released on November 7, he was invited to live with the Robertses as one of the family until his legal troubles were resolved.

Thanksgiving came early at the Robertses' Bel Air home that fall. Brooke had told her family that Joe's favorite meal was turkey, and so, although Thanksgiving was not for several weeks after Joe's release, her mother Lynne decided to do up a huge turkey dinner to celebrate. All four of the Roberts children were there. Joe was welcomed as the newest member of the clan.

During the months that followed, Bobby Roberts treated Joe exactly like one of his own children. He was given a membership in an expensive Century City health club, taken to dinner, and provided with abundant spending money. He was at last living the life of the boys he had so envied at the Harvard School.

After Joe had been granted bail, it was a simple matter for Ben and Reza to get bail also. Soon after Joe's proceedings went so well, bail was set for both of the others by a Redwood City judge for $500,000 each.

Although Ben's family was by no means wealthy enough to have that sort of cash on hand, they moved quickly to secure their son's release. It was inconceivable that he should be allowed to languish in jail for a crime they were convinced he had not committed. Soon after the bail was set, with the homes of his parents and an aunt and uncle in Boston as security for his bail, Ben Dosti was released pending trial, and for the first time in more than a year, the family was reunited.

Reza's family was slower to come through with the money for his release, but finally, after a preliminary hearing found that there was enough evidence to hold Ben, Reza, and Joe over for trial on the Eslaminia murder, an aunt put up Reza's bail. After his release, the young man moved in with Debi Lutkenhouse, who had been working diligently to get him out of jail so he could move in with her.

By spring of 1986, all of the accused murderers except Jim Pittman, who was awaiting a second trial on the Levin killing before he would even be arraigned in Redwood City, were free on bail.

Oscar Breiling was furious. He knew the two prosecutors Wapner and Vance had done their best, but how could any judge think that these guys should be released on bail? From everything he knew of Joe Hunt, Breiling was certain that he would do something hideous while out on the streets. He had already threatened numerous people, after all, and he must know that Dean Karny was by far the most important witness against him.

Oscar knew he must take immediate steps to protect his chief witness, or Hunt and the others might never be convicted at all. By late winter, after spending hours battling complicated bureaucracies, Breiling had arranged for Karny to become part of California's Witness Protection Program. It wasn't much. The program could really only promise someone a driver's license under a new name, and a stipend to relocate. Breiling himself would have to take on the job of seeing that Dean remained safe. He would have to find him a place to live and instruct him about remaining anonymous.

Once he had Karny relatively removed from harm, Breiling turned his attention to seeing what he could do about getting his defendants back in jail.

The young San Mateo County jail inmate was not the kind of person Oscar Breiling loved dealing with. The son of a middle-class Peninsula family, the young man had run with Reza during the Iranian boy's wildest days. The two had done drugs together and bragged of their other dubious accomplishments. In 1983, when the troubled young man told Reza about a burglary he had been involved in, Reza had gone to the authorities. It was now time to return the favor.

By coincidence, Reza's former friend was once again in the Redwood City jail when Reza was brought in on charges of murdering his father. The two were assigned to the same cell. Shortly after Reza's release, the young man let it be known to jail authorities that he had heard some very interesting things from Reza while they were housed together.

After learning about the allegations, Oscar Breiling met with the inmate for several hours. The agent wasn't wild about dealing with a snitch, but he couldn't afford to be choosy. According to the young man, Reza had admitted killing his father. Moreover, he had talked about plans he and others charged in the case had developed for killing a crucial witness. Breiling assumed Reza had been referring to Dean Karny.

Soon after Breiling's conversation with the inmate, John Vance went back into court to argue a motion to pull Reza's bail. The motion was granted, based on the testimony of the informant, and Reza Eslaminia was returned to custody.

Chapter
57

The California court system has been criticized repeatedly for the long delays that often precede criminal trials, and
by the fall of 1986, Fred Wapner was himself becoming very
critical. Time and again, he had been prepared for trial, but
each time as the scheduled date neared, Hunt's lawyers had
requested and received postponements.

But finally, on the morning of November 13, after nearly
two years of delays, the two sides were ready to begin picking
jurors for the trial of Joe Hunt on charges of Ron Levin's
murder. More than a hundred potential jurors were escorted
into the courtroom that morning to begin the grueling process
by which twelve jurors would ultimately be selected to decide
Joe's fate.

Jury selection is at best an inexact science, and all the
lawyers in the Hunt case were painfully aware of the limitations of the process. Technically, they were to try and find
twelve people capable of deciding Joe's fate justly. But in fact

each side was looking for jurors who would be sympathetic to its particular point of view.

The process was cumbersome. First the judge asked jurors which of them would be able to sit for up to three months on the case. Those who legitimately could not were dismissed. Then, because Hunt would possibly face death if convicted, the jurors were grilled to make sure they weren't categorically opposed to California's death penalty law. Just this initial part of the screening process took several weeks and required Judge Rittenband to bring in more potential jurors to have a large enough pool.

Once there was a large enough panel of jurors from which to select, the screening process became more intense. Each side was allowed twenty-six peremptory challenges with which they could dismiss jurors they didn't like without having to cite cause. In addition, the lawyers could argue for the dismissal of a particular juror because of bias that might taint the case. The lawyers knew as they began that the process could take more than a month.

Wapner, Barens, and Chier were all aware of the stakes during the selection process. One bad decision here could mean losing the case. They had all thought long and hard about what information they could glean in twenty minutes of questioning that would tell them how a person might vote in the end. It wasn't easy.

Barens and Chier had been talking between themselves for weeks about who their perfect juror would be. They wanted women, they had decided, since women might well respond positively to their young, handsome client. They also wanted people with compassion, liberals who might see what a waste it would be for a young man with Joe's potential to be sent away to prison. Beyond that, they would go by instinct.

Barens and Chier also viewed voir dire, the process of questioning jurors, as a chance to do a little lecturing. You must remember, they reminded panelists, that Joe Hunt is at this point in time innocent. The burden of proof, the defense lawyers reminded them again and again, was on the prosecution. Even if they thought their client was guilty after the trial, if they still had some reasonable doubts, they were required by law to vote for acquittal.

In between subtle lectures about the responsibilities of jurors, Barens and Chier attempted to discover as much as they could about the people seated before them. What did they like to read? What were their favorite television shows? What did their spouses do? How many children did they have? Seated at the defense table, Joe Hunt, who looked and acted far more like an attorney than a defendant, made detailed notes of the jurors' responses, attempting to build a profile of each person from which the defense team could infer how they would be likely to respond to the evidence.

Fred Wapner had several specific concerns. He was going to have to convince a jury that Joe Hunt had killed a man even though he could produce little physical evidence of a murder having taken place. He had no body, no bloodstained crime scene, and no weapon. It was a daunting task, as he would have to rely largely on circumstantial evidence to make his case. As he faced the jurors, Wapner wanted to make very certain that he discovered how they felt about circumstantial evidence.

"Let's say you have just baked a cherry pie," he would say to jurors, "and it is sitting on your kitchen table. You are home alone with your four-year-old child. You leave the kitchen, and when you come back much of the pie has been eaten, and your child is covered with pie filling. Who ate the pie?" Some of the jurors went around and around with the prosecutor. They couldn't say, they insisted, without having witnessed the act. They would never risk unfairly accusing a child on such flimsy evidence. These were the jurors Wapner excused immediately.

Another primary area of concern to the district attorney was the potential jurors' family ties. To prove that Levin was dead, Wapner would rely heavily on the testimony of Carol Levin. From a very close-knit family himself, Wapner had no trouble believing her assertion that if her son were alive anywhere in the world, he would make contact with her to let her know he was okay. Hunt would be claiming that Levin had merely disappeared. Wapner wanted jurors who would believe he couldn't do that to his mother. "How many times in the last month have you spoken to your mother?" Wapner asked the potential jurors. Did they keep in close touch with their children? With their siblings? These were crucial questions, Wapner felt.

Chapter
58

In the early-morning hours of November 20, 1986, Carmen Canchola had insomnia. The pretty, pampered daughter of a wealthy Tucson family, Canchola was frequently bothered by sleeplessness, and she knew better than to lie awake wishing she were asleep. That morning she made herself turn on a light and picked up a two-month-old *Esquire* magazine she had borrowed from her brother Roger. In the past six months the crimes with which Joe Hunt had been charged had been getting some media attention for the first time. The magazine Canchola picked up that night had an article about the BBC, and the young business student was intrigued.

The story told in detail the tale of Joe Hunt and of the two murders he was suspected of having committed. The young woman was at that time unaware of Joe Hunt's trial, which was still in jury selection four hundred miles away in Los Angeles.

As she flipped through the article's pages, Canchola was

struck by a drawing made from a photograph of Ron Levin, one of the men who had supposedly been murdered by this Hunt. There was something vaguely familiar about the man in the picture, she thought. On another page, she came to a description of Levin. He had been, according to the article, tall, slender, and always expensively dressed. He had been well groomed, with striking silver hair and piercing eyes. He was also, according to the article, gay.

As she read the words, Canchola realized why the man was familiar. She looked back at the drawing. She was virtually certain now. She had seen him in a Tucson gas station about two months earlier. That, she realized with a start, had been some two years after he had supposedly been murdered.

Canchola remembered vividly the night she had seen the man. She was supposed to have been in class at the University of Arizona that night. Instead she had gone out to dinner with her boyfriend, Chino Lopez, a stable and sturdy young man who managed one of the McDonald's restaurants her father owned in the Tucson area. At the restaurant the couple had run into Canchola's parents, and they had ended up dining with them. After dinner, Carmen and Chino stopped in at a gas station near the university. As Chino filled the tank and checked the oil, Carmen idly watched the other customers. There was one in particular who intrigued her.

The man was driving a beautifully restored, cream-colored classic car. He himself seemed regal. He was immaculately dressed in designer jeans and a polo shirt. He had well-styled silver hair. Now, this was a handsome man, Carmen thought. All men should look that good at forty. Chino seemed to be taking quite a long time, but Carmen wasn't bothered. As she watched the intriguing man, a little human drama seemed to be unfolding. He was with a younger man, who was also very attractive. Carmen felt certain that they were gay. They seemed to be arguing. Finally, they left, but before pulling out of the parking lot, they drove close to Carmen's car, staring at her. Apparently they had noticed her interest and were now taunting her with it.

After Chino returned to the car, they spoke briefly about the man. "It looks like he liked you," Chino said somewhat jealously.

"If he liked anybody, it was you," Carmen said. "He was definitely not a man interested in women."

Carmen had forgotten all about the man and the encounter—until she read the piece in *Esquire*. Now she was in a panic.

Carmen thought about talking the situation over with Chino, but she quickly rejected that course of action. She knew what his advice would be. Don't get involved, he would tell her. Forget it. He and her family thought of Carmen as someone who needed protecting. They wouldn't want her involved in anything that would upset her. But she couldn't just forget what had happened. Joe Hunt might be in jail at this very moment, and she believed she had evidence that the person he was supposed to have killed was alive.

The next day at school, Carmen discussed her situation with a classmate, who agreed with what Carmen had already concluded: she had to go to the police.

Fred Wapner heard about Carmen Canchola on a Friday when the court was normally in recess. He realized immediately that he would have to fly to Tucson and talk with her. He would have liked to take Les Zoeller with him, but the detective's wife was already two weeks overdue with the couple's second child.

Wapner viewed his trip as a major annoyance. After nearly two years of examining evidence, he was utterly convinced that Levin was dead and that Hunt had murdered him. The report from Tucson didn't change his mind about that. In fact, he was surprised that there hadn't been more of this kind of sighting. The case had already gotten considerable publicity. Whenever there was an alleged murder without a body, people were going to come forward believing they had seen the victim.

Wapner wished this call had come at some other time. With his first paycheck from the district attorney's office years ago, he had purchased season tickets for the UCLA Bruins football team, and he hadn't missed a game since. Now it looked as if he wouldn't be able to attend the biggest game of the season. His team was playing its crosstown rival, USC. He hated to miss it, but he couldn't possibly be back in time.

Wapner was surprised at how credible Carmen Canchola and her boyfriend seemed. Without hesitation, each had been able to pick Levin out from a photo lineup as the man they saw in the gas station. They never wavered in their stories. Neither could positively identify what kind of car the man had been driving, although Chino, who had agreed to come forward after Carmen told him she had spoken to the police, thought it looked most like a Hudson Hornet. As UCLA slammed USC on the playing field, Wapner interrogated and reinterrogated the couple. At the end of the day, he summed up his feelings. "I think you're sincere," he told Carmen. "I think you believe you saw Ron Levin. I just think you're wrong."

Before notifying the defense of what had happened in Tucson, the district attorney's office needed time to assess the reliability of the statements. Shortly after Wapner's return, he sent two Beverly Hills police officers to Arizona with a mission: to locate the gray-haired man with the classic car. The district attorney realized that the best way to defuse the situation was to locate the man Canchola and Lopez thought was Levin and find out who he really was.

The able detectives worked quickly. First they got as much information from Chino about the car as they could. Next they contacted classic car clubs in the state to try to locate someone with a cream-colored Hornet who also had silver hair. Within days, they had come up with just such a person. He even said he bought gas at the kind of station in which Chino and Carmen had seen their man, although he didn't recall going to the particular outlet they described. But when the man's photo was shown to Carmen and Chino, they responded immediately. This was absolutely not the man they had seen. Defeated, the officers returned to Los Angeles.

Shortly thereafter, Fred Wapner asked for a meeting with Rittenband and the defense lawyers in the judge's chambers. There he revealed what he had heard in Tucson. Arthur Barens and Richard Chier were ecstatic. This was the kind of break defense lawyers usually only dreamed of. If Carmen Canchola couldn't produce reasonable doubt in the minds of jurors, they wondered, then what could?

Chapter
59

On October 18, 1986, a maid at the Hollywood Center Motel had to make a decision. Several days earlier a man had taken Room 304 and left express instructions that he didn't want to be disturbed for a week, no matter what. The run-down motel on Sunset Boulevard in the heart of Hollywood was used to strange requests from its highly transient guests, and the desk clerk had noted the instruction without questioning it. Now the maid had noticed a strong and very foul odor coming from the room. Despite the tenant's request, she decided to open the door and see what was causing the smell.

The maid looked in timidly at first, but the room seemed undisturbed. It was clearly unoccupied. Upon entering Room 304, she could tell the smell was emanating from the closet. There she discovered a steamer trunk from which the odor seemed to be coming. Peeking quickly inside, the maid saw what appeared to be a decaying body wrapped in plastic. She slammed the lid and reported her discovery immediately to her boss.

When officers from the Hollywood division of the Los Angeles Police Department arrived, they inspected more closely. They sent the body off to the coroner and then proceeded to thoroughly search the room. When they were done, they had come up with several items that might prove significant: a syringe, a Diet Coke can, and a discarded gas station credit-card slip. The cardholder's name was Dean Karny.

On October 20 at 11:30 A.M., workers at the Los Angeles County coroner's office performed an autopsy on the badly decomposed body. The pathologist noted three distinguishing marks on the slight young man who appeared to be in his early twenties. His left hand and his left forearm bore tattoos of a cross. On his right shoulder he had a tattoo of a bird sitting on three flowers. The cause of death was found to be asphyxiation.

By October 22, Hollywood detectives Mike Diaz and Robert Rozzi had identified the young man in the trunk as Richard Keith Mayer, a twenty-one-year-old hustler who worked the streets of West Hollywood.

On November 3, the Hollywood Police Department received a stenciled letter in the mail. MEAN DEAN KARNY IS AT IT AGAIN, the terse statement read.

After Fred Wapner was apprised of the situation, he again interrupted the jury selection to request an in-chambers conference with Judge Rittenband and the defense lawyers. As it happened, Arthur Barens wanted to confer as well. He had received a strange letter at his law offices. "Coverup in Hollywood police department," the typed and photocopied note began. "Dean Karny has killed again at Hollywoodland Motel." After Wapner explained what authorities knew to date, the judge placed a gag on the attorneys. They were not to talk about what they had heard to anyone. The transcript of the discussions in chambers would be sealed. Jury selection would be postponed for a few days to give the defense a chance to file any motions it wanted to prepare and to let the prosecutor follow up on his investigation.

Barens and Chier were jubilant. This had to be it, they told each other. Not only did they now have a witness who said that Levin was alive, the prosecutor's chief witness against their client was possibly involved in another murder.

But by the following week the lawyers were considerably less optimistic. Rittenband had ruled that there was no reason to interrupt the case. He would allow the defense to call Carmen and Chino, but he would not allow them to question Karny on the Hollywood murder. He had reviewed the evidence, he told them, and was convinced that Karny had not been involved.

After a search of Karny's apartment and a grueling interrogation, the Hollywood police had dismissed Karny as a suspect in the killing. Although it is still not clear exactly what it was, Karny had an airtight alibi for the time Mayer was killed. Very close tabs had apparently been kept on the protected witness during the period in question.

The feisty Rittenband was not inclined to allow the defense to turn the Mayer killing into an issue in the case pending before his court. He refused to allow the defense to evaluate the evidence so far gathered in the murder investigation. He was convinced Karny was not involved, he told the lawyers sternly. Moreover, he wasn't about to jeopardize an ongoing police investigation by ordering the details of it released prematurely, particularly to Joe Hunt.

In a subsequent police report, the two Hollywood detectives made clear their theory of the case. "It appears that the victim in this case was murdered to discredit Dean Karny, who is a former BBC member and is the state's star witness in two separate murders."

To date, no charges have been filed in connection with the Mayer homicide.

Chapter
60

Oscar Breiling was spitting mad. One afternoon shortly after the Mayer killing, he had been ordered to give a sample of his fingerprints and then to go home. He was not to come in to work for a few days.

At first the whole thing had seemed like a big joke. Breiling had gone to Los Angeles for a briefing by Hollywood police officers Robert Rozzi and Mike Diaz, who were investigating the motel murder. Before the officers arrived, Les Zoeller handed around a composite drawing, which had been made with help from the motel clerk. Oscar was stunned when he looked down at the drawing. It was an exact likeness of him, right down to the beard. The only thing wrong was the sunglasses. Breiling never wore sunglasses.

After laughing with Zoeller and the others over the likeness, Breiling had an idea. From another cop, he borrowed a pair of dark glasses and sat back to wait for Rozzi and Diaz. When they entered the room at last, the two officers were stunned. There was their suspect sitting where they least expected him to be. What was going on here?

But in the end, it hadn't been so funny. To avoid any appearance of impropriety, Breiling was suspended with pay to give the officers a chance to check him out in connection with the murder.

Breiling realized his suspension was necessary. Rozzi and Diaz were simply being good cops. But that didn't make him any less furious. The state investigator was convinced that the likeness was more than coincidence. Whoever rented that motel room, Oscar believed, had been made up to look like him. Somebody had wanted to implicate him along with Dean Karny in the crime.

Breiling was quickly cleared of any connection to the Mayer homicide, but because of his involvement in the Hedayat Eslaminia case, he was prohibited from looking into the matter further. He would probably never know for sure who had done it. But if he had to bet, he knew who he would lay money on. It made him all the more determined to continue gathering information on the Eslaminia murder.

By early January 1987, Fred Wapner had run out of jury challenges. The defense lawyers still had one left. But after interviewing another juror, Arthur Barens rose from his seat. "Your honor," he said, "I'm pleased to advise you that we have a jury."

The jury that would try Joe Hunt was not a typical one. Ten of the jurors were women, only two were men. The four alternates, who would serve if any of the jurors were excused during the course of the trial, were all women. The jury was also much better educated than most. Among the jurors and alternates many were college graduates, and several had advanced degrees. One, Juel Janis, who would later become the foreperson, had a Ph.D. in public health and had served as assistant to the U. S. Surgeon General before becoming assistant dean in the School of Public Health at UCLA.

But before the jury would begin hearing the case, Rittenband informed the jurors, the lawyers had some motions and other matters to attend to. They were to return to court in a week for the beginning of the trial.

Chapter
61

On the morning of January 8, 1987, Oscar Breiling flew to Los Angeles, rented a car, and drove to the Beverly Hills Police Department to begin a highly unusual mission. He had arranged for all the policemen he knew in the Los Angeles area to meet him in Beverly Hills. By the time they had all assembled, there were Les Zoeller, Rozzi and Diaz from Hollywood, and several others they had recommended.

After they had all been seated in a meeting room, Breiling passed around a copy of a search warrant he had brought with him. "We are going to be searching the house of Bobby Roberts on Bellagio Drive in Bel Air," Breiling told the assembled officers. He then urged them to read the affidavit he had filed with the Redwood City court to get the warrant. The affidavit spelled out specifically what the men would be searching for: "papers, documents, photographs, records, and handwritten notes any of which relate to the activities of Joseph Hunt, Arben Dosti, James Graham, Reza Eslaminia, and other members of the staff of the BBC" from January 1, 1984, to October 22, 1984.

After the men had read the documents, Breiling gave further instructions. "This search will be centered in the areas of the house occupied primarily by Joe Hunt," Breiling said. "We'll give only cursory attention to the rest of the house in order to cause the least amount of inconvenience to the Roberts family." It was highly likely, Breiling said, that as soon as the search began, the Robertses would call Joe and his lawyers at the courthouse, where they were making final preparations to begin trial. "Under no circumstances," Breiling warned emphatically, "are you to look at papers unrelated to materials described in the search warrant. This particularly means don't examine anything that pertains to communications between Joe Hunt and his defense lawyers or to plans they may have relating to his defense. If you are in doubt about whether something is defense related, don't read it. Put it aside."

Breiling had battled ferociously to get the search warrant he was about to serve. It was highly unconventional, in fact virtually unheard of, for a law enforcement agency to search the premises of someone currently on trial, as Joe technically was. But in this case Breiling felt it was justified.

A few weeks earlier, Dean Karny had come to him with the contents of a briefcase he had previously forgotten he had. In it were financial records, handwritten notes, and documents that Breiling felt could help him make his case. According to Karny, there were many more similar records that had been in Hunt's possession. The BBC leader probably still had them.

John Vance, after just a little prodding, agreed with Breiling about the search. That's what Breiling liked about the attorney. There was none of the usual "I'm the attorney and I know best" sort of attitude. Vance realized what a talented and smart investigator he had in Breiling and was always willing to listen, even when Breiling wanted to talk about matters of law. Convincing the Special Prosecutions hierarchy had been a different matter.

The defense team was sure to cry foul, Breiling's bosses said. They would say the search was a thinly disguised attempt to learn about defense strategies. A search now could conceivably jeopardize Wapner's whole case, and possibly Vance's as well. The defense might also view the search as a way of trying to get evidence to link Hunt to the Hollywood murder without having to develop a search warrant for that. It was just too risky.

After thoroughly researching the issue, Vance was convinced that the search would not only be legal but would also be a great idea. He decided he would fight for it. With Breiling arguing the need for the search from an investigator's viewpoint and Vance arguing the law, the higher-ups' concerns were eventually overcome, and on January 6, Breiling had driven to Redwood City to get the warrant.

The Robertses' maid Hattie Mullin was surprised when she opened the door to Oscar Breiling at ten-thirty on the morning of January 8. She quickly called upstairs to Bobby Roberts on an internal phone system, and he came down in his bathrobe. After greeting Breiling cordially, Roberts examined the warrant. "We've been expecting something like this," he said to Breiling, "but you won't find anything you're looking for in this house." Roberts went upstairs to inform his wife, who was still in bed, of the situation. Then the men began their search.

Breiling had believed that Joe and Brooke shared the guest house behind the house, but he was informed by Roberts that Brooke alone lived there. Joe occupied a bedroom on the second floor. He used another second-floor room as an office. The officers were amused by the mess in both Brooke's and Joe's rooms. They lived in such beautiful surroundings, the men thought, but they lived like pigs.

Shortly after he had begun the search, Breiling was summoned to the phone. Arthur Barens wanted to speak to him. Breiling informed the defense lawyer about what he was doing. Barens expressed concern about the searchers seeing privileged defense documents, but Breiling assured him they would not go beyond the scope of the search warrant. Shortly after the phone call, a very agitated Richard Chier arrived on the scene. Breiling assured him they were not looking for defense-related documents, but the attorney refused to be placated. After following Breiling around for a short time, he left and went and placed a phone call. A few minutes later, he came back.

"Joe Hunt is right now petitioning the court to represent himself in pro per," Chier informed Breiling. "If he succeeds, then he will be acting as his own lawyer, and this property will be considered his law offices, and you will be prohibited by law from searching in this manner. I would advise you therefore to cease and desist." It was a highly inventive strategy, representing the one sure way to stop the search quickly. But Breiling was unfazed. "I'll stop searching when I am ordered by a court to do so," he said calmly. Chier waited anxiously during the rest of the search for a phone call from Barens ordering a halt to the searching. But the call never came. In court in Santa Monica, Rittenband refused to consider Joe's motion, and so no order was issued.

When Chier noticed Les Zoeller at the Roberts house, he was amazed. "What are you doing here?" he demanded to know. "You're involved in a current trial. There's no way you should be looking at the documents my client has here." Zoeller had known that such a confrontation was likely, and he did feel a bit like a child caught with his hand in the cookie jar. Wapner had no idea his investigator was assisting on the search. Vance and Breiling had discussed whether the district attorney should be informed but had decided against it. Wapner was overcautious, they felt. He would try to stop them from searching. Zoeller had reluctantly agreed not to tell the attorney, but it was not a decision he was completely comfortable with.

In the early afternoon, after a phone call from Chier, Wapner called the Roberts house and asked to speak to Zoeller. "What the hell are you doing there?" he demanded. "I want you to leave immediately." Wapner didn't know what was going on, but he knew he didn't want to be part of it and he didn't want his investigator mixed up in it either. Until the others were finished, Zoeller waited outside.

That afternoon, after the search was completed and the seized items had been photographed and catalogued, Chier objected to the removal of the documents. "You're taking a lot of stuff I need to defend my client," he insisted. Breiling promised to make copies and return things quickly, but the lawyer still was not pleased. Breiling offered to let the lawyer go through the documents to see if he found anything that might involve defense strategy. When the investigator returned, Chier was holding a piece of lined yellow paper dated January 5, 1987. On it, in what appeared to be Hunt's handwriting was the word "Pittman." Below that were the words "Planting snitches."

"This document seems to me to be outside the scope of your search," Chier said. "It bears a date that is long after the BBC was dissolved." Breiling took the paper back. "If you want to fight me in court over that one," he told the lawyer, "I'll be happy to present my justification for taking it." After loading the boxes of documents into the waiting police cars, Breiling and the others left.

As Vance and Breiling had expected, Barens and Chier quickly filed a motion to dismiss the case against Hunt as a result of the search. The defense strategy had been compromised as a result of the search, they maintained. It was impossible to adequately insure that the prosecutor hadn't received information from the search that would give a clue to Hunt's defense. During the next several days, Judge Rittenband heard testimony on the motion. At the end of the hearing, he denied it categorically.

On February 2, Barens asked that the trial be delayed to give the defense a chance to regroup. "We did not bring this catastrophe on ourselves," he told the judge. "We are victims of the catastrophe. It has distracted us from the immediate task of preparing opening arguments. We have no alternative but to ask for a continuance."

But Rittenband was tired of all the delays. "I'm admonishing you now," the judge said. "We're going to go to trial next Monday."

Outside the courtroom, Barens paused to talk to reporters. "Will the trial really begin, then?" a journalist asked.

"Yes," Barens said with defeat. "If this building falls down, we will be meeting with the jurors in the parking lot on Monday."

Chapter
62

Fred Wapner had expected that a fair number of spectators would turn out for the start of the trial. There had recently been a lot of media attention focused on the case. But he was absolutely stunned when he rounded a corner inside the Santa Monica courthouse and saw the huge crowd milling outside Department C on the morning of February 2. Television camera crews jockeyed for position as their producers barked orders. Dozens of onlookers stood by, waiting for the drama to unfold. Ten minutes later Arthur Barens and Richard Chier turned the corner, visibly uncomfortable themselves as they came upon the throng. Only Joe Hunt appeared to take the situation in stride. Flanked by his attorneys, the tall, handsome young man swaggered down the hall to the courtroom, his demeanor suggesting that at last he was receiving the kind of attention he felt he deserved in life.

Inside, the atmosphere was practically festive. A standing-room-only crowd chatted excitedly. Three dozen reporters, some from as far away as Baltimore and New York, exchanged greetings and gossip about the case. Dozens of people crowded the spectator section, including people with vague connections to the case: a former classmate of Hunt's at the Harvard School; a former girlfriend of a BBC member; friends of the witnesses. As Joe and his attorneys entered, they stopped to speak with the Roberts family, who had turned out in their trendiest Hollywood finery for the occasion.

Amid the hubbub, only Ron Levin's parents and brother, sitting silent and grim in the center section of seats, seemed fully aware of the real purpose of the occasion.

Fred Wapner looked nervous as he took his place at the prosecution table in Judge Rittenband's courtroom. The intense prosecutor knew he did not have an easy task ahead of him. In laying out his case, he would have to first convince the jurors that Ron Levin was dead, even though his body had never been found; then he would have to convince them that the quiet, well-dressed young man seated at the defense table had killed Levin.

The defense lawyers, although less visibly anxious, also knew they had their work cut out for them. The jury would be hearing some very compelling evidence. There was the fact that Joe had told ten BBC members he killed Ron Levin; there was the seven-page list; there were well-documented stories of Joe's broken promises to investors. But the defense lawyers were nevertheless convinced they had an excellent chance if the jurors would act according to their instructions. The attorneys planned to put on Carmen Canchola, and wouldn't that be good enough to cause at least reasonable doubt? Only time would tell.

The defense team was quite worried about one aspect of the trial. During jury selection, Judge Rittenband, never one to hide his feelings, had taken a strong dislike to Richard Chier, whom he considered a smart aleck. In the days before the trial began, the judge had stunned both the prosecution and the defense by banning Chier from speaking in front of the jury. He could argue motions, the judge said, and he could feed anything he wanted to Barens. But Rittenband said he felt strongly that Chier's speaking before the jury would not be in Hunt's best interest. The lawyers were being paid by the court, as Joe had been declared indigent. If they wanted the pay arrangement to continue, the judge said, the lawyers would abide by his wishes.

During the long months of preparation for the case, the attorneys had divided up responsibility for different witnesses. Now Chier would not be able to put questions to anyone. It was a blow, both to the defense case and to the aggressive lawyer as well. "I came in here a rooster," Chier complained to a reporter, "and he's made me a capon."

Before the jury was brought in, Chier and Barens filed several motions in a last-ditch effort to delay the trial. But after hearing brief arguments, the judge spoke gruffly: "The motions are all denied. All right. Let's get the jurors in and start this trial at long last."

Fred Wapner looked terrified as he rose from his seat and strode to the podium. Wearing a conservative, well-cut gray suit, he plunged straight into his opening statement, explaining carefully and methodically, if nervously, the case he planned to present. "The first part of the case will begin with this man, this Ron Levin," Wapner said, his voice quavering slightly as he held up a picture of Levin for the jury to see. He then told them for the first time about the events of June 7, 1984, that necessitated their being in the courtroom.

Next Wapner addressed one of the biggest problems with his case head on. After hearing the evidence, he cautioned the jurors, they might think Levin had been a very unsavory character. "Ron Levin was, by his own admission, a con man," Wapner said. "He told almost everyone that he came in contact with that he was a con man." In addition, Wapner said,

"He was [facing charges of] ten counts of grand theft and a count of receiving stolen property and one count of writing a not-sufficient-funds check" at the time of his disappearance.

But none of this, Wapner told the jury, should be construed as indicating that Ron Levin had engineered his own disappearance. The prosecution's case would clearly show that Levin had strong ties to Beverly Hills and would never have left willingly. It would show that Levin, a man acutely concerned with money, left without taking much of the cash he had available. In addition, Wapner said, "He was very, very close to his mother, and wherever he was, he would call her" if he was alive.

The second part of the case, Wapner said, would "shift gears" and examine the activities of Joe Hunt and his BBC. Hunt, he said, acted as the founder and uncontested leader of the group. To help control his followers, Hunt used Paradox Philosophy, about which Wapner said, "I don't pretend to understand it in any way, but what it really comes down to is situational ethics. You can say anything, do anything, if it is right for you at the time. Black is white, white is black."

Next, Wapner explained how Levin had tricked Hunt and how Hunt had shortly thereafter begun to plan Levin's murder. Finally, he described the murder. "After getting the contract signed, Joe Hunt and Jim Pittman took Ron Levin into the bedroom, he was put on the bed, and he was shot in the head."

Wapner concluded his opening with a dramatic flourish very different from his otherwise dry statement: "The people from the BBC will tell you that when Joe Hunt was talking to them at the meeting on June twenty-fourth, he said, 'We have committed the perfect crime.' Well, I will submit to you, ladies and gentlemen, he did not commit the perfect crime, and when you put this case all together, all of the circumstantial evidence, the list that was found, the statements that were made, you won't have any reasonable doubt at all that Joe Hunt is guilty of first-degree murder. Thank you."

By the end of Wapner's hour-long statement, the jury had

an excellent sense of the case the prosecutor would present. It would be a case very like Wapner himself, thorough and careful but not always scintillating. But would it be enough? Many in the audience wondered whether the prosecutor's flat style would be able to carry the jury through the long months of the trial.

After lunch Barens rose before the television cameras to make his statement. Wearing a custom-made suit of his own design with a white, three-point handkerchief, the short, dapper lawyer began a very different kind of presentation. With the folksy but histrionic style of a Baptist preacher, the defense lawyer opened his speech: "Good afternoon, ladies and gentlemen. I bet you are all surprised after all you heard that I came back after lunch. But I think we probably have some things to talk about."

During the next forty minutes, Barens presented his view of the case: that Levin was not dead at all, but had disappeared to escape his pending legal problems. The facts, he suggested, pointed less to "an adventure in murder" than to "an adventure in illusion" by a master con man who had engineered his own disappearance. "This is going to be a case," he told jurors, "about tension between Ron Levin and Joe Hunt, and where the tension took them."

If Wapner's opening statement had seemed flat, Barens's seemed almost too slick. His carefully scripted speech was peppered with dramatic metaphors. "Like a lion in the Serengeti desert that moves on after exhausting the prey in that area," Barens told the jury, "so too, Levin moved on to more fertile grounds." But, there was nothing spontaneous beneath the superficially chatty style.

Other defense lawyers in the room were surprised at one aspect of Barens's remarks. The attorney had made a lot of promises to the jury, and some of them might be difficult to keep. Several weeks before the trial began, Arthur Barens had speculated about his opening remarks. "I'm not going to put on much of an opening statement," he said. "One thing I learned from the Pancoast case is never promise jurors anything you can't deliver."

Despite the lessons he claimed to have learned, Barens assured jurors that he could explain everything. "The defense will bring forward witnesses that will verify for you where Joe Hunt was the night in question and what he was doing," Barens promised. Later in his speech, Barens focused his attention on the incriminating seven-page list. "I submit to you that the list is not a recipe for murder," he said, looking straight into the eyes of the jurors. "This list means what it says, and Hunt is going to talk to you about that and we will see if it is a list for murder or was intended for another purpose."

In one dramatic statement Barens had promised the jury not only that the list could be explained, but also that Hunt would take the stand in his own defense. To underscore the point, he later told jurors, "Joe Hunt is not going to hide from you. He is not going to try to disappear. He is going to answer all of the questions." Time would tell.

For better or worse, by 2:30 P.M. on the first day of trial, both sides had laid out for the jury the outlines of their cases as they envisioned them.

Chapter
63

Fred Wapner knew that the beginning of the trial would be the toughest part for him. During the first few days, he would have to introduce the jury to his victim, and Ron Levin had been a cheat, a liar, and a criminal. But the con man had also had a lot of charm, and many people had cared deeply about him. Wapner simply had to hope that by putting Levin's friends and family on the witness stand, he would develop in the jurors some real sympathies for the eccentric man's many good qualities.

Despite Wapner's hopes, the first part of his case seemed less like a murder trial and more like a celebrity roast. Levin's closest friends, while they had clearly been very fond of him, described a man with wild eccentricities. Fashion designer Tere Tereba recalled on the stand her first meeting with Levin in which, she said, "I asked him what he did. He told me he was a thief."

Dean Factor, one of the two young men with whom Levin

had planned to go to New York on the morning of June 7, 1984, described how Levin had once taken him to the UCLA Medical Center and talked his way into the cadaver room by posing as a doctor. Later he told Dean he had dissected a corpse, just to show he could get away with it. "Ron loved attention and he loved to be seen. He loved creating a scene," Levin's friend Mark Geller testified. "I think there was a period of about a month or two in the late Seventies when Ronnie insisted that he be the only one that was allowed to eat lunch on the second floor [of L. A.'s exclusive Bistro Gardens restaurant] where they don't typically serve lunch. . . . He said that he didn't want to sit downstairs with all of the little ladies having lunches."

It was hard to tell exactly what effect the anecdotes were having on the jurors, but the defense lawyers were clearly enjoying themselves. If Wapner didn't elicit enough strange stories during his questioning, Barens took over on cross-examination. The observers seemed delighted with the testimony, and the courtroom frequently broke out in laughter. Fred Wapner was quite worried. This was not the reaction he wanted. And so, on February 10, the sixth day of the trial, he called Ron's mother, Carol Levin, to the witness stand.

Since the opening day of trial, the attractive, carefully made-up Beverly Hills housewife had found it too painful to sit in the courtroom, leaving that to her husband or her son Robert. She returned only for her testimony. After Carol Levin seated herself before the court on the first morning of her testimony, it was doubtful whether she would be able to speak. When she finally did, her voice was small and trembling. If Levin's friends had been amused and sometimes annoyed by their friend's dishonesty, his mother had been unaware of it. She knew, of course, that he had served some time in jail—she had visited him there frequently—and she knew that he was facing new criminal charges, but Ronnie had told her he was innocent, and that was enough.

The face Ron Levin showed to his mother was squeaky clean. He doted on her, she said, calling her frequently and always making her welcome when she dropped in on him. For her court appearance, Carol Levin brought with her photos of the numerous bouquets her "Ronnie" had remembered her with on special occasions over the years, as well as many greeting cards. She nearly broke down as she came to one dated March 6, 1971. " 'Doubt that the stars are fire,' " Carol Levin read aloud with a trembling voice. " 'Doubt that the sun does move. Doubt that truth be a liar. But never doubt I love you. Love, Ronnie.' "

Mrs. Levin, fighting to keep back the tears, testified that her son called frequently, even when he was out of the country. In the twenty-four years since he had left home, she said, he had never gone more than a week without calling her—until June of 1984. Wapner ended his direct examination on that point. "Since you spoke to him on June sixth in the evening, you haven't spoken to him?" Wapner asked.

"No."

"He hasn't called you?"

"No."

"Have you heard from him in any way?"

"No."

"I have nothing further," Wapner concluded.

Joe appeared to be enjoying himself during the trial. The immaculately dressed, attractive young man took an active role in his defense, scribbling notes all day on a yellow legal pad, whch he pushed over for his attorneys to read. Often he fed them questions or whispered strategies in their ears. It was as if Joe had found a new BBC, a bunch of guys all working closely together with a strong sense of purpose. His demeanor seemed inappropriately cavalier for a twenty-six-year-old standing trial for murder.

At times Arthur Barens's cross-examination seemed more like argument than questioning. Often when witnesses made points Barens agreed with, he underscored them for the jury, much to Wapner's annoyance, by saying, "Quite so." Other times, when a witness made a point Barens considered beneficial to the defense, he would rephrase his question several times to elicit the same answer to make sure the jury understood its significance. Once in a while, his technique backfired.

One day early in the trial, Barens held up a photograph of Levin's bedroom and asked Wapner's witness James Foulk to examine it. Foulk, a very handsome Hollywood hopeful, had worked as Levin's assistant after the two men met in a bar. Foulk had been in Levin's bedroom to confer with his employer late on the day of Levin's disappearance.

"Do you notice anything unusual about this photograph?" Barens asked Foulk. The photograph had been taken by police investigators after Levin was reported missing, and in it the bedspread on the bed was the unfamiliar one that had caused Levin's housekeeper and two young friends concern on the morning of June 7. Foulk described a few things he thought might be out of place, but did not mention the bedspread, which had presumably been changed after Foulk last saw the room.

"Anything else?" Barens asked, underscoring for the jury that the bedspread didn't look odd to Foulk.

"Not really."

"Anything at all?"

"No."

"Nothing looks different?"

"Not that I can see."

"You're sure?"

"Well," Foulk said slowly, scrutinizing the photograph more carefully, "that bedspread doesn't look familiar. Ron always had a white comforter on his bed, and that one looks green."

Amid laughter from the jury and audience, Barens turned to Rittenband and said with rueful good nature, "Life is difficult, Judge."

"You shouldn't have asked that last question," Rittenband responded with equal good humor.

Judge Rittenband was not always so good-humored in his exchanges with the defense lawyers. It was apparent from early on that the judge had strong feelings about the case, and his sympathies were not with Joe Hunt. Occasionally, when the judge didn't like the direction a line of defense questioning was taking, his face would grow stormy and his bushy eyebrows would rise. In terse tones, he would make an objection himself rather than waiting for Wapner to do so. Other times, the judge virtually ordered the prosecutor to step in. During a sensitive portion of Barens's cross-examination of a witness, the judge interrupted. "I have no idea how this is relevant," he said testily. Then he turned to Wapner. "I'll sustain an objection if you make an objection."

Both the defense and the prosecution were troubled by the impatient judge's actions. Barens and Chier worried that Rittenband's seeming prejudice might bias the jury against them. Wapner felt that the judge was, in a sense, emasculating him before the jury, creating an impression that the prosecutor was so weak that he needed the judge's help.

Wapner had another concern as well. When he left the courthouse each day, the attorney fretted privately that the judge, in his zeal to have the truth come out, might allow things to happen in the trial that an appeals court would consider improper. The last thing he wanted was to win now only to have the verdict overturned later. He realized he must watch not only his own actions, but also those of the judge.

During the early days of the trial, Arthur Barens adopted the habit of answering a few questions from the press in the hallway outside the courtroom, in effect giving a brief news conference after each day's session adjourned. The reporters tried to get Wapner to do likewise, but every day his response was the same. "I have no comment. I believe cases should be tried in the courtroom, not in the media."

Although Rittenband was fully aware of the press conference being conducted outside his courtroom, he took no action for several days. Then, after the noon break on February 5, the judge called all the lawyers into his chambers. Sitting behind his imposing desk in the oak-paneled office, Rittenband was clearly displeased.

"I just got a telephone call from a friend of mine in Las Vegas who was listening to a broadcast on CNN, and you were being interviewed in the hallway after the trial had ended yesterday," the judge barked at Barens. The broadcast had left Rittenband's friend "with the definite impression that it was extremely humiliating about me, the remarks you made." The judge seemed unconcerned about the larger issues of whether it was appropriate for the defense to comment on the day's proceedings, but he was furious that Barens had said negative things about him. Without further ado, he issued a decree. "I am ordering you under no circumstances to talk to the press or be interviewed by anybody outside in the hallway. Do you understand that?" Barens meekly agreed, and the daily press briefings ended.

Once Wapner had established who Ron Levin was, he moved on to examining business and financial data he hoped would convince the jury that Levin hadn't left town willingly. He demonstrated, for example, that Levin had been expecting a ten-thousand-dollar cashier's check, which in fact came a few days after his disappearance. He called witnesses who testified that Levin had paid various bills, including car leases, which he probably wouldn't have paid if he had planned to skip town. He had recently invested money in a securities account, which he didn't withdraw before leaving. The testimony was often very tedious, and put at least one juror to sleep, but the district attorney felt it was all necessary.

Wapner strongly wanted the jurors to see Jim Pittman. It

might be difficult for them, he felt, to believe that the well-dressed, almost effete-seeming Joe Hunt sitting in front of them was capable of murder. He wanted them to see the powerful bodyguard.

The prosecutor couldn't just call Pittman to testify, since he was facing charges of his own. So instead Wapner arranged for him to be brought into court to be identified by security people from the Plaza Hotel. Getting Pittman before the jury did not turn out to be as easy as the prosecutor had hoped.

On February 12, Wapner arranged for Pittman to be brought into the courtroom during the lunch recess. The strong man looked ridiculous. The defense lawyers had been concerned that his appearing in jail clothes might prejudice the jury and so had requested that he be provided civilian clothing. But the bailiff had been unable to find clothes to fit Pittman's massive frame. He was wearing a Hawaiian-print shirt with buttons that looked ready to burst. His pants wouldn't close fully and revealed his blue jail suit beneath.

But the biggest problem was Pittman himself. Almost immediately after being brought in, Pittman began protesting that he didn't want to be in court without his attorney. Ignoring his protests, the defense lawyers expressed concern about the jury seeing Pittman's handcuffs, which were soon removed.

"You couldn't stop me anyway if I wanted to go," Pittman told the bailiff good-naturedly. "I'll stick around, though. I like the scene."

Finally, annoyed that his requests to have his attorney present were being ignored, Pittman yelled out, "When I stand up, I will tell people I'm in jail!" The lawyers ignored the outburst and continued making plans. Chier, concerned about Pittman's wristband, a clear indicator that he was in jail, offered his watch to cover it. "Why should I wear that? I'm going to tell them I'm in jail anyway," Pittman said, more adamantly this time. It finally sunk in. Wapner looked at Barens and Chier. They tried to reason with Pittman, but he would have none of it, and was in the end taken away from the courthouse. Wapner was just too worried that an outburst by Pittman might cause a mistrial.

On the following day a polite and compliant Pittman was returned to court in his jail clothes, this time with his attorney present. After he was identified by Joe Vega, security supervisor at the Plaza, the jurors spent some time sizing him up. Joe Hunt, sitting with his back to his former cohort, didn't acknowledge the bodyguard.

As the trial progressed, Judge Rittenband began increasingly to jump in and play prosecutor. If he thought Wapner had not asked an important question, he spoke up and asked it himself. If a witness made an important point, the judge emphasized it to the jury by asking a follow-up of his own. It all made Wapner very nervous, as the judge sometimes delved into subjects the prosecutor felt were best left untouched.

Two weeks into the trial, Martin Levin was called to testify about searching his son's apartment after his disappearance. During his direct examination, the judge jumped in with something that left both the prosecutor and the defense lawyers stunned. After Martin Levin told about having found the seven-page list, Wapner put up a large, cardboard blowup of the list for the jury to see. But Rittenband apparently felt the blowup was insufficient.

"I think the clerk made copies of them for the jury, if you want to distribute them so they can look at them," the judge said with barely contained self-delight. "Some of them might be a little nearsighted and can't see it from that distance." It was a clear statement from the judge to the jury: This evidence is very important; study it.

The lawyers approached the bench to ask the judge why he had taken the highly unusual step of deciding himself to pass out an item of evidence to the jury. Barens pointed out that the list hadn't even been introduced as evidence yet. Wapner argued that none of the jurors seemed to have a problem reading the blowups he placed on the bulletin board.

"It is a procedure that we have followed throughout the whole trial. I don't see why all of a sudden—"

"He [Wapner] is objecting to it?" the judge interrupted. "All right. I will overrule the objections." The jurors kept their lists.

Later that day, the jury finally got what it had been waiting for—a look at one of the BBC boys. Among the boys, Jeff Raymond was an excellent choice for Wapner to call first. Handsome, likeable, and relatively uninvolved in much of the BBC's operations, Raymond looked like the kind of boy any of the jurors would have been proud to have as a son. In addition, Raymond decided immediately after the June 24 meeting to go to the police.

During Raymond's testimony, Hunt appeared acutely uncomfortable for the first time during the trial. As Raymond described Hunt's confession to the BBC boys, Hunt tried to busy himself writing. Occasionally he would look up at Raymond with a mixture of arrogance and contempt that the jury, facing Hunt, couldn't fail to notice.

At the end of the day, "60 Minutes" cameraman Wade Bingham, filming for an Ed Bradley segment, looked up from his camera. "I'd convict him," he said.

"Because of what you heard here today?" a reporter asked.

"Nope. Because of what I've seen through here," he replied, pointing to his camera lens. "I've been watching people through this thing for thirty years, and this guy is guilty."

In the middle of Tom May's testimony a few days later, a group of seventeen well-dressed teenage boys filed into the courtroom and quietly found the few remaining seats. In the hall during a break, they told reporters they were visiting from the Harvard School. It was Career Day, and these were the boys who wanted to become lawyers. When asked about the school's infamous alumnus sitting at the front of the courtroom, one earnest, dark-haired young man replied soberly, "Everybody has his cross to bear, and Joe Hunt is Harvard's cross."

As the testimony of the BBC boys proceeded and as Wapner prepared to begin calling Joe's investors, he was feeling much more confident about the case. Hearing the testimony in the courtroom crystallized for him the strengths of his case. The BBC members had all been quite good. He only wished he knew what the jurors were thinking.

During the prosecutor's case, the friction between Chier and Rittenband seemed to increase daily. The judge would yell at the plump, red-headed Chier; Chier would file a motion for mistrial; the judge would dismiss the motion out of hand. But the constant friction was taking a toll on Chier. His wife, pregnant with the couple's first child, urged him to try and ignore the judge, and Chier did make an effort. But the impetuous, irreverent lawyer had never much liked authority figures, and Rittenband could get under Chier's skin like no one else in the world. Shortly into the trial, the attorney hit on an idea. Each morning just outside the courtroom door, he paused, took a deep breath, and chanted to himself, "This man is not my father." It helped, he said, get him through the long days.

But despite Chier's efforts, six weeks into the trial the simmering tension between Rittenband and the defense lawyer erupted again into a full boil. Barens and Chier had submitted a motion to the judge requesting that they both be allowed to address the jury during the closing arguments of the trial. When the motion was argued that morning, Wapner rose to speak in support of his opponents' position. Saying first that he had "no objection" to the defense request, Wapner went on to argue that the law as he read it specifically allowed two lawyers to argue for the defense. "I am concerned about what appears to be the specific dictates of section 1095 of the penal code," he said to the judge, "which . . . seems to be fairly mandatory on the issue. . . ."

First Rittenband dismissed Wapner's argument. Then he turned his attention to Chier. "I think that it was for the best interests of this defendant not to have [Chier] in any way appear before any jury in this case and argue anything before them. That includes making concluding arguments."

Chier was unable to remain silent. "I have been slandered here, Your Honor," he said icily. "I would like to respond."

After some give and take, the judge got even more personal. "Mr. Barens is ten times the kind of lawyer you are, and he can best represent this defendant. . . ," Rittenband said. "You want me to deny the motion because you want to take another appeal. That is what you have been doing, appealing, appealing, and appealing. Always running crying to the court of appeals or the Supreme Court. Go ahead and do it again. I am going to deny your motion."

The whole incident disgusted Arthur Barens. "I never thought I'd be coming to court to do battle with the judge instead of the prosecutor," he said after the day's session.

After weeks of trial, the jurors were acting like old friends. When several of them began complaining of stiff backs, another brought pillows for everyone. Each day at lunch they went off in large bunches to nearby restaurants or to the local shopping mall where they browsed or had a meal at one of the fast-food restaurants. They seemed willing to make the best of their long stay in Department C, laughing at any attempt at humor and somehow staying cheerful through the tedious days. Until Dean Karny took the stand.

In previous court proceedings, Karny had been a credible but wooden witness. When he had first testified about the horrific actions of Hunt and others, including himself, it was as if he was talking about what he had eaten for dinner the night before; his recitation had seemed utterly emotionless. But the Karny who was escorted by armed guards into Rittenband's courtroom on March 17 was a changed witness. His gaunt face was punctuated with dark circles under his eyes, as if he hadn't slept in weeks, and he seemed visibly upset at being in the courtroom. As he was seated, Hunt stared at him intently. Karny looked away, but then looked back. Finally the eyes of the former best friends locked for several seconds, until Hunt looked away. Karny sighed and settled himself in his seat for his ordeal.

The jury must have realized that Karny's testimony was crucial even before he began to speak. That day, for the first time, Patrick, the affable bailiff whom the jurors adored, was wearing a gun. And although Karny was escorted in and seated before the jurors came into the courtroom, they had to notice the four armed guards stationed around the room. When Karny began to testify, the jury stopped smiling and began listening more intently than ever before. Soberly and with seemingly heartfelt emotion, Karny described how he had helped plan Levin's murder, assisting Joe in drawing up the seven-page list on the pages of a yellow legal pad. All the while his former lieutenant spoke, Hunt made notes on the yellow legal pad before him, occasionally looking up in seeming disgust at what he was hearing.

Eventually, Wapner had Karny describe to the jurors what Hunt had told him about the murder. "[Hunt] said that he had disfigured the body with a shotgun, that he had shot it so that it wouldn't be recognizable even if it was found," Karny testified, speaking slowly as he tried unsuccessfully to keep his emotions in check. "He said that at one point, Ron Levin's brain jumped out of his skull and fell on his chest. . . . He seemed like he thought it was kind of neat in a weird way."

The court was perfectly still and silent as Karny described the murder in detail for the first time; the large clock above the courtroom door seemed to be the only thing moving. It got to be 3:00, 3:10, 3:15, and still Rittenband didn't call for a break, as he always did at precisely three o'clock. Finally Wapner asked the court if it wasn't a good time for a brief recess.

"Would the ladies and gentlemen of the jury like a

break?" the judge asked the jury. To a person, they shook their heads no, and the proceedings continued.

What was perhaps the trial's most powerful moment yet came on the third day of Karny's testimony. Wapner was taking Karny through the list point by point, asking him to explain various items. Wapner made a joke.

"[Joe] didn't put anything on the list, did he, about 'take list with you'?" Wapner asked, referring to Joe's apparent mistake in leaving the list behind. The packed courtroom and jurors began to laugh. Then Karny looked up at them, his haunted eyes scanning the courtroom in shock, as if he couldn't believe anyone could find humor in the events he was describing. The laughter stopped.

When Karny realized his testimony would not be concluded before the weekend, he decided to go home and return on Monday to resume testifying. He felt too nervous in Los Angeles. But when he picked up his airplane ticket from the district attorney's office, he was appalled. Not only had the ticket been purchased in his real name; he was to fly directly to the northern California location where he had been in hiding. Any good investigator for the other side would be able to trace him easily.

For Karny, the incident underscored the inadequacy of the California Witness Protection Program. His attorney and Oscar Breiling had been working for months to get the Federal Witness Protection Program to take him, as the U.S. Marshal's office was far better than the state at keeping witnesses safe. But so far the talks had always bogged down over money issues. The federal government balked at footing the whole tab for a witness in a state trial; the state had little interest in paying additional money for the care and feeding of an admitted murderer.

Finally, though, it looked as if there were breakthroughs. Karny learned during his testimony that he could probably be taken into the federal program. One afternoon during the trial, he met with federal agents and heard about their stringent rules: he could tell no one his story; he could only call people from his past life from pay phones, and then never collect. Worst of all, he could never see his family, except when he was brought in to testify in a trial, and then only if the program could arrange a safe meeting. He would be given a new identity, money to get started, and assistance in getting a first job. But it would be a lonely life. If he violated even one of the program's rules, he would be booted out. Nevertheless, Karny did not have to think long before accepting the government's offer. As soon as he concluded his testimony, he would become the responsibility of the feds.

Barens and Chier had an important decision to make in their cross-examination of Karny. In his opening statement, Barens had touched briefly on Karny's testimony. "Witness Karny is about the only witness that is going to come into this court that we totally disagree with," Barens told the jury. "And who is Karny? Karny is a well rehearsed, professional witness. A witness who is here pursuant to an immunity grant. . . . They have let Dean Karny go from a murder he admits he committed in the Bay Area." It had been a calculated attempt on Barens's part to leave the jury with the impression that Dean alone had committed a murder in northern California.

Rittenband had felt Barens's opening remarks were misleading about Karny's involvement in the other murder. Several days before the key witness was scheduled to testify, the judge took the defense lawyers into his chambers and warned them to restrict their exploration of Karny's immunity deal to the Levin case only. If they brought up his bargain in the Eslaminia case, Rittenband warned the defense, he would allow the prosecutor to "go into all of the details and the involvement, if any, of your client." With that in mind, the defense lawyers had to decide whether they would leave the subject alone entirely or risk raising the specter of their client's alleged involvement in another murder.

Barens and Chier decided to confront the issue straight on. Within two minutes of beginning his cross-examination of Karny, Barens opened the door on the Eslaminia murder. "Isn't it a fact that what really happened was you went and got an immunity for a murder you confessed to in San Mateo . . . ?"

Barens hoped he had left the jurors with some serious doubts about Karny's integrity. If they were also a little mystified about another murder, so be it. Several days later, when the defense was nearly finished grilling Karny, the lawyers met with the judge. Wapner indicated that he planned to walk through the door Barens had opened by asking Karny more details about the Eslaminia murder. He definitely wanted to elicit from Karny the names of the other participants.

Barens and Chier argued the point, but when the judge ruled against them, they decided to try and mute the issue by asking the pertinent questions themselves. Barens had hoped that concerns about an appeal would prevent Wapner from exploring the Eslaminia matter at all. But if more facts were going to be brought out, he definitely didn't want the jury left with the impression that he had been intentionally hiding something from them.

"Now, as far as the defendants who are existent in the northern California case," Barens began when his cross-examination resumed, "the defendants would include Joe Hunt, would they not?"

"Yes," Karny replied.

"Reza Eslaminia?" Barens continued.

"Right."

"Ben Dosti?"

"Right."

"Jim Pittman?"

"That's right."

When Wapner began his redirect examination of Karny,

he wanted to make sure the jury had understood Joe's involvement, so he had Karny again name the other participants. At that point, he was satisfied, but the judge couldn't resist going further. "Who is Reza Eslaminia?" Rittenband asked, ignoring Barens's quick objection.

"Reza Eslaminia is the son of the man who was killed," Karny said, letting the jurors know that the alleged killing involved patricide.

And the end of Karny's testimony, Wapner rose. "The prosecution rests," he said.

Chapter
64

Arthur Barens wasted no time presenting his defense. Rather than calling minor witnesses to dispute small points raised by the prosecutor, he plunged right in, calling Brooke Roberts as his first witness. And in two days of testimony, she provided the crux of Hunt's case.

Brooke was dressed immaculately, her pale blond hair held back by a wide peach-colored ribbon; she looked like anything but a murderer's moll. As the pretty young woman told her strange tale, she spoke easily and at times almost flirtatiously to the judge and jury.

Brooke's first job was to discredit Karny, whom she portrayed as having a jealous, protective, and almost unnatural relationship with Joe. "At first when I met Dean, I thought they were very good friends," Brooke testified. "Then the more I got involved in the household, it seemed like I knew that Dean didn't want me to be there. It seemed like he was almost in a way obsessed with Joe."

Brooke said she was often made to feel like odd man out by Dean. "Everything I would want to do for Joe, like his laundry and things like that, he would always get in the way. . . . If I wanted to buy him some clothes or something, he picked out Joe's wardrobe, and he made it very clear to me that that wasn't my position. . . . I felt he was very jealous of me and like in love with Joe."

In a further attempt to discredit Karny before the jury, Brooke told about an incident she claimed had happened in March of 1984. She and Joe had just returned from Hawaii, she said, and they got home and went into Dean's room to say hello. "We jumped on Dean's bed," Brooke testified, "and we heard clanking, and we didn't know what was going on. Joe reached under the bed and he pulled out handcuffs. He said, 'Dean, not this again.' " Karny, she said, turned white and screamed at her to get out of his room. Then he "ran to the bathroom and started vomiting."

When asked if she had seen Dean with handcuffs at any other point, Brooke said yes, that she had seen a picture with Dean Karny, Evan Dicker, and a girl in it, and they were handcuffed. In the hallway later, the girl in the photograph, a former girlfriend of Karny's who had happened to come to court that day, was furious. "That picture was taken at a Halloween party," she said. "It was a joke. We were all in costumes, and it was clear from the photo."

In the middle of Brooke's first day of testimony, an elderly juror suffered a convulsion in the jury box. Although she was quickly revived and insisted she was able to continue, the judge decided after an interview the next day to dismiss her from the case. The woman's medical problems had prompted other jurors to come forward and say the ill juror had been reading about the case and telling the other jurors what she read. Rittenband had given strict instructions prohibiting the jurors from reading or watching any reports of the trial, and he was furious.

Soon after she left Department C, the juror was reached by reporters, who asked her how she felt about the case to date. "I was leaning strongly toward not guilty," she said. "I just don't think the prosecutor has proved his case." If the woman's views were representative of the jury as a whole, Wapner was in big trouble. The defense hadn't even had its say, yet the woman was still leaning toward Joe.

With the elderly woman's departure, the makeup of the jury changed considerably. Already, one juror had gotten permission to go back to work, and his seat had been filled by Kathleen Keenan, a bright and well-educated IRS appeals officer. For the new vacancy, the court clerk drew from a hat the name of Juel Janis, the former assistant dean of the UCLA School of Public Health. The jury now had only one man, and it had considerable brainpower. Wapner had to hope the change was good for the prosecution.

Back in the courtroom that afternoon, Brooke Roberts came through for Joe. She gave him an alibi. On the night of the murder, she testified, she had gone to see the movie *Streets of Fire* with Karny and others. When she arrived home alone at about 9:45, Joe was dressed for bed and was brushing his teeth in the bathroom. She said he told her excitedly about how earlier in the evening he had consummated a $1.5 million business deal with Levin, and he showed her a check for that amount.

The two were so excited, Brooke said, that at around tenthirty they called her mother, who was supposed to be arriving home from Alaska that day. "I told her, 'Guess what, we have great news. Joe got a big check from this guy,'" Brooke testified. Next, she said, her mom asked to speak to Joe, and they talked for a couple of minutes. It was a significant story. If Hunt had really been killing Levin, he couldn't have been home by 9:45.

Brooke also explained away one of the biggest problems facing the defense: if Joe didn't murder Levin, why did he tell BBC members he did? Joe was very upset, Brooke testified, that the Levin check had bounced and worried that he would lose control of the BBC. One time she had found him face down on his bed sobbing. When Brooke finally got him to tell her what was wrong, he confessed that Levin's check had bounced. "How could Ron be so cruel?" Joe sobbed, according to Brooke.

Shortly thereafter, Brooke said, she overheard a strange conversation between Joe and Dean. "I was walking to the kitchen," Brooke testified, "and I heard them laughing and planning something. It was all muffled, but the first thing I heard was Dean talking, saying, "Well, who could we say did it?" Later, she said she heard Dean say, "I know, I know. You could say that you killed Ron."

Just then, she said, Joe discovered her listening at the door and she demanded an explanation for what she had overheard. Joe told her that he thought the boys would respect him more if they thought he had murdered someone, and that it would bind the group together. "He said not to worry. He said it was just for effect. He said he didn't want to lose the BBC," she testified.

Brooke said she had disapproved of Joe's plan from the beginning. "I told him not to say that," she wailed to the jury, shedding a few tears. But the courthouse audience seemed unmoved. When Brooke asked the judge for tissues, there was general laughter in the courtroom.

With Brooke Roberts, the defense had drawn a clear line. The jurors could believe Dean Karny, or they could believe Brooke Roberts, but they could not believe them both. In case anyone had missed the point, Brooke underscored it for the jury. In response to a question from the judge, she turned pertly toward him. "Are you believing me or are you believing Dean?" she asked.

Wapner's first question on cross-examination was short and to the point. "What is your current profession, Ms. Roberts?" he asked. After some stalling, Brooke admitted that she had been working as an actress.

Brooke's mother, Lynne Roberts, took the stand next, to corroborate her daughter's story. The gracious, attractive, clearly affluent housewife was very convincing. She had spoken to Joe, she recalled adamantly, and he had told her about his deal. It was at around 10:30 P.M.

Wapner took the same tone in cross-examining Mrs. Roberts that he had with Brooke. He was aggressive, almost combative, and acted as if he didn't believe a word she said. It seemed to many in the audience that the prosecutor was being unnecessarily harsh on a woman who came across as sincere and believable. But during his long, tough questioning, Wapner elicited one very important point: Mrs. Roberts had relied on Brooke to remind her what day she received the phone call.

"They had all the information when he was supposed to have committed this crime," Lynn Roberts testified, "and Brooke said, 'Remember, Mom, that was the day of the check. Remember, we called you about the check? And they are saying Joe did this crime that night.' " Wapner then asked her if she had an independent recollection of the date of the phone call. "No, I didn't until, you know, we talked about it."

Fred Wapner had been dreading the appearance of Carmen Canchola, who took the stand on April Fool's Day. She might very well provide a juror or two with reasonable doubt.

Canchola seemed dignified and self-possessed when she took the stand, her privileged and sheltered upbringing clearly showing in her demeanor. She told her story simply, the same story she had told Wapner earlier. She had seen a "very, very attractive" man in a Tucson gas station, and had watched him for perhaps fifteen minutes while her boyfriend Chino had worked under the hood. The man had made a powerful impression on her. Two months later when she read the *Esquire* article, the accompanying picture had "looked familiar." After reading a description of Levin in the article, she looked back at the picture, she testified, her voice filling with emotion, "and I tried to picture it with silver hair and the eyes and everything, and I thought, 'God, that is the guy that we saw.' "

While it was unclear whether or not the jurors believed Canchola had seen Ron Levin, they were certainly sympathetic toward her. When she described her confusion over what to do, several jurors smiled and nodded encouragement, trying to help her through testimony that was obviously difficult for her. It seemed clear that Carmen at least believed she had seen Ron Levin.

Wapner came on even stronger with Canchola than he had with the Robertses. He grilled her ruthlessly about small details, refusing to pause even during several occasions when she started crying. Wapner was trying to point up certain things for the jury: Canchola had only seen the man for a short time; she had seen him two months before she read the article; she had not immediately recognized him from his picture.

Wapner's tough style with Canchola was a gamble. He hoped that he could show that the young woman was not as self-assured as she had at first seemed, that she had a hysterical edge. But the strategy could easily backfire in light of the jury's obvious sympathy for Canchola.

After Carmen Canchola's testimony, the defense had a big decision to make. They had already provided Joe with an alibi. They had, they hoped, raised doubts in the jurors' minds that Levin was dead. Should they do more? Most important, should they put Joe on the stand?

Barens and Chier slept little over the weekend of April third, as they examined and reexamined their options. Joe was articulate and persuasive; if the jury got to know him, could they possibly believe he killed someone? On the other hand, Joe had a lot of explaining to do, and Wapner had proven he could be very aggressive on cross-examination. Moreover, Barens and Chier were worried about any future appeals. It was well known among defense attorneys that cases in which defendants testified were far less likely to be overturned on appeal. Finally, the attorneys worried about the jury's reaction if Joe didn't testify. They had been promised Joe Hunt; would they feel betrayed if they didn't get him?

Department C was packed for the first time in several days after lunch on April 5. Word had gotten around the courthouse that Joe's testimony was imminent, and none of the dedicated court watchers wanted to miss it.

But immediately after the break, Arthur Barens stunned the courtroom. He rose, paused, and then said solemnly, "The defense rests." Joe Hunt would not take the stand in his own defense.

Chapter
65

It is prevailing wisdom in California courts that murder cases without bodies are won or lost in closing arguments. One story, perhaps apocryphal, has a defense lawyer winning his case with the following ruse. As he finished his closing remarks, he turned toward the courtroom door and shouted the victim's name. All the jurors quickly turned in their seats to see whether the supposedly dead man had actually walked into the courtroom. He was not there. "Now, that is reasonable doubt," the defense attorney concluded.

Neither Wapner or Barens had any such tricks in mind, but both sides had agonized over their closings. Wapner went first, meticulously reminding the jury of the points his witnesses had made in earlier weeks. He referred frequently to large charts that he posted for the jurors to see, as he took them back through the weeks of prosecution testimony. His argument was simple: Ron Levin would never have disappeared on his own, and Joe Hunt had murdered him. Other-

wise, Wapner asked, why would Hunt have claimed credit for
the murder? Why would Pittman have gone to New York with
Levin's credit cards? And finally, why was the list in Hunt's
handwriting found at Levin's house?

When his turn came later in the day, Barens approached
the podium carrying a large black notebook. Hundreds of
hours of preparation had gone into Barens's closing remarks,
with Chier, Barens, and Joe himself all contributing heavily
to the four-hundred-page script that Barens now began reading. By four-thirty, when court adjourned for the day, he had
barely made a dent in the notebook, and it was clear the jury
was finding his remarks tedious. When Barens returned the
following morning, his speech had been greatly condensed.
Parts of almost every page were marked with thick black
lines.

In cutting his speech, Barens had freed himself up for a
more dramatic delivery. Toward the end of what had still been
several hours of summary, Barens's voice got soft and he
looked straight into the eyes of the jurors. "If [Joe Hunt] can
be in this courtroom judged guilty of murder, then it is my
fault as his counsel. My limitations would be responsible. If I
could be so inept in showing you people of this jury the
innocence of my client, which is so obvious, then how could
I face Lynne and Brooke Roberts, who gave me this case and
the proof to save him? How could I tell them that I wasn't
enough, even with the proof sent to us by a greater power in
the form of Carmen and Chino? If I cannot make this point,
if I cannot utter a single truth and be understood, then
condemn me rather than this young man. For I would be the
only one guilty of the crime of murder in this courtroom."

Then, stirring himself still further, Barens continued.
"Fifty years ago, Irving Berlin wrote a song, 'God Bless America.' Its words are an anthem for our country and for our
generation. In the words of that song, I see the same country
you do. I see a country that is willing to forgive this young
man his ambition; to forgive him for being Ron Levin's fool.
Forgive him for attempting to exploit Ron Levin's disappear-

ance. This country, long on justice, bars from its gates mere suspicion. Joe Hunt has paid for his immaturity. He paid for his failed dream." Barens's voice became more intense as he spoke. "Do your duty," he concluded. "Set him free. Set Joe Hunt free." The jury remained impassive.

When the defense lawyer had finished, Wapner stomped back to the podium for his final rebuttal. The attorney had gained confidence during the long months of the trial, and his last speech was by far his best effort. "Forgive Joe Hunt for his immaturities?" he began furiously. "We are talking about murder. This isn't immaturity."

It was toward the end of his rebuttal, however, that Wapner made his strongest and most stirring speech of the trial.

The jurors, he said, should closely examine the defense reaction upon first hearing of Carmen Canchola. "Put yourself in Joe Hunt's position," Wapner urged the jurors. "You are innocent of a crime you didn't commit. No murder ever happened. And now you are presented with evidence that says that the man you are alleged to have killed is in fact alive in Tucson, Arizona. What is the very first thing that you are going to do? You hotfoot it down to Tucson, Arizona, with as much manpower as you can muster. You send people all over the city and you find this guy. You didn't kill him and somebody says that he is alive. You are going to get to Tucson immediately. You are going to put fliers all over the city. You are going to take out ads in the paper. You are going to put things on television. . . . Do you see a word of that? Nothing."

Barens, Chier, and Hunt looked outraged during Wapner's final remarks. It was all they could do. The defense got no further chance to address the jury.

Back in Rittenband's chambers after the final arguments, the lawyers and judge hammered out what instructions would be given to the jury before it began deliberating. The defense had a major strategy decision to make. Rittenband had left it up to them whether or not they wanted to have the jury instructed about the possibility of returning a verdict of second-degree murder, which carries less severe penalties than first-degree murder. On the one hand, such an instruction might result in the jury voting for the lighter sentence, but on the other hand, a jury might be able to get a compromise consensus on a vote of second-degree murder when they otherwise might not be able to agree on any verdict.

Chier asked the judge politely whether he might use Rittenband's cloakroom to discuss the issue privately with his client. But Rittenband seemed unwilling to forget his feud with the attorney. "The bathroom, that's an appropriate place for you," the judge answered.

At three o'clock on the afternoon of April 16, nearly two and a half months after the complicated trial began, the jury received its final instructions. The defense had opted for all or nothing, so a verdict of second-degree murder would not be among the jurors' options. Hunt's fate was now in their hands, and even the most seasoned court watchers and reporters were uncertain what the verdict would be.

At eleven o'clock on April 22, the jurors sent out a message from the jury room. After only two and a half days of deliberations, they had reached a verdict. It would be read at one-thirty.

By noon, many of the trial's major participants had gathered at the courthouse. Wapner waited nervously in his office down the hall with his mother and Les Zoeller. Television crews worked furiously laying cables and jockeying for the best spots. Upstairs in the cafeteria the Levins waited, tense and silent, for a verdict they fervently hoped would at least lessen their pain. Barens and Hunt arrived together twenty minutes before court was scheduled to convene. Hunt seemed calm; Barens intensely nervous. When Chier arrived moments later, the two attorneys embraced, clinging to each other for support.

At one-thirty, the twelve jurors filed solemnly in to the

packed courtroom and took their accustomed seats in the oak-paneled jury box. "Have you reached a verdict?" Diane, the court clerk, asked. Jury foreperson Juel Janis nodded solemnly and held out a sealed manila envelope for the bailiff to take to the judge. Rittenband ripped it open and quickly scanned the contents, his face revealing nothing. He then handed it to the court clerk, who prepared to read it.

The tension in the courtroom was tangible. No one felt certain about what the jury had decided. During the long weeks of trial, both sides had been like Kremlin watchers. Prevented by law from discussing the case with the jury, the lawyers and court personnel had instead watched and noted gestures and reactions during the long trial. Certain jurors seemed to like and respond to Barens, others to Wapner. But no one was willing to try and translate a few facial expressions into a verdict.

Finally, the clerk began reading. "We the jurors in the above entitled action," she read steadily, ". . . find Joseph Hunt guilty of murder in the first degree."

There was a muffled roar in the courtroom as one hundred and fifty people gasped simultaneously. Few even heard the clerk continue. The jury had also decided that special circumstances applied in the murder, which meant he could be sentenced to death.

Joe Hunt showed little emotion as the verdict was read. When the clerk had finished, he turned to look at Brooke Roberts and shrugged his shoulders, as if to say, "Oh well." Moments later, he answered questions from the press for the first time during the trial. "I think it's a tragedy," Hunt said of the verdict, "because Ron Levin is alive. I'm sure he'll be found in the next couple of years, with the sort of visibility he's had recently." Then, claiming that "Ron Levin did not die by my hand that night," Hunt calmly noted that the verdict was "just one of those unfortunate circumstances of compound error. My only responsibility is to keep my chin up, and that's what I do best."

Before the defense lawyers had time to compose themselves after what had been a major blow, they were called up to the bench. "When do you think you can begin the penalty phase?" Rittenband asked.

Chier lashed out. "When you pay me for the guilt phase," he said, referring to what he believed was the deliberate withholding by the court of his court-approved fees for defending Joe.

"You're fired," Rittenband said. "Mr. Barens will be much better off in the penalty phase without you."

As Chier left the courtroom minutes later, perhaps more discouraged than he had ever been, a cameraman pushed Chier aside. "Get out of the way," the man said, "the lawyer's coming. We've got to get shots of the lawyer."

Chapter
66

⋆

When Arthur Barens went to his closet on the morning of May 11, he chose a black suit to wear to court. It was an appropriate expression of his mood. Only two weeks had passed since the jury came back with a guilty verdict; now Barens must go before the same jury and ask that they spare his client's life. Barens felt there was little cause for optimism.

The penalty phase of the trial would take about three weeks. First, Wapner would have a chance to present evidence of aggravating circumstances—other violent acts Joe had allegedly planned or committed—in an attempt to convince the jury to recommend a sentence of death. Then Barens and Chier, whom the judge had agreed after all to allow to continue in the case, would try to convince the jury to spare their client, presenting evidence that might make Hunt's actions understandable, or put him in a more sympathetic light. At the end, the jury would sentence Joe either to death or to life in prison without possibility of parole.

If the defense lawyers were somewhat subdued after their defeat, Fred Wapner also seemed changed on the first morning of the penalty phase. After two weeks off, the prosecutor appeared more confident and calm than he had at any other time during the trial. He had won the biggest case of his career; now he could relax. He would argue strenuously for the death penalty, but he would still consider the trial a victory even if he lost in the penalty phase.

But by far the biggest change that day, at least in appearance, was in Joe Hunt. During the guilt phase of the trial, Hunt had turned out each day immaculately dressed in expensive suits. Now he was wearing an ill-fitting jail-issued jumpsuit. It was a none too subtle reminder to the jury that each night when they went home to comfortable beds, Hunt went back to his jail cot. The judge had objected to Hunt's attire in chambers, and he clearly didn't want Hunt manipulating the jurors, but the defendant had insisted on wearing his jail clothing. After bidding the jury good morning, Rittenband addressed the issue of Joe's apparel. "You will notice that the defendant is dressed in jail blues. That is at his own election and desire."

Although Hunt's clothes had changed, his spirits remained high. After the jury left the courtroom at the end of the day, Joe was positively playful. He asked Patrick, the bailiff, if he could go to the back of the courtroom for a drink of water, and Patrick agreed. As the convicted murderer made his way to the fountain, Los Angeles *Daily News* reporter Ron Ostroff, who had covered the trial daily from an aisle seat in the front row of the press section, quipped to the bailiff, "We have this all planned out, Patrick. I'm going to kick open the door, and Joe's going to run for freedom."

Joe turned around and grinned at Ostroff, who during the course of the trial had shown himself to be conscientious and very meticulous. "Ostroff," he said with mock disdain, "you wouldn't cross the street against the light."

*   *   *

During the penalty phase, Wapner could bring up alleged acts of violence for which Hunt had never been convicted or even charged. This meant that Wapner could fully explore, without having to worry about reversal by a higher court, the Eslaminia killing, the car laboratory shoot-up, and the alleged attack on Bruce Swartout in Irvine. During an opening statement of several minutes, Wapner explained to the jury a little bit about each of the three incidents and promised them fuller explanations during the next week.

Arthur Barens made no attempt to hide his disappointment in the verdict during his opening statement. Saying he would be "less than candid if I didn't tell you how difficult it is for me to come and speak to you again," Barens told the jury frankly, "I don't expect a lot." He continued with an impassioned argument against the death penalty, citing his personal opposition to capital punishment. "I can remember as far back as high school writing papers decrying the death penalty," Barens said. He then cited the Klaus Barbie trial, which was beginning that day in France. "They'll never hear a discussion of the death penalty in that case," Barens said, pointing out that the United States is the only Western country that still had death penalty laws. In closing, Barens asked the jury to "consider the tragedy that has already occurred in Joe Hunt's life and don't add to that tragedy by the state-sanctioned murder."

Wapner presented his evidence on Joe Hunt's other offenses in his usual straightforward style. Observers, BBC members, and police officers testified to the Swartout and car lab matters.

Dean Karny was re-called to tell the full story of the Eslaminia murder. His testimony was extremely powerful, and the jurors were deeply affected. That night, one juror woke up screaming. She had dreamed that someone had given her all of Eslaminia's bones. In her nightmare, she had known that if she could only figure out how to assemble them correctly, he would come back to life. But she could never put them together quite right.

During his case, Wapner had painted Joe as an emotionless and calculated killer. Now the defense had its turn to try and show otherwise.

Barens and Chier first called several members of the Bellagio Drive clan, in hopes that the glamorous Robertses could convince the jury that Joe wasn't so bad after all. Michelle Beranek, the pretty, soft-spoken, self-possessed fiancée of one of the Roberts boys, spoke of visiting Joe in jail prior to his release on bail. "We couldn't touch," she said of her visits, "but we would raise our hands to, you know, the glass." Later, when Joe was released and went to live at the Roberts house, Beranek said, she and he had shared a special bond, in that they had both been taken into the family from outside. Joe frequently said to her, "God, Michelle, aren't we lucky? Isn't this great?"

In describing Joe's personality, Beranek said he was always "even-tempered, bordering on stoic." But, in the one strange note to her testimony, she said he had recently become more open and sentimental since completing a course at Lifespring, a New Age self-improvement program. Joe had participated in the course after his release from jail at the urging of the Robertses, most of whom had become involved in the program. She and Joe had spoken only once about the course, Beranek said, and he had told her "that he was aware at times that he was very reserved," but that through Lifespring, "he had gotten in touch with himself more as far as feelings and vulnerability."

Todd Roberts, the second oldest of the three Roberts boys, acknowledged that the family's support of Joe had caused some raised eyebrows. "People avoid you. People ridicule you in public. A lot of people said, 'Well, you guys will be moving out soon because he is going to skip bail because he is guilty.'

But the fact was that we believed in his innocence so much, we all said that he wouldn't go anywhere."

Even before their testimony, the Robertses had been very much in evidence at the trial. Almost every day at least one member of the stylish family attended, and often two or three came. In conversation, Joe referred to the Robertses as his family, and they claimed him as one of their own. But until the penalty phase, Joe's real family never attended the trial.

Kathy Gamsky, Joe's mother, began coming to court during the second week of the penalty phase. She refused to speak to any of the reporters who requested interviews. She wouldn't even give her name. But it was clear she was Joe's mother. Her face, though far more careworn and drawn, was essentially Joe's face. Her tall, thin, straight body was a female version of Joe's. When she watched Joe, which she did throughout the long court days, her face reflected the sadness of a mother watching her son's life coming to a tragic end.

Joe's sister, Kay Hunt, a large, pale young woman who accompanied her mother to court each day, was the first of Joe's family to take the stand. Her testimony was perhaps the most moving of the trial. She began, often tearfully, describing her family, her tyrannical father and her meek mother. Joe, she said, was always the one who tried to mediate disputes and keep the family together.

It was clear from Kay's testimony that she could in no way reconcile the things people were saying about Joe with the big brother she had known, and she was determined to show the jury her Joe. When they were kids, she told the jury, Joe had gotten a paper route. But the first couple of times Joe was paid, his father, always short of cash, had taken the money. The next time, she said, "when he knew he was going to get paid, he decided to take me to Toys 'R' Us and spend the money, and then we went to Farrell's [ice cream parlor], and we had to walk four or five miles to get there. But we had a big day, which he had all planned, and he spent practically all the money on me." Kay sobbed as she told the story, turning in her seat and addressing her remarks straight to the jurors, who would decide her brother's fate. At least one of the jurors cried with her.

Greg Gamsky, Joe's older brother, described the often bitter family battles that took place before his parents split up. His father, Greg said, had pushed Joe relentlessly in hopes that Joe would make money for him. "My father is like a Fagin in the story *Oliver Twist*. He uses children. He started with my brother at an early age to start up a pattern that my brother would do for him and provide." It was Joe's devotion to his father, Gamsky said, that caused the six-year gap in relations between Joe and his brother, sister, and mother.

Kathy Gamsky's intense guilt about losing touch with her son was clear as she described her search for him. "I would write to Joe [after he moved to Chicago with his father] and never get a response, and then I would try to call there, but they had moved," Mrs. Gamsky recalled. "So I called some of Mr. Gamsky's relatives and asked them if they knew where Joe was, because I was very concerned about him, and they told me they didn't know where he was." By now Mrs. Gamsky was weeping. Another time, she said, she approached someone she thought looked like Joe, "because he was in a phone booth right next to our apartment building, right down the street, and I thought finally maybe Joe came back and he was trying to call me." At some point during her testimony, she looked up at the jury. "This is very painful for me," she said, "because I love Joe a lot and I miss him a lot, and I feel very badly about ever letting him go to Chicago."

Mrs. Gamsky also described to the jury how she had finally found her son on Sunday morning, November 2, 1986. "I got a phone call . . . from my oldest son. In the Los Angeles *Times* there was an article showing that Joe was in prison and this whole thing about the BBC or the Bicycle Club or whatever it is. . . . We had at that point no idea that Joe was in any kind of situation and that he had been in prison." Mrs. Gamsky said that her son Greg immediately called Arthur Barens and that she was reunited with Joe shortly thereafter. He had asked her not to come to court for the guilt phase of his trial because he wished to spare her. "I told him that I had this feeling like I wanted to put him in my pocket and never let him out of my sight again."

Fred Wapner seemed to have no sympathy for Kathy Gamsky, and he tried to put her in a different light with the jury. In his cross-examination, he hammered at her about why she hadn't been in touch with her son for so long. After all, he pointed out, she had known where he worked while he was in Chicago.

"You didn't think about calling the Chicago Mercantile Exchange and asking?" Wapner asked.

"I did think about it," Mrs. Gamsky replicd.

"But you didn't do it?"

"No," she said resignedly. "I did not do that. You see, you have to understand. I was also getting pressured by the other two children, Greg and Kay, who wanted absolutely no contact with their father."

Steve Solomon, a clean-cut Jehovah's Witness who worked as a personal fitness trainer at the exclusive health club where Joe and the Roberts family worked out, provided perhaps the most bizarre testament to Joe's character. Solomon said he was initially drawn to Joe after meeting him at the club because "I am a very moral person. I study the Bible a lot. And the majority of the people I come in contact with, they would swear a lot, talk about drugs a lot, talk about women a lot, and Joe didn't seem to have any of these typical male characteristics, so we started communicating."

Their friendship grew, Solomon said, partially because of a shared interest in Pac-Man and other video games. "When he would come in [to the club], we would work out and have a little practice, have a protein shake, and play some Pac-Man.

You know, fun stuff." Solomon had so much respect for Joe, he said, that "he was one of the few people that I wanted my parents to meet when I had them out for last Memorial Day weekend. . . . There is a lot of uncleanliness, so to speak, in L.A.; I wanted them to have the right impression that their son was not about to fall off the deep end."

Solomon said that about six months into his friendship with Hunt, Joe approached him. "He said, 'Steve, you are the last one of my friends to know about this. I have to tell you something. I am on trial for murder.' " After that, Solomon said, his feelings toward Joe remained unchanged. "I was friendly with him before I knew it. There was no reason not to be friends afterward."

From all the character witnesses, one thing had become apparent. Joe had made very positive impressions on all the people who testified to his character, but few really seemed to know him. They all had noted that Joe was very interested in their lives, and that he was an excellent listener. But he rarely, it seemed, opened up about his own life. To the Robertses he had barely spoken about his real family, and the Roberts boys had little sense of even such things as where Joe had gone to school, or what his business had been.

In the weeks since the guilt phase of Joe's trial had ended, several more spottings of Ron Levin had been reported. The final witness put on by the defense was one of the sighters, a legal secretary, whom the defense called in hopes of exploiting any lingering thoughts the jurors might have that Ron Levin could be alive. Although the jury had convicted Hunt, Barens and Chier felt that some might have nagging doubts about sentencing him to death when it was still remotely possible Levin could resurface.

The final defense witness, a petite, flirtatious blonde with a slight Southern accent, told a simple story. She had worked as a secretary in a Beverly Hills office with Levin for a couple of years during the mid-Seventies. She hadn't seen or thought of him again until early 1987, she said, when she had a conversation with a woman who had also worked in the suite with Levin. "She said, 'Remember Ron Levin?' I said, 'Well, the name rings a bell. I can't place the face at the moment.' And she said, 'Well, you know he is missing and they think he was murdered.' And I said, 'No, I didn't know that,'" the witness testified.

Then, in February of 1987, just a few months before her testimony, the secretary said, she saw Ron Levin in a Century City high-rise office building. "I was leaving the office. He was coming in from the outside, and he was near the security desk," she said. "He was walking facing me." The secretary said that although she recognized the face immediately, she hadn't realized until she was driving home that the man was Ron Levin, and that Ron Levin was supposed to be dead. A few days later, she saw a story on television about the Hunt trial, and she took down the lawyer's name and eventually called Richard Chier.

During cross-examination, Wapner established that in fact the secretary couldn't have seen the man in question for more than a few seconds, that she had never actually spoken to Levin during the time they'd worked in the same office in the mid-Seventies, and that she hadn't seen Levin in years.

Wapner thought he had probably discredited the secretary's testimony sufficiently, and he planned to let his penalty phase case rest. But then Les Zoeller, just before court was scheduled to begin the next morning, reached the other secretary from whom the defense witness had supposedly learned about Ron Levin's disappearance. After speaking to her, Zoeller and Wapner decided to bring her into court as a rebuttal witness that morning.

The new witness's story was quite a bit different from the secretary's. In several minutes of direct examination, Wapner elicited testimony from the woman that she had never met Ron Levin and that she had never discussed his disappearance or possible murder with the defense witness. It was doubtful the jury would take the first secretary's claims very seriously now.

After this witness's testimony, both sides rested.

If the jury had found it relatively easy to decide on Joe's guilt, they seemed to be agonizing over what his penalty should be. For the first time since they were empaneled, the jurors seemed to be having serious disagreements. By the third day, ragged emotions were evident on the faces of all the panelists leaving and entering the jury room. After the noon break, one juror was led back into the chamber crying hysterically. Another wept as she left the courthouse later in the day. But by midafternoon on the fourth day of deliberations, the jury had decided on a penalty. Joe Hunt would spend the rest of his life in jail.

After the verdict was read, the judge leaned forward and addressed the jurors sincerely. "In my twenty-six years on the bench, I can't remember a jury that has so intelligently carried out its duty," Rittenband said. "You are discharged with my thanks for a job well done."

For the defense, the sentence was a hollow victory. While they had certainly argued against the death penalty, the defense lawyers were aware that in some ways their chances for a reversal on appeal would be better if Hunt had been sentenced to die in the gas chamber. And the jurors made it clear that they had not been swayed by sympathy for Hunt. "We thought death would be too light a sentence," juror Pat Robles said during an impromptu news conference after the verdict. "We thought he needed some time to think about his actions," Dean Rutherford, another juror, added.

Joe Hunt's sentencing by Judge Rittenband on July 6 was a mere formality, as the judge was required by law to impose the sentence recommended by the jury. But Rittenband used the sentencing as an opportunity to express his feelings about Hunt. "Perhaps, as expressed by several of the jurors, it will be a greater punishment for you to be confined to the state prison for the rest of your life rather than suffer death, which could also have been appropriately imposed," Rittenband said sternly.

Rittenband was not the only person who had words for Joe that day. Under California law, a victim's relatives have a right to speak at the sentencing, and Martin Levin chose to do so. "I have anger and contempt for this man who killed my son, our son," Martin Levin said, looking at his wife, who sat in the front row. "I just hope he stays in prison for the rest of his life and feels the things we feel."

In requesting to speak, Levin had told a probation officer, "My wife will never get over it. [She] wakes up in the middle of the night on a regular basis and asks me, 'Do you think he suffered much before they brutally murdered him? Do you think he was dead before they buried him? Was he tortured before they killed him?' If I had my way," Levin continued, "[Hunt] should be killed. Why should he live and my son die?"

For Martin Levin, addressing the court was something of a catharsis. Almost every day for the preceding six months, he had been in court; now perhaps he could put things behind him. Bob Levin, Ron's younger brother, was not quite ready to let things rest. "So long, Joe Hunt," Levin called out as Hunt was being led from the courtroom in handcuffs. "I hope you have a good time while you're there. I hope they do to you what you did to my brother."

Lynne Roberts leapt to Hunt's defense. "When your brother shows up, what will you say then?" she shouted back, expressing the one small hope Hunt's supporters still nurtured.

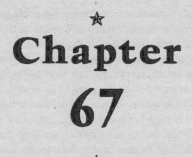

Chapter
67

John Vance sometimes wondered what he was doing in a line of work like this. By nature, the prosecutor was a thoughtful intellectual. He liked to think and to read. In his spare time, not that there had been much of that lately, he made wine in his basement. The best year of his life was probably the one he spent at the London School of Economics pursuing a master's degree in law. Now he was spending his life immersed in truly awful crimes.

Some days Vance found himself wondering just how much longer he could continue in this kind of work. How could he ever explain his job to Caroline, the three-year-old daughter he adored? Right now she was too young to really understand. But what about when she grew older? He sometimes felt an overwhelming desire to shield her from even knowing about the existence of the kinds of cases he worked on every day.

Despite his deeper philosophical questions, Vance also loved his work. He loved examining the chain of evidence that would eventually make a convincing case. He got satisfaction out of matching wits with the defense lawyers. He even liked solving the discrete legal problems of motion work. Most of all, though, he loved the sense of justice that came from getting criminals convicted. He felt that he went into court as the representative for the victims. He could never hope to make them whole again, but he could make the legal system work for them instead of for the criminals.

Vance had plenty of experience getting convictions. He had tried dozens of felony cases, first as an assistant district attorney out of Solano County north of San Francisco and then with the California Attorney General's office, and he had won a lot of them. He was confident, although cautious, that the trials stemming from the Hedayat Eslaminia murder would also result in convictions.

Vance had already fought some hard battles in the cases long before the first ones were even scheduled for trial. The defense lawyers representing Ben Dosti, Joe Hunt, and Reza Eslaminia were all excellent, and they had filed motion after motion to make the prosecution's case more difficult. The toughest one had been over the documents belonging to Hedayat Eslaminia that the CIA had seized. The defense had argued that what was in those documents might help their cases. Who could know, they asked, that the documents didn't contain vital information that would point the finger at someone else?

To bolster their argument, the defense lawyers had attached to their motion two documents that had apparently been mistakenly left behind by the CIA. The documents appeared to be some sort of funding proposal for insurgency teams, presumably to launch an offensive against Khomeini. The papers talked of two groups of men, an A team and a B team. Each would need about one million dollars, weapons, and training. If this was what the agency had left behind, the defense lawyers pointed out, what had they taken?

After hearing the motion, the judge had refused to throw out the case. But he was reserving the right to issue sanctions on the prosecutor at a later date. The whole thing made Vance nervous. He was left wondering when and if a sword would drop.

Vance had won hands down on the motion he cared most about. Originally, he had hoped to try Pittman, Hunt, Dosti, and Reza Eslaminia all together. But when Hunt's trial in Los Angeles had dragged on so long, it was clear Hunt's defense could not be put together quickly enough that he would be ready with the others. Pittman, too, was clearly out of the picture. Because of legal proceedings in Los Angeles, he had not yet even been arraigned in Redwood City. His retrial down south would probably be going on at about the same time as the first of the northern California trials.

But Vance desperately wanted Ben Dosti and Reza Eslaminia to be tried together. True, he would be going up against two defense teams instead of one, but there were nevertheless definite advantages. It would be difficult for one defendant to point the finger at the other as easily if they were both in court. If their stories differed substantially, and they would almost have to, Vance would in effect be getting help from one defense lawyer against another. In addition, Vance hated even to think about having to try four separate cases. He couldn't imagine how he and his witnesses could remain fresh through that many proceedings. The defense lawyers argued furiously to the judge for a severance, saying that they had conflicting defenses and were therefore entitled to separate trials, but Vance argued equally hard. In the end the judge ruled in favor of the prosecutor. The first of the trials for Eslaminia's murder would begin without further delay.

Chapter
68

Nineteen eighty-seven had been a good year for Tom Nolan, Ben Dosti's lawyer. His Palo Alto practice was thriving, and he was really beginning to be recognized as a top attorney. A recent book naming the top one hundred defense lawyers in the country had included Nolan's name. In addition, he had been named president of the California Attorneys for Criminal Justice, a real feather in his cap. But Nolan was too good a lawyer to let the accolades go to his head. Trying a good case required old-fashioned hard work no matter how great a lawyer you were.

The Dosti case, he knew, would be difficult. On the surface, the case seemed like a slam-dunk for the prosecution. They had a body and they had an eyewitness who would testify that Dosti had been a key participant. But Nolan knew that his client had a reasonable explanation for everything. It was his job to present Ben's side of things and to poke holes in Vance's case. After that the jury would decide whose version was correct.

Nolan had known from the time he entered law school that he wanted to be a defense lawyer. Part of it, he believed, was his finely honed sense of fairness. Always large, and somewhat overweight, Nolan had been picked on often during his childhood. It had left him with a sense of outrage at persecutors that he now channeled very effectively into defending others in court. He didn't always agree with everything his clients represented, but everyone, he believed, was entitled to a good defense. Part of the job of a defense lawyer, the way Nolan viewed it, was to protect his clients' right to be different or nontraditional and not to let some rookie cop decide what was acceptable behavior. It was inherent in the American system.

Nolan had been brought in on the Dosti case by Richard Hirsch, the lawyer first retained by the Dostis. With his practice and family in Santa Monica, Hirsch hadn't felt he wanted to try a lengthy case so far from home. The Dostis wanted the best, and Nolan was the best on the Peninsula, Hirsch had told them. The case had appealed to Nolan immediately. Ben Dosti seemed like a nice kid. His family was terrific. The case would be a tough one, but it was exactly the kind of challenge Nolan loved. Because of the nature of the case, Nolan was allowed a court-appointed attorney to assist him. For that job he would have Richard Keyes, a bright, intensely organized young lawyer who would make the lead attorney's job much easier.

Nolan spent the week before the Dosti trial alone in his Monterey beach house, an hour south of his home in Palo Alto. He needed time and solitude to read over all the evidence in the case and to pull his thoughts together. It was an important time for the thirty-seven-year-old lawyer. He had spent months getting in top shape, exercising and dieting rigorously. Already he had lost fifty pounds. No one could say he was overweight at this point, although his six-foot-five-inch frame was definitely imposing. In Monterey he had a strong sense that his months of vigorous training would pay off. He felt ready for this trial.

Jury selection took only a few days. Then it was time for opening statements. Vance's was simple and straightforward. He told the jurors the basic facts of the case, explaining how he would prove each. He wanted them to go into the case knowing what he would be getting at with each witness. It helped, he felt, to have the jurors aware ahead of time what they would be hearing.

Nolan went next, laying out for the first time the basic strategy of Ben's defense. He wanted to make sure that any evidence they heard wouldn't be interpreted solely the way the prosecutor wanted it to be. In fact, he told them, the actual story of what had happened on July 30 was very different from the one John Vance had just told them. Ben, he said, had been told by Joe Hunt that Reza's father was in trouble and needed help. He was being watched by the Ayatollah's people, and he needed help getting out of town. Joe had told Ben that Hedayat had gone to the BBC boys and asked if they would help by staging a kidnapping. After they got him away, they would hide him in a house down south until he could make arrangements to live somewhere else. Ben hadn't actually gone to Eslaminia's apartment on the day of the abduction, so if there had been foul play, he wasn't aware of it.

It was an interesting story. Most of the details the prosecutor would put forth could be explained both by Ben's version of events and by Vance's. It was a question of which version the jury would believe.

Neither Gary Merritt nor Joe Allen, Reza's court-appointed lawyers, made opening remarks. There was no reason, they felt, to tip their hand early in the trial. They believed that in most cases it was far better to surprise the prosecutor late in the case with the defense. Why give the other side any longer than necessary to take aim?

The tall, gray-haired Merritt, Reza's lead defense counsel,

had tried hundreds of cases, always as a defense lawyer. This one was perhaps more interesting than some, but in most respects it was just another trial. He had one responsibility: to fight to the best of his ability for his client. The American justice system was, in Merritt's view, essentially an adversary system. His job was to beat the prosecutor, and he believed in doing his very utmost to win.

The seasoned Merritt, although he would never lose sleep over a case, retained a lot of passion about his work. Early in his career he had come up against a couple of dirty cops and a prosecutor or two who were willing to bend the law to get a conviction. It had illustrated clearly what he had always known in his heart: just because someone was accused of a crime didn't mean he was guilty. It was then that Merritt had started viewing the prosecutor as the enemy, and although Vance was affable and seemingly honest, he was an enemy nonetheless.

Merritt was known on the Peninsula as an excellent attorney, although he had a reputation for very aggressive courtroom behavior on occasion. His colleagues particularly loved to tell the tale of the armed robber whom Merritt once defended. The case was seemingly hopeless. Merritt's client had allegedly badly assaulted a nun during a hotel robbery. Before trial began, Merritt filed a motion to keep the nun from testifying, knowing that her words might be what swayed the jury. The nun, he argued to the judge, was clearly incompetent. After all, Merritt said, "we have here a fifty-two-year-old Catholic virgin who believes she's married to a poor itinerant Jew born two thousand years ago who was an admitted felon in his own time. Can this woman really be believed?" Merritt's tactic failed, as he had felt certain it would, but he believed in pushing the justice system to its limits.

Merritt planned to be as tough as he needed to be in Reza's defense, but there would be plenty of time for that later. As the trial began, Merritt and his cocounsel focused on the job ahead.

*   *   *

Vance called Dean Karny early in his case, and it was then that he first got a taste of the difficulty of going up against four lawyers. In Santa Monica, the jurors had loved Karny. Nolan, Keyes, Merritt, and Allen intended to keep that from happening here. Nolan raised objections to virtually every statement Karny made. If the witness mentioned a meeting, Nolan objected on grounds of vagueness. He wanted to know the date and time of the meeting as well as who was present. He didn't want his client painted black by a broad brush.

During cross-examination, which lasted for several days, both Merritt and Nolan tried to score points. They had both studied all of Karny's previous testimony and tried to point out contradictory statements. The tactic wasn't particularly successful, since the lawyers were left with only tiny contradictions about specific dates and orders of events. Nothing substantive was effectively challenged.

But they were more successful than anyone who had yet examined Karny in presenting his worst face to the jurors. Through their persistent questioning about such things as Karny's asking for the prosecutor's assistance in getting admitted to the bar, they were able to show the star witness as a stool pigeon who still held fast to the belief that by ratting on others, he himself could live an untouched life. The lawyers also succeeded in making Karny angry, which also lessened his attractiveness. John Vance tried to console himself. The jury didn't need to like Karny, he reasoned, only to believe him. Time would tell about that.

Dean had laid out clearly, in his usual articulate fashion, all the events surrounding Hedayat Eslaminia's abduction and death. The rest of Vance's case was essentially corroboration. During the next several weeks, he called witness after witness to substantiate Dean's testimony. A clerk from the Villa Motel confirmed that Ben Davis (a name used by Ben Dosti) had taken two rooms for the night of July 29. A U-Haul clerk testified that Dosti had rented a large truck on the thirtieth. Hedayat Eslaminia's friends testified that he had not been close to his son. The Swiss banker testified about the two boys trying to withdraw funds.

By the end of the prosecution's case in mid-November, Vance had laid out a compelling set of facts. But observers in the courtroom were reluctant to lay odds on a conviction. Karny had seemed a little weasly, many thought. How could you really believe him? And he was the only one who could say that Ben and Reza had been involved in a kidnapping. Most of the court employees, lawyers, and random observers who were dropping in on the trial frequently felt it was just too early to tell. They were waiting to hear the other side.

Debra Lutkenhouse held her head high as she walked to the stand to testify as the first witness in her fiancé's defense. She wanted the jury to see from her manner that she was a smart and together young woman. If I believe in Reza, she hoped her composure would say, so should you.

If the jury was to acquit Reza, Merritt realized, it would need to get a sense of the boy's troubled, even pathetic, past. Merritt himself had certainly come to have sympathy for the young man as he had gotten to know him. But the jurors would also need to see that Reza had grown beyond the chaos of his early life, and that he was clearly now someone who would be incapable of murder. Debi's role was cut out for her.

She began by explaining her romance with Reza. At first, she said, he had been a braggart, always claiming to have more money and better prospects than he did. But finally, Debi had just confronted him. "I said, 'Stop being a jerk. You don't have any money; stop putting on these airs.' " He had been much better after their talk, she said. For long periods, Reza had gotten on very poorly with his father. Many of the disputes, she said, were over money. Reza had been very distraught when his father had left the Lutkenhouse family with bills for more than ten thousand dollars in a failed business deal. It had caused a serious rift between them. But Reza had always loved his father.

*   *   *

On November 24, it was Reza's turn to take the stand. Reza's testimony would clearly be the crux of his defense. In the end, the jury would evaluate what he said in light of what Dean had said and what Ben would say. But despite the gravity of the situation, Reza looked positively cocky as he took the stand. Each morning after he was brought up from the jail, Reza had been allowed to put on a suit for his trial. On the first day of his testimony he wore his best clothing, a dark blue pinstripe suit. His hair looked freshly shampooed. As he seated himself in the witness stand, he smiled broadly, first at his lawyer, then at Debi, and finally at the jury. At last, he seemed to be saying, I've got my chance.

Reza's slightly accented speech was soft and respectful as his attorney led him through a sequence of questions about the events of July 1984. Joe Hunt had known, Reza told the court, that Reza and his father were not speaking, and that this fact bothered Reza very much. Joe had offered to intercede. He would go to Belmont personally and try to persuade Hedayat to speak to his son.

On Monday, July 30, Reza said, he had been in the Bay Area after visiting Debi for the weekend. That afternoon, he had gone to his father's building at a time previously decided on with Joe, who had come to town to try and arrange the reconciliation. Reza said he waited outside for a time in Debi's gold Porsche, and then Dean Karny came out of the security building with the message that Reza's father refused to see him. Disappointed but not surprised, Reza had gone back to Debi's. Shortly thereafter, he had returned to Los Angeles.

The first he knew of his father's abduction, Reza told the court, was when he got back to Los Angeles and visited his mother. She had heard that his father had disappeared and urged him to take charge. That afternoon, he said, he had approached Joe Hunt for help and advice about what to do. At some point during his meeting with Joe and Jim Graham, who happened to be there, Joe had admitted that Hedayat was dead, and that he was responsible. Reza said that his reaction had been disbelief, that he assumed the others were kidding. But, he said, continuing his highly unbelievable testimony, Graham had quickly dispelled that notion by punching Reza hard in the chest and shouting, "Listen, motherfucker, no one's kidding! Your father's dead as a doornail, and you may be next." Reza grew excited as he described the scenario.

Joe, Reza testified, had been somewhat calmer. "Look, Reza," he claimed Joe had told him, "Your father's dead. We didn't mean to kill him. It just happened, but he's dead nevertheless. Your only concern right now should be to keep yourself alive and your family alive." The others, Reza said, had gone on to threaten him, his family, and Debi. If he told, they might all die. Reza said he had believed Hunt without question. "In his eyes, you could tell the guy was serious," he said. All of his subsequent attempts to lay hands on his father's assets had been motivated by fear.

John Vance was flabbergasted. The story Reza had told on the stand was clearly going to be contradicted by Ben. The defendants would be pointing their fingers at each other, which would, with luck, leave the jury convinced that both boys were lying. It seemed difficult to believe that the jury could believe Reza, the prosecutor thought. He had appeared too cavalier on the stand. To Vance it had been obvious that Reza was making things up as he went along. He hoped the jury had gotten the same impression.

Vance was more worried about how the jury would react to Ben Dosti. The dark-haired, serious-seeming young man had put on a little weight recently, and the case had clearly aged him, but he was still quite nice-looking. The worst thing for Vance was Dosti's family. Every day his mother and sisters, and often his father, when he could take time off from work, had been seated in the front row of the courtroom watching the proceedings. Their pain was touching. Ben's sisters were both beauties, his mother and father handsome and well-dressed. Everything about them spoke of good breeding. Could the jury actually believe that a family like this had spawned a cold-blooded murderer?

At eleven o'clock on the morning of December 1, Ben Dosti looked as if he would rather be anywhere else on earth than on the witness stand in the Redwood City courtroom. With his head slightly bowed, he breathed deeply, as if gathering his courage, and slowly scanned the room. He looked respectful, somber, and very, very scared. It was the proper demeanor for someone accused of murder—much better than Reza's offhand smirking.

Ben's story explained virtually every point made during the prosecution case except the testimony of Dean Karny. Yes, he admitted, he had gone to the Bay Area to scout around; yes, he had rented a motel room in Belmont the night before the abduction; yes, he had rented the U-Haul; yes, he had gone to Palm Springs looking for remote houses. But he had not had any idea what was really going to happen.

According to Ben, Joe had told him that their mission was to smuggle Hedayat Eslaminia out of his apartment without the Ayatollah's people getting wind of it. They would take him to Los Angeles and help him muster his assets so he could start a new life. In return, Eslaminia would compensate the BBC generously.

On the actual day of the abduction, Ben testified, they had finished their preparations early. Having nothing else to do, the boys had all decided to take a nap in their motel room. The five boys had sprawled out on the beds and floor. At some point, Joe Hunt had awakened Ben and told him he wasn't going to be needed for the operation. Ben said the others left and he then went back to sleep. Some time later, Joe returned, claiming everything had gone perfectly. Ben and Joe had ridden back to Los Angles in the pickup, Ben said, and they had no trunk with them. He had no idea what had happened to the U-Haul.

The next day, Ben said, Joe informed him that Mr. Eslaminia had died en route to Los Angeles. Dean, he said, had panicked and dumped the body beside the road in Soledad

Canyon. Ben said he had been too scared to go to the police at that time. "I was afraid," he said, breaking down and crying for the first time since taking the stand. "There was a body discarded, and I knew about it." He had instead decided to keep quiet and help Reza in his search for his father's assets. He hadn't had any problem with that, he said, because Reza, as the eldest son, was entitled to his father's assets now that he was dead.

In cross-examination, Ben told Merritt that he had come to believe that Joe Hunt killed Ron Levin. Later, under cross-examination by Vance, he said, "It's my belief now that Mr. Hunt may have had something to do with the death of Eslaminia." He based his belief, he said, on the testimony he had heard. Did that mean on Dean Karny's testimony? Vance asked. "In part," Dosti replied. Vance was amazed at the answer. If Ben thought Karny was a hideous liar who had implicated him falsely in a murder, why would he believe what Karny said about Joe Hunt? He hoped the jury picked up the implications.

Vance was pleased overall with the testimony of the two defendants. Could anyone really believe, he wondered, that in the middle of an exciting mission to rescue a beleaguered political refugee, the participants would all curl up and take naps? Privately, Vance and Breiling referred to Ben's story as "the sleeping beauty defense." And could the jury possibly put any credence in Reza's claim that he had arranged for Joe to be a mediator? Why in the world, Vance wondered, would Reza have picked Joe for the role instead of another Iranian? His father barely spoke English. The mission would have been doomed to fail. Moreover, the prosecutor told himself, there were several points the defense attorneys simply hadn't addressed adequately. Why had Reza written in mid-July in his appointment book, "They think I shouldn't be seen. Cause more fear"?

Perhaps the most criticial question unanswered by the defense was about Dean Karny. Why would Dean lie about the involvement of Ben and Reza? If there had been no foul play, Dean wouldn't have needed immunity. If things had happened as he described but without Ben or Reza, why would he have implicated either boy? Hunt would have been enough to make the authorities happy.

Chapter

69

Tom Nolan finished presenting his case just after Thanksgiving and now he desperately wanted to send it to the jury quickly. Common legal wisdom holds that juries are more sympathetic and forgiving around the holidays, and Nolan felt his client was in an excellent position to benefit from the spirit of the season. The jury had seen Ben's family. Perhaps they would be reluctant to return a conviction that would put him into prison just before the holidays. But Nolan didn't prevail. Judge Miller gave the jury a choice of hearing closing arguments immediately or waiting until early January. They unanimously voted to wait.

All the lawyers had spent hours on their closing speeches, and by the time court reconvened on January 5, they were ready. Vance's closing remarks were straightforward, taking the jury back through testimony from the beginning of the case, which Vance reasoned had now receded in their memories. Gary Merritt went second, reminding the jury about what his client had said. Tom Nolan brought up the rear. That was the way he liked it. He only wished the prosecutor didn't have a chance for rebuttal.

As soon as Merritt finished, Nolan and his assistant counsel, Richard Keyes, sprang into action, dragging out easels, a drawing pad, an overhead projector, and two boards covered with Velcro. Nolan had a lot to tell the jurors, and he didn't want them to be bored. After giving each juror a notebook containing pieces of evidence he felt to be particularly important, Nolan began. The lawyer's arguments took several hours, but they were brilliantly presented. Nolan was asking the jurors to trust him. Throughout the trial, he had sent them subtle messages that he liked Ben. Whenever he had leaned over to whisper to his client in the courtroom, he had put his arm around him. In the hallway he was chummy with Ben and the rest of the Dostis. I believe in Ben, his actions seemed to say. Now he was telling jurors why they too should believe.

After building up Ben Dosti and discrediting the prosecution's witnesses, Nolan turned his attentions to Dean Karny. Could they believe this admitted murderer who had cut such a cushy deal for himself? he asked the jurors. After talking about Karny's instability and reasons for lying, Nolan turned to the jury one last time. "Are you willing to walk arm in arm with Dean Karny? Because if you are, you're betting Ben's life on it."

After Nolan finished on the afternoon of December 7, it was time for Vance's final rebuttal. The trial had been agony for Oscar Breiling. He felt, he said, like a gunfighter who had spent months preparing for a big duel and then had his guns taken away. In the courtroom, Vance was the one to present the evidence. He was the lawyer. And although Vance was better about soliciting his opinions than any lawyer Oscar had ever worked with, Oscar was nevertheless frustrated. He knew exactly how he would present the case, yet he had been forced to sit silently on the sidelines. By the time of Vance's rebuttal, the frustration had become almost palpable, and Oscar could hardly listen to Vance's words. He looked straight ahead, breathing deeply. In three and a half years of working on this case, Oscar had become convinced that these boys were not only guilty, they were monsters, a perfect example of what happens when kids are raised without morals. He couldn't stand the thought that they now, because of good lawyering, might get off. Months ago, he had made a promise to his God that he would leave the case entirely in His hands, but sitting in court he realized how hard that would be. He just cared too much.

Vance's rebuttal emphasized again and again why the jury should believe Karny. In his testimony, Vance said, Karny had repeatedly been willing to accept blame himself as well as to implicate others. He had no reason to lie. After two hours, the case was over. It was now up to the jury to decide.

After seeing the closing arguments, the trial's most faithful observers were in agreement about a couple of things. Reza, they felt, would probably be convicted. His demeanor on the stand had suggested that he was lying, and his story was just too hard to believe. Besides, there were crucial questions Reza had not answered; such as the meaning of his diary entry about not being seen. Ben, they felt, was a different story. It was unlikely the jury would acquit him—there was just too much evidence against him. But could all twelve jurors really agree on a conviction? Most of the spectators thought it unlikely. Nolan had been too good. As one court employee said in the elevator after hearing the arguments, "I believe in my heart that Mr. Vance's version is correct, but Mr. Nolan was very persuasive."

No one expected a quick verdict for such a complicated case, but the lawyers and defendants were nevertheless extremely anxious. Each day during the deliberations, the various attorneys checked in with the court clerk several times, asking whether there had been any stirrings, any smoke signals indicating that the jury was nearing a verdict.

After lunch on January 14, nearly a week after deliberations began, the jury sent out to the clerk several notes asking for clarification from the judge on certain issues. Upon hearing about the requests for assistance, the lawyers hurried to the courthouse to read the notes and try to discern from them clues to what the jury was thinking.

The group had previously been instructed that as part of its deliberations it must decide whether Hedayat had died as a result of some gratuitous infliction of force by an abductor. Now the jury wanted to know if "confinement in a trunk and/ or suffocation" could be considered such force. The question seemed to be a good sign for the prosecution. It seemed that at least some jurors were convinced that Eslaminia's death was caused as a result of his being locked in a trunk. The jurors must then also accept that at least one of the defendants had been involved in placing him there. The judge instructed the jury that yes, that would be considered gratuitous infliction of force.

Another juror posed a question that seemed to be a positive sign for one or both defendants. His question was, "If a defendant joined the conspiracy after Hedayat's death with the purpose of stealing Hedayat's assets, is it required that they also know the purpose of the trip to northern California in order to find them guilty of conspiracy to commit grand theft?" Clearly the juror was taking seriously at least one of the defendant's assertions that he had never been told the real reason for going to Belmont.

What gave Vance the most cause for optimism was a question from one juror who wanted to know whether, if she found a defendant guilty of one part of count 1, she must automatically find him guilty of another section of the count. At least one juror seemed to be leaning strongly toward a conviction. The same juror also requested a rereading of the testimony Ben Dosti had given after the morning break on

December 1. The lawyers all scurried for their copies of the transcript to see just what he had said at that time.

Judge Miller had initially intended to answer the jurors' questions the next morning, a Friday, but one of the jurors was sick. The lawyers would have to sit on pins and needles through a long weekend. Monday was Martin Luther King Day.

First thing Tuesday morning the judge began answering the jurors' questions. Yes, he told them, confinement in a trunk constituted force. Yes, a defendant must have known the purpose of the trip to be guilty of conspiracy. Yes, if a juror found a defendant guilty of one part of the count, then he must also be found guilty of the other part. The jury listened intently as the judge instructed them. But they listened most carefully as John Vance and Tom Nolan took turns reading back the requested Dosti testimony. They had wanted to hear the most crucial part of his statement—his version of the events of July 30, 1984.

By the time the somber jurors left for their lunch, their questions had all been answered, and the lawyers thought it seemed clear that the jury was near a verdict. John Vance predicted they would return by four that afternoon, and Nolan and Merritt thought that sounded like a good guess. But juries operate at their own pace, and by the end of the day, no verdict had been reached.

By the next afternoon, journalists and spectators began gathering outside Judge Miller's court, clearly expecting a verdict momentarily. Downstairs in his temporary quarters in the District Attorney's office, Vance jumped each time the phone rang, unable to believe that the jury wouldn't return a verdict that day. But at three o'clock, more than an hour before their usual breaking time, the jury foreman announced to the court clerk that it was pointless for the jury to deliberate any longer that day. The jury was obviously having a hard time reaching a consensus. A mistrial, at least on some counts, was beginning to seem inevitable.

John Vance had reservations in Yosemite for the weekend

of January 22. The trip had been planned as a way for him to unwind with his wife and daughter after the grueling trial. But by late Thursday it was beginning to look doubtful that he would be out from under the case by the weekend.

On Friday the jury sent out another question. If they found that Hedayat Eslaminia had committed suicide in the trunk, should they still convict one or both defendants of murder? Vance and Breiling found the question unbelievable. There had been a tiny bit of testimony during the trial that Dean had heard Hedayat shout *"Vye, vye, vye"* while in the trunk. When he had heard about this, Reza had told Dean the unlikely story that the cry was an Iranian suicide chant. Perhaps, he had suggested, his father had killed himself. It was testimony Vance hadn't even bothered to address. It had seemed so ludicrous. Could the jury really be taking that, of all things, seriously? Judge Miller instructed the jury on Monday morning that no, if Eslaminia killed himself, the murder charge would not be applicable.

Vance had braced himself for a hung jury, but after lunch on Monday, January 24, he got a call from a clerk. "They have a verdict," she said.

"An actual verdict?" Vance asked, disbelieving. "Not a mistrial?" The clerk assured him that no, it was not a mistrial, the jury had reached agreement.

Vance boarded the elevator to the eighth floor with a heavy heart. Based on the question the jurors had sent out on Friday, they were very far away from convicting. If they had reached a verdict, it was probably an acquittal. He didn't even have Breiling for moral support, as the investigator had remained home that day with back pain. Perhaps it was for the best, Vance thought. Oscar cared so much about the case it would be terrible for him to be in the courtroom for an acquittal.

After all the parties had arrived at the courtroom, the clerk took the envelope to the judge. He opened it and read the verdict silently before handing it back to the clerk to be read aloud. Finally the clerk began. Vance listened to her read for several seconds before her words sunk in. *Guilty*. She had read the word *guilty*. The jury had convicted Dosti on all counts and Eslaminia on all but one. The jury had not concluded that he intended in advance to kill his father, and therefore had not convicted him of conspiracy to commit murder, but on all other counts they had been certain.

Ben was immediately taken into custody in the courtroom. The Dostis, all of whom held up well except one of Ben's sisters, bid Ben goodbye and left quietly. Reza was led back to jail by the bailiff.

By the next day, Ben and Reza were planning their appeals. In April both boys were sentenced by Judge Miller to life in prison without possibility of parole.

Chapter 70

It was not until the northern California trial of Ben and Reza was winding down that Joe Hunt decided to end his self-imposed silence about the BBC. On December 12, 1987, in an interview room at San Quentin prison, where Joe was serving his sentence for Levin's killing, he spoke to Ed Bradley of CBS's "60 Minutes," trying out publicly for the first time the story he had planned to tell at his trial in Los Angeles. In a series of rambling, inarticulate, and often bizarre answers to Bradley's questions, Joe attempted to vindicate himself in the Levin murder and to dispel what he felt were myths that had grown up about the BBC. He succeeded at neither.

From the beginning of the interview, most of which never aired on television, Joe refused to let any unflattering image of the BBC escape his attention. The group, he insisted, had never been called the Billionaire Boys Club, even in jest, until Tom May started slinging the term as part of an attempt to market a movie about the group. Joe had never consciously sought out affluent boys for membership in the group, he said. He looked rather for people who shared his vision.

With regard to the group's philosophy, Joe seemed determined to dispel any notions that it was based on sinister principles. But his revisionist explanation of the BBC's guiding theory often bordered on the absurd.

Paradox Philosophy had been characterized as epitomizing situational ethics, he acknowledged, but in fact nothing could be further from the truth. "Now, 'black is white and white is black and all the shadings in between' is a phrase that you'll find over and over in books on philosophy," Joe said, not naming any specific books. "The first time I encountered it was in a book, a pamphlet on racial discrimination suggesting that there was, should be no color concept between human beings. But when I read it, it struck me that it was true in a lot of other ways."

As he refined his beliefs, Joe said, Paradox Philosophy became a sort of prescription for thinking positively, for turning adversity into prosperity; not at all a means for justifying heinous acts. "Even something as terrible as a holocaust," Joe continued. "There's no question that it's a hideous, horrible thing that is black in every sense of the word when . . . you attach an ethical presumption to the word 'black.' But if it is kept in our minds, and if people never forget that sort of cataclysm and the horror of that, then it can stand as a bulwark against that happening in the future. In that sense, black is white, white is black." Joe's explanation ignored the testimony of virtually every other BBC member about what the philosophy had involved.

Next, Joe addressed the financial problems that arose in the group. The BBC's troubles had not sprung from malfeasance, he insisted. Rather, they demonstrated that "there was some gross rank immaturity going on. There was no real wisdom. There might have been some intellectual wisdom, but as far as application, ability to apply it, it was severely lacking."

Preliminaries aside, Bradley went to the heart of the matter. "Did you kill Ron Levin?" he asked.

"No, sir," Joe replied solemnly.

"Are you capable of murder?" Bradley pressed.

"In defense of my country—I think of that sometimes as murder because you're up against someone who's drafted by the other side, sort of a political murder. But you know, it's not even something that even comes up in a person's life on a level that I was leading it. Somebody might owe you money; you might have an argument with somebody, but it doesn't go to that in your mind."

When Bradley asked Joe about the seven-page list found in Levin's apartment, he had a ready, if complicated, explanation. It had all started, Joe said, sometime during the late spring of 1984. The BBC had persistently tried to get Levin to pay money the group felt he owed as a result of the Clayton Brokerage scam, but Levin had consistently refused to do so. Then Joe thought he saw an opportunity to get money from Levin in a different way.

"I had been talking to Ron about Microgenesis," he said, "and one day he says to me, 'Joe, there is a possibility that I can [sell some rights to] the Microgenesis technology. Can I have some paperwork on it? It's an opportunity for me to pay back the money that I owe you and make up for some of the damage.' "

Soon, Joe told Bradley, he began to suspect that Levin was planning once again to scam the BBC, and he became very nervous that Levin would tarnish the name of Microgenesis, a company Joe still had high hopes for. "That put me back on my heels again, and I [started] thinking that there had to be some sort of way to just get this man out of our lives entirely, and that's what the [list] was about. I went back and I talked to some of the guys, and we started brainstorming about how to back this guy out of our lives, and we decided to try and scam the scammer."

Joe claimed he met with several BBC members about the Levin situation. "Our brainstorm was that we would create this list. I would go over to Ron Levin's house and I'd use it as a prop to try and scare him off. I'd say, 'Ron, look, things have gone so far that this is what some of the guys are thinking about, and I'm coming to you because I can't handle the level that this has been taken to. You have to leave Microgenesis alone. Don't proceed with any fraud that you've got planned there.' " The list, he said, was intended only to frighten Levin into thinking the boys had come up with an extortion plan. No one had ever intended to put the plan into action, and even the phony plan had not been for a murder.

Shortly before Levin disappeared, Joe said, he put the scare plan into action. "I walk in and I say, 'Ron, you know you're really walking on thin ice here, and there are some things you don't know about our group that you really should. Some of these guys are involved with some people that play very rough, and they've gone to them with the problems we've been having with you, and they said, well, the thing to do is get leverage on the guy. And then I met with them, and I took some notes about what was discussed.' "

Next, Joe told Bradley, he brandished his list with its notations to "Kill dog" and "Handcuff Levin." "It was supposed to be taken seriously by Levin," Joe said. "Unfortunately, it wasn't. After I went through my entire spiel about this with him, he said—I'll never forget it—'Don't teach your grandfather to suck eggs. Don't con the con man, Joe. This is ridiculous.' "

The day after his failed attempt to frighten him into backing off on any Microgenesis dealings, Joe said, Levin called him up. Levin assured Joe that he had real investors lined up who wanted to purchase some rights to the Microgenesis rock-pulverizing technology. He intended to do an absolutely straight deal. The BBC's cut would be $1.5 million if all went according to plan. Eager for money to put things back together at the BBC and to repay investors, Joe was interested in what Levin had to say. After all, he said he reasoned, what could he possibly lose? "I'm thinking, all I have to do is deliver some paperwork. Either the check's good or it's not."

On June 6, the last day Levin was seen alive, Joe went to the con man's house. There, he said, Levin signed an option agreement with Microgenesis and in exchange gave Joe a check for $1.5 million drawn on a Swiss bank. Ron said he was going to New York the next day to consummate the deal with his investors. That, Joe said, made him a little nervous. "I said, 'Well, Ron, you know I'm uncomfortable because of everything we've gone through. I'd like to have a representative of the BBC there to make sure that this deal is not derailed at any point into something else.'" Levin's first response was negative, Joe said, as he didn't want "one of those snobby little brats you run around with." But when Joe promised him Jim Graham, Levin agreed. If Joe would send Graham over, Levin would make plans with him and provide him with the financial means to get to New York.

His business with Levin finished, Joe said, he went home, where Brooke found him brushing his teeth when she got home from the movies.

The next day, Graham, a.k.a. Jim Pittman, went as planned to New York, Joe said, but Levin never came.

If Joe didn't kill Ron Levin, Bradley asked him, then why did he announce that he had to a BBC meeting on June 24? Things were really moving at that point, Joe said, toward a big deal involving Microgenesis. A Canadian company was interested in putting up significant sums of money, which the group now needed desperately. But, Joe said, by that time his stock as leader of the group had fallen drastically with the other boys. Several were involved, he said, in trying to wrest Microgenesis out of Joe's hands. He decided to take drastic action. "So I called this meeting, and I said, 'You know that list we created? I actually ended up using it for a different purpose. I knocked off Ron Levin.'"

Joe's announcement, which he maintained was a lie, was intended to accomplish two things. "I'm looking first to scare them into leaving the technology alone for just another month or so until I can close this deal and settle accounts. Second, I'm interested in saying it in such a way that they won't immediately go to the police." Because the other boys had been involved in drawing up the list, Joe believed they would be too scared to bring the police in. In the end, he said, he had been right, as none of the boys had reported the meeting for more than a month.

The meeting on June 24, Joe insisted to Bradley, was motivated by noble concerns. "Joe Hunt is just trying, in a way that turns out to be catastrophic, to stand up for these eighty investors and see that the money gets back to them," Joe said, referring to himself in the third person, as he often did during the "60 Minutes" interview. "There's precious little chance of that at that point, but it was my responsibility to try."

If Joe didn't kill Levin, as he maintained, then what happened to him? Bradley asked Joe. "Levin had basically exhausted the territory in Beverly Hills," Joe maintained. In addition, he was facing twelve felony counts for one of his frauds and stood a chance of serving significant time in jail. Levin decided on his own to skip town, Joe maintained, and "then along comes Joe Hunt and gives Levin a very terrific opportunity to assemble an escape from the situation where he doesn't have to worry about people hounding him. . . . He has a seven-page piece of paper which is tailored to order. He maneuvers Pittman into a situation [where he] goes to New York. . . . In doing so, he creates the situation which circumstantially looks extremely sinister." In fact, Joe speculated, Levin had left town to escape his difficulties and was living happily somewhere else.

Joe's explanation of the events surrounding Levin's disappearance covered most of the nagging points except for one: if no murder had occurred, then why would Karny have made up such a horrendous story?

On that point Joe was bitter. "Dean Karny is a person with severe, unrecognized problems," he said. Dean felt himself to have some exposure with regard to Hedayat Eslaminia, a matter Joe had told "60 Minutes" in advance he could not discuss because of his pending trial for Eslaminia's murder.

Moreover, Joe said, Karny had been connected to a "third homicide," the Hollywood motel murder, that the police were refusing to make full disclosures about. "I'm sitting here in a chair in prison," Joe complained, "and it's so clear that Mr. Karny's the common denominator in the problem here at this point."

Despite his claim of innocence, Joe said he was not surprised that a jury convicted him of murdering Ron Levin. The trial, he said, had been so skewed by the judge's actions that he had been unable to put on a full defense, or to take the stand as he had desperately wanted to do. "When I heard the call that they had come to a verdict," Joe said, "I went into my bathroom and I got my toothbrush, and I got my shoes and my pants and forty dollars because that's what's allowed in these jails. I put all those things in the car and said good-bye to the family. I didn't say I thought that verdict was coming, but it was absolutely so apparent, long before the defense even took the stand, that there was no other possible outcome."

Sometimes, Joe told Bradley, he tries to piece together exactly how he ended up where he did. When he does that, the blame falls everywhere but on Joe Hunt. "It's almost like a multicar collision," he said. "In other words, a variety of different things on all sorts of levels going wrong. I think the final answer is in the people that I was with at the time, and a blindness on my part to recognize the characteristics of certain people as being so ingrained that they couldn't be changed. Specifically, that's true of Ron Levin. And also, in a very tragic sense, it's true of Dean Karny."

With hindsight, Joe said at the end of the interview, "I recognize I made a series of blunders that perhaps will keep me here for the rest of my life. But I didn't kill anybody. So I don't want to put my head down. There's no shame. When I go up in San Francisco and face the death penalty again, I hope I'll do it with my head up, because I did my absolute best. . . . I tried to do my best for those people. I got caught up in a situation with people [and] I didn't understand their motivations or the level of their games."

Epilogue

Five years after Ron Levin's murder, the story of Joe Hunt and the Billionaire Boys Club is far from over. Motions must still be argued, murder cases tried, and appeals heard. The legal process set into motion in 1984 will not be completed for perhaps another decade. And until the last motion is heard and the last appeal duly considered, the lives of dozens of people will stay wrapped up in that eventful summer.

Joe Hunt, as might be expected, has remained the most flamboyant participant in the legal battling. Early in 1989, no longer happy with his very competent court-appointed counsel for the Eslaminia case, Parker Kelly, Joe decided to become his own attorney for the Redwood City trial, keeping Kelly on to assist him. Since then, he has kept John Vance and Oscar Breiling busy, filing dozens of motions and winning many of them. His legal work to date has been ambitious and often very good, although he does occasionally suffer setbacks in court.

During arguments for one motion, Joe insisted that, as his own attorney, it was imperative that he be allowed the same latitude as the prosecutor to move freely around the courtroom, approaching witnesses and the like. He would, after all, be acting as his own attorney, Joe insisted. After letting Joe make his points, the judge finally made his ruling.

353

It was not Joe Hunt the attorney the judge was worried about, he said in denying the motion. It was his client.

Joe's trial is currently scheduled for mid-summer 1989, although it may well be delayed until late in the year or even until 1990. He is appealing his conviction in the Ron Levin killing.

For the other BBC members who became defendants in the murder trials, life moves more slowly. Reza Eslaminia and Ben Dosti are roommates in Folsom Prison, one of California's most brutal high-security prisons. They too are appealing their murder convictions.

Like Joe, Jim Pittman is incarcerated in the San Mateo County Jail. His preliminary hearing on the Eslaminia murder will follow Hunt's trial. Because of his familiarity with the case, Pittman's lawyer from his Los Angeles trial, a top-flight Beverly Hills criminal specialist named Jim Brody, has been appointed by the court to represent Pittman in Redwood City. Pittman's trial will probably not begin before mid-1990. Should Pittman be acquitted, he will go free.

John Vance and Oscar Breiling are occasionally daunted at the prospect of facing the back-to-back trials. Breiling would like to retire. Vance would like to move on to other cases. But both men are committed to prosecuting the two remaining people they believe killed Hedayat Eslaminia. Above his desk, Breiling still keeps a photograph of Eslaminia's bones. "That's who I'm working for," he tells visitors to his office.

For the rest of the members of the BBC, life has slowly returned to normal. Most are beginning to move ahead in careers they might have started on several years earlier had it not been for their involvement with Joe Hunt. Some have become very successful. And they are all trying, with varying degrees of success, to put the BBC behind them. But it is not easy. For many, knowing they will be called several more times to testify keeps Joe Hunt very much a part of their lives.

Only for Ron Levin and Hedayat Eslaminia is the story of the BBC really over. And they have left behind family and friends who will remain permanently scarred by their encounters with the Billionaire Boys Club.